The Lambeth Cholera
Outbreak of 1848–1849

The Lambeth Cholera Outbreak of 1848–1849

The Setting, Causes, Course and Aftermath of an Epidemic in London

Amanda J. Thomas

McFarland & Company, Inc., Publishers

Jefferson, North Carolina, and London

LIBRARY OF CONGRESS CATALOGUING-IN-PUBLICATION DATA

Thomas, Amanda J., 1960–
    The Lambeth cholera outbreak of 1848–1849 : the setting,
causes, course and aftermath of an epidemic in London /
Amanda J. Thomas.
      p.   cm.
    Includes bibliographical references and index.

    ISBN 978-0-7864-3989-8
    softcover : 50# alkaline paper ∞

    1. Cholera — England — London — History —19th century.
2. Cholera — England — London — Epidemiology.   I. Title.
[DNLM: 1. Cholera — epidemiology — London.   2. Cholera —
history — London.   3. Disease Outbreaks — history — London.
4. History, 19th Century — London.   5. Rivers — London.
6. Vulnerable Populations — London.   WC 11 FE5 T454L 2010]
RC133.G6T46   2010
614.5'1409421— dc22   2009039036

British Library cataloguing data are available

On the cover: J.D. Wingfield, *Doughty Street, Lambeth, 1848*,
the proposed site of the Lambeth Ragged School, watercolor
(courtesy Lambeth Archives department)

Manufactured in the United States of America

McFarland & Company, Inc., Publishers
  Box 611, Jefferson, North Carolina 28640
   www.mcfarlandpub.com

To the memory of my aunt,
Hilda Wraight (1921–1976)

Contents

Acknowledgments

Centre for Kentish Studies, Maidstone, Kent.
City of Westminster Archives Centre, London.
General Register Office, England.
Friends of Medway Archives and Local Studies Centre, Strood, Kent.
John Snow Public House, Soho, London.
John Snow Society.
Kent Archaeological Society.
Kent Family History Society.
King's College London, Archives and Corporate Records Services, Information Services and Systems, London.
Lambeth Archives Department, Lambeth, London.
London Borough of Lambeth.
London Metropolitan Archives, London.
London Transport Museum.
Medway Archives and Local Studies Centre, Strood, Kent.
Museum of London.
National Portrait Gallery.
Ordnance Survey.
The Royal College of Physicians.
The Royal College of Surgeons of England.
St. Bartholomew's Hospital, Archives and Museum, London.
Verulamium Museum, St. Albans.
Wellcome Library, London.

Susan Algar; Roy Beaufoy; Dr. Iain Boulton, Project Officer (Communities and Education), Parks and Greenspaces, Environment, Culture & Community Safety, London Borough of Lambeth; Heather Burnett; Stephen Dixon, Archive Service Manager, Essex Record Office; Dr. Sandra Dunster, University of Greenwich, and Kent Team Leader for the Victoria County History's *England's Past for Everyone (EPE)*; Elaine Gardner; Chris Green, Museums and Heritage Officer, St. Albans Museums; Dr. Andrew Hann, Senior Properties Historian, English Heritage; Kenneth V. Iserson, M.D.; Lee Jackson, *The Victorian Dictionary*; Laurence Marsteller, M.D.; Cindy O'Halloran, Ms. Alyson Russen, Head Teacher, Millbank Primary School, London; David Thomas; Georgina Thomas; Joe Tenner, Handspring Design; Alison Turner-Rugg, Special Projects Officer, St. Albans Museums; my family and friends.

Special thanks to my son, Alexander Thomas, whose help and advice have been invaluable.

Preface

Lambeth is situated on the south bank of the River Thames in London, opposite the Houses of Parliament and Millbank. My interest in Lambeth and the cholera epidemic of 1848–1849 began with a family history question about the Osmotherlys, relations of my six-times great-grandmother and who had migrated from the Medway Towns in Kent to Lambeth for work. I was asked why I thought three of the family had died within such a short space of each other. While illness seemed an obvious answer, I was still surprised to discover there had been a cholera epidemic at this time; the only outbreak I had knowledge of was the famous 1854 outbreak and Dr. John Snow's discovery that the Broad Street pump in Soho was its source.

My first trip to Lambeth Archives to try and discover more followed, and there the crisp and unfaded pages of the 1848 Lambeth District Sanitary Reports gave vivid accounts of life in the filthy, narrow streets of the south bank of the River Thames. Having been brought up near Rochester, Kent, and just down the road from Higham, where Charles Dickens had lived for many years, I was familiar with the famous novelist's descriptions of life in nineteenth century London. However, nothing could have prepared me for the reality of the depravation in Lambeth. Page after page contained matter-of-fact descriptions of dark, marshy streets filled with muck, no sanitation and sewage spilling out of overflowing cesspools, a lack of running water, cows kept on patches of wasteland, pigs kept in cellars, and butchers disposing of carcasses and entrails in open ditches. All the while the people took their drinking water from the River Thames into which the detritus of their life freely flowed. There was no doubt in my mind that the people of Lambeth could not have failed to succumb to any epidemic which might have erupted in this period.

The attitude of the District Sub Committee members in the reports appeared sympathetic, yet it was evident that little was being done to alleviate the poverty in Lambeth. I noticed also that several of the reports contained repetition, and wondered if some of their visits had even taken place at all, or if the Sub Committee members had put together their later reports in the safety of their own offices, away from the stinking marshland and industries of the waterfront.

Next I visited the waterfront area itself, though by this time I had already started to read a little more about the history of the area. I approached Lambeth from Westminster Bridge, a wonderful vantage point to savor the Houses of Parliament and the spectacular view of London and the River Thames. I then turned right and walked south of the old County Hall and the London Aquarium, onto the Albert Embankment which at this point mirrors the leafy Victoria Embankment on the opposite shore. However, once past Lambeth Bridge the Embankment opens up to a wide, open thoroughfare. Here I attempted to orientate myself, to work out how today's streets correlate with those of the nineteenth century. The only reference point was the railway line and from that I was able to work out the exact position of Great Lemon Court, the first courtyard tenement the Osmotherlys called home which today sits directly underneath the ballroom of a luxury hotel.

London and Lambeth. Reproduced by permission of Ordnance Survey on behalf of Her Majesty's Stationery Office. Crown copyright © 2009. All rights reserved. Ordnance Survey License number 100048998.

The building of the Albert Embankment in the 1860s eradicated all traces of what had once been the industrial centre of London. In Southwark, just ten minutes' walk back up the Embankment, the old winding streets had been preserved, and I wondered why this had not happened in Lambeth. Had the authorities wanted to eradicate all evidence of their ineptitude? And why was there no reference to the two thousand who had died in the cholera epidemic of the 1840s? Even in the burial ground in Lambeth High Street there was no mention of that two-year period when mass graves spilled over with the bodies of the victims of the disease.

I realized that the episode had been forgotten. The waterside area had been razed to the ground because it was simply not economical to try and restore the area. The houses and factories had been built on marshland which flooded continually, and the Albert Embankment was above all else a flood barrier. I decided to find out more about how Lambeth had developed, and why some of the most important figures of the industrial age had come here to set up factories. However, most of all I wanted to find out why so many people had died, and why they had not been important enough to remember. They at least deserved some sort of memorial; hence, this book.

Introduction

By 1848, Lambeth, a district on the south bank of London's River Thames, had become one of the most important industrial centers in England. Its proximity to the main bridges and highways of the capital was essential to its development, as was its distance from residential areas and the regulations of the City of London. Throughout the 1800s, laborers from deprived farming communities migrated to America, Canada and Australia, but some decided to try their luck closer to home, attracted by the jobs available in the newly industrialized areas like Lambeth.

One such migrant worker was James Osmotherly, born in 1807 in the village of Cliffe, Kent. James was the eldest son of James and Charlotte (née Mairs), and a descendant of John, born in Rochester in 1691, a parish clerk and bell ringer at the cathedral. The Kent Osmotherlys probably originated in Cumbria in the north of England and were dispersed during the Civil War in the late 1600s, when a branch took up the Parliamentarian cause. Why the family should have come to Rochester remains a mystery, but it may have had something to do with the Church. John's Protestant sympathies were noted in the cathedral records when he received "ten shillings for ringing on the thanksgiving day. For the blessing of God upon His Majesty's councils and arms in suppressing the late unnatural [Jacobite] rebellion ... 1716." John performed similar duties at St. Helen's Church at Cliffe which is situated within the diocese of Rochester.

An ancient settlement, Cliffe lies at the tip of the Hoo Peninsula separating the River Medway to the south and the Thames Estuary to the north. From 1776 until 1857, these malaria-ridden, bleak marshland waters were the mooring place for prison hulks and their cargo of convicts awaiting transportation to Australia, and the setting for Charles Dickens' *Great Expectations*. The Medway area has always had a close relationship with London, given its geographical proximity. The Roman Watling Street bisects the Medway Towns linking Lambeth's neighbor Southwark to Canterbury and Dover, whilst the River Medway joins the Thames at the western end of the Hoo Peninsula.

Like many other migrant workers, James Osmotherly left Cliffe in about 1830. In the days before the railways, he probably walked to London, however, he may have left by boat from the port of Gravesend, about 12 miles from Cliffe. Perhaps, like many of his cousins, he considered boarding a ship to America, but instead he took the shorter, and cheaper, route up the Thames to Lambeth.

By the end of 1831, James was well established in Lambeth, married to Ann and celebrating the birth of Emma, the first of seven children. He had changed his surname to Osmer, probably because it was simpler to pronounce, and also because it would have been easier for employers calling out the names each morning of laborers waiting for work. James was a coal laborer, essential work in a Lambeth full of factory furnaces needing constant stoking. No doubt James felt fortunate to have a job, however, while history would have us believe that this was an age of political agitation with reforms which put the working man at the top of the agenda, the reality was very different. Wages were low and living conditions so appalling, they make the well-known descriptions of London life by Charles Dickens seem utopian.

Between 1801 and 1901, Lambeth's population grew from 28,000 to 302,000, and in 1849 the population was already approaching 135,000. The waterfront area of Lambeth was lined with wharves and factories housing steam engines fueled by coal-fired furnaces producing such items as glass, pottery, soap and lead shot.

A list of occupations in the 1841 Census gives a clear picture of this bustling, industrial community: malt roasters, distillers, potters, fishmongers,

Boats on the River Medway, 1830, Upnor, Frindsbury Extra, close to Chatham Dockyard. From the Medway Archives and Local Studies Centre, Couchman Collection: Print from engraving entitled Upnor Castle, near Chatham, Kent, *drawn by T.M. Baynes, engraved by T. Garner and published by George Virtue, 26 Ivy Lane, London, DE402/25/p.10 (U). Reproduced by kind permission of the Director of Regeneration, Community and Culture.*

The Thames foreshore at Lambeth circa 1860 showing R. Bain boat builders, Lambeth Rice Mills and the potteries Stiff's and Smith's; the gasometers of the London Gas Works are just visible in the background. From the Woolley Collection, photographed by William Strudwick, ref., 446. Reproduced by kind permission of Lambeth Archives department.

saddlers, coal merchants, lime burners, coopers, pork butchers, barge builders, tailors, blacksmiths, brick layers, engineers, excise officers, seamen, milk dealers, dressmakers, hairdressers, and, of course, laborers.[1]

Terraced housing and back-to-back courtyard tenements were rapidly erected for the growing working population on the low-lying marshland, butting onto factories engaged in dangerous industrial processes. In the Lambeth District Sanitary Reports, compiled in 1849, members of the Sub Committee for Division 4 noted, "At ... Fore Street there were bone crushing factories, the smell complained of as a great nuisance; the bone bugs creep through the wall into the next house."[2]

In the waterfront area there was no sanitation and no running water. Sewage was disposed of in the streets and into the River Thames, which was also the source of the district's water supply.

Asiatic Cholera had already struck London in 1832, claiming around 7,000 lives, and at the time it was the common belief that such diseases were transmitted through the air and in the particles of foul smelling *miasma*. Sir Edwin Chadwick (1800–1890), who played a pivotal role in social and health reform and who was Public Health Commissioner from 1848 to 1854, famously declared, "All smell is disease."[3]

The scientist Dr. John Snow (1813–1858) is credited with the discovery that cholera is a waterborne disease, having closely observed the cholera epidemic of 1848 to 1849 in Lambeth, and returning there during the subsequent outbreak of 1854. He noted that the residents of Fore Street took their water from the Thames in buckets and realized that there was a correlation between cholera and drinking river water contaminated with sewage: "Now the people in Lower Fore Street, Lambeth, obtained their water by dipping a pail into the Thames, there being no other supply in the street ... when the epidemic revived again ... the first case ... was in Lower Fore Street."[4]

Snow's observations in Soho in 1854 confirmed his findings, but the real breakthrough was the difference in mortality rates in Lambeth between those who were supplied with river water taken downstream by the Southwark and Vauxhall Water Company and those who were supplied by the Lambeth Waterworks, which had moved to Thames Ditton in 1852, taking its supply from the less contaminated waters upstream. Despite his meticulous research and logical argument, Snow's findings were not universally accepted, however, following the 1854 epidemic, improvements did begin on London's sanitation and water supply. Work on the existence of the cholera bacillus, *Vibrio cholerae,* was also published in the mid 1850s by the Italian Filippo Pacini (1812–1883), but its existence was only accepted in 1884 with the work of the German scientist Robert Koch (1843–1910).[5]

Sir Edwin Chadwick was also convinced living conditions and disease were interlinked and saw his role as Royal Commissioner on London Sanitation as an opportunity to improve living conditions for the urban poor, especially in London. Unfortunately his dictatorial approach and arguments over the role of local government and finance were not conducive to rapid change. The Royal Commission on London Sanitation began its work in September 1847, and presented its findings in 1848. While there is no direct reference in the *First Report* of the Commission to the Lambeth District Sanitary Reports, they were likely conducted with a view to submission to the Royal Commission, or as a fact gathering exercise for the Parish of Lambeth. The Lambeth Vestry Committee Minutes and District Sanitary Reports are held at Lambeth Archives and show that in the first months of 1848, the authorities were aware that the living conditions of the Lambeth population were severe enough to fear a second cholera outbreak. In January 1848, Mr. J.W. Weeks of the Sanitary Subcommittee reported: "We fear there is every reason to apprehend, should it please God to visit us with that awful scourge the cholera."

As it was thought cholera was transmitted through the air, the reports focused on the foul smells the Subcommittee encountered:

> We first visited Jurston Street ... a large portion was covered with stagnant water, quantities of mud composed of ashes and decomposed vegetables and all kinds of refuse thrown into the street by the inhabitants — within a few yards ... is a large open drain ... open nearly the whole distance from Christ Church work-house to the Westminster Road. In this part the sight is most revolting — dead cats and dogs and filth of every description, and although it was a cold morning, such was the offensive effuiva [sic] emitted as to render a speedy retreat most desirable ... in a small yard we found a number of pigs, the stench was so great that we could scarcely remain near the spot for the

inquiries ... [in] Hooper Street ... several cesspools overflowing ... most offensive smells ... one family generally occupies only one room. We next visited Harriet Street ... the very worse street in the whole district, the dirt of all kinds have been left to accumulate for years ... thrown up into great heaps ... no drains — and cesspools in a bad state. [In] Gloster [sic] Street ... we found one man had ten pigs in the cellar, on opening the front door the stench was dreadful. In Short Street we found a cow yard and ... without any drain whatever ... in heavy rain, the place is regularly flooded.[6]

Such were the living conditions for the residents of Lambeth. The Osmotherly family lived at 11 Princes Street, next to Lower Fore Street and the river, with no running water and no sanitation, wedged between a series of industrial buildings; by the end of 1849, James, Ann, and their youngest child, Lucy, would all be dead.

1

The Catalysts for Change and Reform

The last years of the eighteenth and the early years of the nineteenth centuries in Britain were a time of great political and social unrest, a watershed between an economy based mainly on agriculture and one with an increasing emphasis on manufacturing. An emerging middle class of factory owners, merchants and bankers, made wealthy by industry, new technology and commerce, were only too aware of their lack of power and rights compared to the landed aristocracy. Less than three percent of the population had the right to vote, which depended on ownership, moreover, all Members of Parliament had to be landowners.[1]

Some within this new emerging middle class could sympathize with the plight of the working population as a result of their own experience, yet real progress for workers' rights was only achieved in the twentieth century, and it was not until 1928 that both men and women over the age of 21 were able to vote. In Lambeth and many other industrial centers, the working and living conditions of laboring families were ignored by the factory owners, whose prime concern was profit. In the cities and new factory towns, families lived in single rooms with no running water, ventilation or sanitation, and communal privies, which served whole blocks of tenements, spilled over into the courtyards and streets. In the countryside the old traditional ways were swept aside and agricultural laborers struggled to find a stable job. For all, hunger was a constant companion.

In the years following the Napoleonic Wars (1799–1815), the population of Britain swelled. In 1750, the population of England had been around 5.74 million,[2] by 1801 this had risen to an estimated 8.3 million, 10.5 million including Scotland and Wales,[3] and by 1851 the population of England had risen to 16.8 million.[4]

New developments in machinery in both the country and town meant that the traditional skills of many craftsmen had become obsolete. Workers now obeyed the rhythms of machines, they lost control of their working day, and had neither the right to complain nor any way to vote for a different system. War and revolution shaped British politics and the economy, speeding up the process of change brought about by mechanization. Successive governments were reactionary to the possibility of revolutionary fever spreading to Britain's shores.

British Monarchs and their Prime Ministers[5]

King George III (1738–1820), reigned 1760–1820
William Pitt the Younger (Tory) 1783–1801
Henry Addington (Tory) 1801–1804
William Pitt the Younger (Tory) 1804–1806
William Wyndham Grenville, Lord Grenville (Whig) 1806–1807
Duke of Portland (Whig) 1807–1809
Spencer Perceval (Tory) 1809–1812
Robert Banks Jenkinson, second Earl of Liverpool (Tory) 1812–1820

King George IV, formerly the Prince Regent (1762–1830), reigned 1820–1830

Robert Banks Jenkinson, second Earl of Liverpool (Tory) 1820–1827
George Canning (Whig/Tory Coalition) 1827
Frederick John Robinson, Viscount Goderich (Whig/Tory Coalition) 1827–1828
Arthur Wellesley, Duke of Wellington (Tory) 1828–1830

King William IV (1765–1837), reigned 1830–1837

Charles, Earl Grey (Whig) 1830–1834
William Lamb, second Viscount Melbourne (Whig) 1834
Sir Robert Peel (Tory/Conservative) 1834–1835
Lord Melbourne (Whig) 1835–1837

Queen Victoria (1819–1901), reigned 1837–1901

Lord Melbourne (Whig) 1837–1841
Sir Robert Peel (Conservative) 1841–1846
Lord John Russell (Whig) 1846–1852

The roots of political unrest may well lie in the American War of Independence (1775–1783). Certainly losing America was a terrible blow to George III and his government, and it signaled the beginning of turbulence in Europe. The War of Independence showed that it was possible to overthrow a regime and start afresh, and while it has long been debated if there was a direct link between this and the French Revolution,[6] it cannot be ignored that the American struggle influenced European minds, and gave hope to the radical movements of the time.

The French Revolution of 1789 to 1799 was a bloody and violent realization of many of the ideals of the Enlightenment movement, its philosophy on how to improve society was perpetuated by French writers such as Voltaire (1694–1778) and Jean Jacques Rousseau (1712–1778).[7] In Britain, similar ideas had been explored by Thomas Hobbes (1588–1679) and John Locke (1632–1704). Hobbes, who had written during the English Civil War, saw the government and the monarchy's role as one of controlling the population to achieve order in society. Locke contradicted this view, arguing that all men had a right to "life, liberty," and if the government failed to recognize this "contract"[8] then the people would be justified in removing them by rebellion. The idea that the people had a right to rebel and that a government's power was conditional was revolutionary in itself.

The intellectual minds of Britain, inspired by this philosophical lead and the fact that it had been put into practice in America and France, were increasingly frustrated with Parliament. At the time of the French Revolution, the Tory government of William Pitt the Younger was deeply concerned that the troubles across the English Channel would spread, and while they could not be certain that the laboring population would not rise up, their main focus was on quashing an increasingly radical — and predominantly middle-class — movement. By the end of 1792, the government was so concerned that reports were put out in the pro-government press that they had discovered and curtailed the plans for an insurrection. Whether this was propaganda or true, it gave the government an excuse to bring troops into London and a royal proclamation was made to call out the militia of ten counties.[9]

The government set up The Alien Office in 1792, on the back of the Alien Bill (the Aliens Act was passed the following year), to monitor French refugees, though Pitt's spies were also keeping an eye on London's radicals.

One such radical was John Thelwall (1764–1834), a journalist, poet and political lecturer,[10] who became an associate of the medical elite practicing at Guy's Hospital in Southwark, close to Lambeth. As a journalist and intellectual, Thelwall was most concerned by the government's suppression of free speech and through his own public speaking preached democratic change. Many of those Thelwall mixed with in medical circles had been trained at Edinburgh University (see Chapter 2), including the leading surgeon and anatomist, Astley Cooper (1768–1841). As a result of his friendship with surgeons at Guy's such as Cooper, Thelwall became a member of the hospital's Physical Society and was invited to speak. His brilliant lecture on *Animal Vitality*, the thrust of which focused on "the physiological basis of life," caused great discussion among the surgeons of the day.[11]

It is easy to see how the charisma and brilliance of radicals like Thelwall could influence not just London's middle-class elite, but the population at

The House of Commons 1793–1794, *by Karl Anton Hickel, oil on canvas, 1793–1795; NPG 745; National Portrait Gallery, London. Prime Minister William Pitt is standing at the center of the painting. Notes from the National Portrait Gallery catalog include the following: "William Pitt was groomed for the role of Prime Minister by his father who had himself held office between 1756–1761 and 1766–1768. Pitt the Younger, as he became known, became Prime Minister at the age of twenty-four. On 12 February 1793, [King] George III sent a message to the House of Commons announcing that France had declared war on Britain and Holland. This painting, which was exhibited at no.28 Haymarket in 1795, is by the Austrian artist Hickel (whose country was already at war with France). It was probably inspired by one of Pitt's addresses following the outbreak of war, although most of the portraits were not painted until summer 1794. It is set in St. Stephen's Chapel, later destroyed by fire."*

large. Thelwall had been a member of the Southwark Friends of the People[12] and had also started a Society for Free Debate, which had been closed down. However, by 1792 The London Corresponding Society (one of many in the country) was attracting more and more interest under the leadership of Thelwall with Thomas Hardy, a shoemaker, and John Horne-Tooke.[13]

The aim of the Corresponding Societies was to educate by staging public speeches and by the promotion of democratic literature, but their bases were republican.[14] A key text for the societies was Thomas Paine's *Rights of Man*, which was sympathetic to the French cause; the societies also wanted to encourage a more widespread belief in the need for parliamentary reform.[15]

Perhaps spurred on by the execution of Louis XVI in Paris in 1793, in

January 1794, Thelwall organized a meeting of The London Corresponding Society in which they decided they were ready — should conditions dictate — to call a General Convention of the People, in short, a revolution. By May that same year, knowing Hardy had already been taken to the Tower of London, Thelwall was also arrested, and his papers confiscated by Prime Minister Pitt's secret committee. Pitt subsequently instructed Parliament to suspend habeas corpus, and, in all, twelve radicals were arrested, including Horne-Tooke. With the prisoners' rights suspended, Pitt deliberately worked slowly to bring them to trial, presumably to inflict as much discomfort as possible. Thelwall was eventually tried for treason in October, the punishment for which was hanging. The government's view was that the only way to overcome the threat of revolution was to eradicate the agitators.[16]

Following an anonymous article in the *Morning Chronicle* which challenged the government's interpretation of treason, the lawyer Thomas Erskine was appointed to defend, using a similar argument. The reprinting of the article in pamphlet form and reporting by the press fueled interest in the trials and crowds gathered at the Old Bailey, creating a public hero out of Erskine. Hardy was acquitted, as was Tooke, leaving Thelwall as the government's scapegoat. But Pitt had not reckoned on Thelwall's skill at public oratory. Erskine advised Thelwall not to conduct his own case, but Thelwall was determined, prepared to die for his cause if necessary, and in the end the jury acquitted him as well and the government's case collapsed.[17]

Thelwall was not alone in sympathizing with the French insurrection. Many organizations known as Revolution Societies were set up for the rich and the educated who saw the struggle as similar to that of the English a century earlier, in what was known as The Glorious Revolution,[18] the ousting of the Catholic King James II and his replacement with the Protestant William of Orange, subsequently King William III. Associations known as Reform Clubs were set up with a similar purpose and along similar lines, though these were established by the skilled craftsmen who were angered by the mechanization of the Industrial Revolution. Also of note were the Hampden Clubs, set up in 1812 by Major John Cartwright to bring together activists within both the working and middle classes.

The trial at the Old Bailey shocked Thelwall into silence for some time, but by 1795 he was back on form and made a return to public speaking. In October he addressed a vast crowd in the neighborhood of Copenhagen House (or Fields) in Islington, north London; three days later, on his way to the State Opening of Parliament, King George III's coach was attacked by a mob.

The government reacted swiftly with the Act for the Safety and Preservation of His Majesty's Person and Government against treasonable and Seditious Practices and Attempts, and the Act to Prevent Seditious Meetings and Assemblies. These Acts ensured that the practices of the radical societies were on a par with treason and that any activity designed to incite revolution would be punished by hanging. In addition, Pitt publicly linked the attack on the King's coach to Thelwall's Islington meeting, and a royal proclamation confirmed this. Membership of the radical clubs became less fashionable.[19] In addition, some of the radicals had been able to travel to France and witnessed first-hand the bloodshed taking place. The reality of revolution made many of them realize that violent insurrection may not be the way forward.

However, for some, the struggle continued. The influential radical Thomas Spence (1750–1814) came from a working background and wrote a pamphlet called *The Real Rights of Man* which included a proposal for common ownership of land, and the division of wealth for the local good. Spence spent six months in Newgate Prison in the 1780s, and his philosophy attracted a significant following. In 1816, at Spa Fields in Islington, North London, Spence's followers held a series of meetings against the government with a

John Thelwall shaking his fist as he addresses the crowds. Copenhagen house *(John Gale Jones; Joseph Priestley; William Hodgson; John Thelwell; Charles James Fox?) by James Gillray, published by Hannah Humphrey; hand-colored etching, published November 16, 1795; NPG D12546; National Portrait Gallery, London.*

view, in effect, to revolution. The leaders, including Arthur Thistlewood, stirred up the crowds to such an extent that an armed mob marched on the Tower of London. Thistlewood and the leaders were arrested, but later released.

In 1799, and 1800, Pitt's government passed the Combination Acts to prohibit collective bargaining by workers and the forming of trades unions. Francis Place (1771–1854) was one of the greatest opponents of the restrictions imposed on the working population by these acts, though they did not entirely succeed in suppressing the union movement. Influenced by Thelwall, Hardy and Horne-Tooke, Place joined the London Corresponding Society and became its chairman when the leaders were imprisoned. Place was also a supporter of Sir Francis Burdett (1770–1844), a representative of the radical cause in Parliament, and it was through Burdett that Place was introduced to the social reformer Jeremy Bentham (1748–1832) and Joseph Hume (1777–1855), who had studied medicine at Edinburgh University and had worked as a ship's surgeon with the East India Company. Place and others argued that a repeal of the Combination Acts would help to balance the rights of workers and employers and there would be no need to form trades unions.[20]

In January 1817, the Prince Regent's coach was mobbed on his return from the State Opening of Parliament, which the government again saw as an act perpetrated by a radical group. Then, in March of the same year, three working-class radical reformers in Manchester, John Johnson, John Bagguley and Samuel Drummond, organized a march to London with a petition for the Prince Regent that highlighted the plight of unemployed spinners and weavers and the plight of the cotton industry in general. Known as the March of the Blanketeers, participants covered their shoulders with blankets and met at St. Peter's Field in Manchester. Around six to seven hundred set out, but many were arrested and only one man, Abel Couldwell, managed to get to London to present the petition.[21]

In 1820, following the death of King George III, Arthur Thistlewood and his associates hatched another plan. Known as the Cato Street Conspirators, they once again plotted revolution and the murder of the government. The government's spy network was still well in place and the conspirators were duly arrested. Thistlewood and four others were later hanged.[22]

Francis Place's campaign against the Combination Acts finally worked in 1824 when the acts were repealed, and a brief period followed of growth, strikes, and violence within the movement, which resulted in the passing of a new Combination Act the following year. The act of 1825 legalized trades unions but made it illegal to "threaten or to take strike action, to boycott non-union labour or picket peacefully."[23] Nevertheless, many of the radicals saw the trades unions as a way to further their cause.

While the effects of war were a catalyst for insurrection, the mechanization which was occurring in the countryside and the towns also caused considerable disquiet. *Luddite* is a name still used today for those averse to change and innovation. The Luddites of the eighteenth century were groups of artisans who smashed new machinery because they saw them as the cause of the eradication of traditional crafts and trades. The Luddite movement started in 1811 in Nottingham, in the north of England, and spread rapidly over the next couple of years. Yet problems had been brewing for some time, and it is possible that the burning of the Albion Flour Mills near Lambeth in 1791 was the work of a Luddite group, though it may have been a protest about the price of grain. In Nottingham, protests initially came from the makers of stockings, or stockingers, whose livelihood depended entirely on a master from whom they rented their machines and acquired their thread. The finished garments were then given back to that same master to sell. From 1811 to 1812, these workers smashed around a thousand machines in protest. Subsequent attacks and the burnings of mills meant that the government, once again, was obliged to put legislation in place.

There are theories that Luddites were provoked by *agents provocateurs* and that they were not smashing machines because they opposed progress but rather because they were averse to the free market and the abolition of set prices.[24] The Luddites were not a national organization and they were not set up in the same way as the radical groups, moreover there was no real political motivation behind their activities. However, their activities were unsettling. Their attacks on machinery, particularly in the north, in Lancashire and Cheshire, took place alongside the protests over food prices, and radical revolutionary plots and conspiracies.[25]

The Napoleonic Wars which followed the French Revolution when Napoleon Bonaparte took power in November 1799 put a tremendous strain on Britain's resources. Napoleon's "Continental System" deliberately set out to destroy Britain's trade.[26] The needs of the military and a growing domestic population also highlighted an urgent need for British agriculture to become more efficient and more productive. The development of new mechanized methods, such as Jethro Tull's seed drill in the early 1700s, speeded up agricultural processes and made them less labor intensive, though the uptake of mechanization was a slow process. Science also played a part in transforming the rural landscape, as a better understanding of soil fertilization revolutionized crop yields and variety by adopting a four-field rotation system, which meant that fields were no longer left fallow. The four field rotation was introduced by Viscount Charles Townsend, or "Turnip Townsend," who divided fields up to grow four different types of crops. The cultivation of oats, barley or wheat would be followed the next year by clover and turnips.

The latter replaced the soil's nutrients and were also used as cattle fodder; grazing also effectively fertilized the ground with the manure the cattle produced.[27]

Since medieval times agricultural land had been divided into narrow strips, an inefficient and labor intensive system. In the average English town, strips of land belonging to a single farmer were not even necessarily next to each other, having been passed down through families by marriage and sometimes swapped from one person to another. For many years it had been recognized that consolidating and enclosing land into larger chunks would improve drainage, crop yields and general efficiency. Crops in larger fields could be rotated more effectively, fertilized more precisely, and seeded and harvested faster using the new mechanical processes.

While many landowners tried to consolidate and enclose land on a local basis, from the 1760s, most land enclosure was achieved through a series of Acts of Parliament which applied to each local area. Legislation required three-quarters of landowners to be in agreement, with notices being posted on the church door. Larger landowners had more votes, and more money to force smallholders to sell; those who owned no land lost the use of much of the common land, which was absorbed into the larger plots.[28] The unfairness of the system led to enormous disquiet in agricultural communities, and some rioting.[29]

Commissioners from London visited parishes whose land was to be enclosed and attempted to settle any disputes, but the upheaval in most local communities was significant. Radical commentators of the day, such as the writer and journalist William Cobbett (1763–1835), made much of the detrimental effects of the enclosures on the laboring population,[30] however, in reality, many of the small communities adapted to the changes, if only because there was no other choice. Migration statistics uphold this and show that in the latter part of the eighteenth century, there was more mobility between rural locations a short distance apart than mass migration to the newly industrialized urban areas. Migration from rural to industrialized areas did not increase until later in the nineteenth century.[31]

During the Napoleonic Wars, the restrictions on trade and a series of bad harvests caused corn prices to rise. Between the years 1795 and 1801, sporadic food riots broke out across the country and the poor were on the brink of starvation.[32] In January of 1795, at Lamberhurst in Kent, some 40 people gathered outside the local mill, accusing the miller of causing "a great scarcity and a sudden rise in prices in that part of the country." They demanded that prices should be lowered.[33]

The London Corresponding Society made much of these riots, highlighting the poverty and lack of rights and suffrage for the ordinary working population. In May of the same year, the Speenhamland System was set up by a group of magistrates in Berkshire, worried that should bread prices remain so high, famine would surely follow.[34] The System, which spread throughout the south of England, introduced a subsidy, in effect a type of poor relief, which means tested workers and topped up their wages to enable them to afford bread when prices rose. The Berkshire magistrates decided that each man would be given the equivalent of the price of three gallon loaves a week (a gallon being eight and a half pounds) and an additional one-and-a-half gallons for a wife and for each child.[35] In effect, the system caused more problems as employers were able to pay workers less, knowing that the parish would make up the shortfall in their wages; some also thought it made the poor idle and complacent.[36] The system remained in place until it was abolished by the Poor Law Amendment Act in 1834.

Enclosure and mechanization changed the English countryside. The introduction of machinery on farms created a loss of some traditional jobs and skills. Enclosure meant that many in the countryside lost their land and became dependent on the owners of the new consolidated and enclosed farms for work. Agricultural laborers also lost the right to graze cattle on common land, and as farmers adopted the new ways the old practice of hiring laborers for a set period and giving them farmhouse lodging began to die out. At the end of the Napoleonic Wars the situation worsened as the labor force swelled further with returning servicemen and an influx of Irish immigrants, moreover, grain prices fell. More and more laborers became dependent on parish relief and while the Speenhamland System to provide bread had been widely adopted, it was not sufficient. The harvests of 1828 and 1829 were meager and by the summer of 1830, laborers in Kent began smashing threshing machines. At first anger was focused in the south and east of England, where agricultural laborers also burnt hay ricks and maimed cattle, but the so-called Swing Riots spread, encouraged by letters sent to local men in authority, such as magistrates, by a ringleader called "Captain Swing." The letters were of a threatening nature, calling for higher wages, a lowering of tithe payments and an eradication of threshing machines. The government once again dealt harshly with the rioters, hanging nine of them and transporting around 450 to Australia.

When the Napoleonic Wars ended in 1815 and trade resumed, grain prices fell rapidly. To prop up the depressed domestic market, the government of Prime Minister Lord Liverpool introduced the Corn Laws. The legislation stated that no foreign grain could be imported until the domestic price reached 80 shillings per quarter pound. The aim of the law was to protect the production of grain, which greatly benefitted the landowners, many of whom were the Members of Parliament who had introduced the law in the first place. For the ordinary working man, the legislation was extremely unpopular, and there was unrest outside the Houses of Parliament when the law was being passed. Those living in the newly industrialized regions, such as Lambeth, who could not produce their own food, had to pay more for their bread, and as prices rose, so people had less to spend on other things, including manufactured goods. To make matters worse, rents were also higher in urban areas.[37] Opponents of the new law felt that it had been drawn up by ministers and members as a conspiracy to enable landowners and grain merchants to make more money.[38] The ordinary working population felt alienated by a government of aristocratic landowners who, in their opinion, did not appear to care or even understand that the poor could not afford to buy bread.

William Cobbett had much to say about the situation in the English countryside. After living in America for a few years, where he became well known for his criticism of political systems, he returned to England in 1800. Following a period of imprisonment in Newgate Prison for his treasonous views, he fled back to America, returning to England again in 1819. Cobbett longed for the England which had existed — if only in his own imagination — pre-mechanization. He believed that the capitalist system, where commercial interests overrode those of the worker, was the cause of Britain's widespread problems. Parliament needed reform and the corrupt Rotten Boroughs (those with excessively small numbers of constituents), Pocket Boroughs (those under the influence of landowners) and the Corn Laws should be abolished. Cobbett also believed that the ordinary working man in Britain was not interested in changing society, but simply wanted food on the table and work: "I defy you to agitate any fellow with a full stomach."[39]

Nevertheless, the National Union of the Working Classes organized a distribution of bread and meat in March 1833. The 14,000 who filled Finsbury Square in London were, according to *The Times* newspaper, "miserable, half-starved and wretched [but] ... they remained extremely peaceable, good-humoured and well-conducted." The food distribution did not occur, and while there was some unrest, the crowd did disperse.[40]

The economy in the 1830s continued to cause social problems. The Corn Laws did little to stabilize the price of grain, and trade worsened throughout the decade, creating great hardship for ordinary people. In addition, the introduction of the Poor Law Amendment Act of 1834, which was supposed to alleviate hardship, created an underclass fearful of ending its days in the workhouse. The new law changed the system of poor relief, though not all outdoor relief was abolished until the 1840s. Outdoor relief was the system of providing money, food, and clothing, in effect any assistance needed, to alleviate the plight of the poor. The main concern of the Poor Law Commissioners, and Sir Edwin Chadwick (1800–1890), its Secretary from 1834 to 1847, had been to resolve in the Act the old system of allowances and Speenhamland.[41] The new law saw the workhouse as the solution to poverty, as it was felt that the poor would do everything they could to avoid going there. In reality, many of the poor had little choice.

In 1834 Robert Owen (1771–1858), a friend of Francis Place, set up the Grand National Consolidated Trades Union (GNCTU), uniting the many groups which had been established and gaining rapid popularity.[42] The government was concerned, and the Home Secretary, Lord Melbourne (1779–1848), decided to make an example of one of the groups. The Friendly Society of Agricultural Labourers had been set up in Tolpuddle, Dorset, by George Loveless, an agricultural laborer. The group was mainly concerned with the lowering of their wages, which had fallen from nine to six shillings. The members agreed they would demand a wage of no less than ten shillings. In March 1834, George Loveless, his brother James, James Brine, James Hammett, George's brother in-law Thomas Standfield and his son, John Standfield, were arrested under the Unlawful Oaths Act, which had been set up to prevent mutiny onboard ship. All were transported to Australia for seven years.[43] Robert Owen led a campaign against the arrest of the so-called Tolpuddle Martyrs, but Melbourne ignored the protest and, by August 1834, the GNCTU had collapsed. The trades union movement did not die, and in the short term much of its energy was rechanneled into the Chartist movement.[44]

In 1837, the Anti–Corn Law Association was established in London by Joseph Hume, Francis Place and John Roebuck (1802–1879) in London, but the greatest opposition to the Corn Laws came from the north of England and the mill workers.[45] The Association formed branches in Leeds, Liverpool, Preston and Huddersfield and, in 1839, changed its name to the Anti–Corn Law League. Richard Cobden (1804–1865) and John Bright (1811–1889), both industrialists from the north of England, emerged as two of the leading figures within the organization; George Wilson was President and administrative head. All succeeded in becoming Members of Parliament, using their positions to lobby the new Prime Minister, Sir Robert Peel (1788–1850), over the issue. Cobden was a particularly skilled orator and was the only Member of Parliament to defeat Peel in a debate.[46]

The rise of a franchised middle class who had made their money from the new technology and factories challenged the traditional monopoly the landowners had in political power, and the very people who had put the Corn Laws in place. Members of the League argued for the Laws to be repealed in order to stimulate free trade (which Peel supported) both in Britain and abroad. This would in turn lower prices, stimulate employment and make British agriculture more productive. They also believed that the unleashing of trade in this way would promote better relations with foreign countries.

The League was a successful and well-run organization, populated by a wealthy membership who paid £500 to join. It was the financing of the League by membership fees and fund-raising events which helped it to be so successful. The organization even purchased property to give certain members the franchise, and in all managed to secure the election of 24 Members of Parliament, including Cobden in 1841. The Anti-Corn Law League achieved what Prime Minister Grey had tried to stop, a coming together of the working and middle classes; the League even attracted the support of the Irishman Daniel O'Connell (1775–1847), the great campaigner for Catholic emancipation.

Pressure to repeal the Corn Laws came from all sides, and the bill was finally repealed in June 1846. The potato blight and famine in Ireland, a population unable to afford grain, and a poor European grain harvest in 1845 all had an effect. Peel bought cheap American wheat and proposed the removal of import duty on grain. He was certain that the repeal of the Corn Laws was the only way forward, though this was not the view of the majority of the Conservative Party. Fellow Conservative, Benjamin Disraeli (1804–1881), made a bitter attack on Peel in the Parliamentary debate that ensued, but with the help of the Whig opposition, Peel managed to push the bill through to repeal the Corn Laws. Disraeli reacted quickly and, with Lord George Bentinck (1802–1848), rallied support to defeat the Irish Coercion Bill. Peel resigned and the split Conservative government fell.[47]

The system introduced by the Corn Laws, which appeared to favor landowners and merchants and, in effect, those in authority, exacerbated the calls for reform, and not just by the Anti-Corn Law League. Protests were more acute in the north, where there was the highest accumulation of working people in the mills and factories. Many of these areas were not properly represented in Parliament as they had grown and developed since constituency boundaries had been put in place. In August of 1819, there was a gathering of a crowd estimated to be between 30,000 and perhaps over 100,000 in St. Peter's Field, Manchester, to hear the radical reformist Henry Hunt of the Manchester Patriotic Union. Magistrates, perturbed by the gathering of such a huge crowd, called in the militia and had Hunt and his associates arrested before they were able to speak. In the melee, a mounted soldier knocked a child from its mother's arms. The child was killed and there was panic. Believing a riot to have started, mounted soldiers were ordered in, who slashed at the crowds with their swords. As news of the so-called Peterloo Massacre spread throughout the country, many saw similarities to the storming of the Bastille and in some areas public meetings were banned.[48] Following the Massacre, the government introduced a series of acts, the so-called Six Acts, which ensured that any radical meeting was deemed as treasonable; this also had the effect of gagging the newspapers.[49]

By the summer of the same year, the government was aware that another plot was brewing in the north, specifically in Derbyshire. Unfortunately the government's network of spies was only paid if they managed to uncover a plot and many became *agents provocateurs*, inciting unrest. Such was the case at Pentrich in Derbyshire, where eventually six men were hanged thanks to the work of William Richards, known as Oliver the Spy.[50] In 1831, the Whig government and its Prime Minister, Lord Grey, proposed an act to reform the electoral system in England and Wales, indeed Grey had accepted the role of Prime Minister on this condition.[51]

Sir Francis Burdett was one of Parliament's greatest supporters of reform. In 1831 he had set up the National Union of the Working Classes (NUWC), a radical organization initially similar to a trades union, but which later became more political and the main aim of which was universal male suffrage.[52] In the same year, Francis Place and Joseph Hume set up the National Political Union (NPU), "not a Union of the Working Classes, nor of the Middle Classes, nor of any other Class, but of all Reformers ... a Union of the People."[53] The Union was against the aristocracy but for a Reform Bill and political economy, and was more conservative than Burdett's organization.

In Lambeth, a meeting was held at Prockter's Hotel, Bridge Road, on November 16 "of a few Friends favourable to Reform in the Commons House of Parliament."[54] The group which formed called themselves the Lambeth Reform Union, the Chairman of which was Mr. John Moore, and the Honorary Secretary Mr. H. Saunders. The organization declared itself for the monarchy and for a reform bill and its aims were:

1. To obtain a full, free, and effectual Representation of the People in the Commons House of Parliament
2. To support the King and his Ministers against a corrupt Faction, in accomplishing their great measure of Parliamentary Reform
3. To join every well-wisher to his country, from the richest to the poorest, in the pursuit of such important object.
4. To preserve peace and order in the parish, and to guard against any convulsion which the Enemies of the people may endeavour to bring about.
5. To give opportunities, by frequent public discussion, for eliciting the best means by which the above objects may be carried into execution.[55]

It is not recorded how many attended the meeting or how much support the new organization had, however, the 1831 Council of the National Political Union had several members in Lambeth, including John Collinson of New Cut; Thomas Hall, 7 Royal Street; Edward Lockett, 29 Isabella Street; and William Manwaring of Marsh Gate.

In 1832, the balloting list for the Council of the NPU included the following "of the working class." F.A. Augero, teacher, 26 Hercules' Buildings, Lambeth, proposed by William Carpenter; John Grady, attorney's clerk and student at law, 6 Pratt Street, Lambeth, proposed by John Hunt. The following were "not of the working class." George Fall, accountant, Doris Street, Lambeth, proposed by John Grady; John Hunt, soap boiler, Broad Street, Lambeth, proposed by Emanuel Dias Santos.[56] The balloting lists included the following annotation in Francis Place's own hand: "List made by one and agreed to by several in the hope of excluding the dishonest men who would destroy the Union — viz Augero, Grady, Lovett, Cleave, Dias Santos, Fall, Hunt," and "Rotunda list made by Dias Santos, Grady and Fall."[57]

The Reform Act was passed in 1832 by the House of Commons but defeated by a Tory majority in the House of Lords, provoking riots across the country, worst of all in Bristol. Grey persuaded King William IV to create some new Whig peers, and used this as a threat to the Tories, but in the end this was not necessary and the bill was passed.[58] It was known thereafter as The Great Reform Act, and support for organizations such as the NUWC and NPU fell away somewhat.[59]

While the Act did not propose universal suffrage, it changed representation in the so-called Rotten Boroughs, where the ratio of Members of Parliament to voters was grossly disproportionate, and in areas such as Manchester, which had expanded in the Industrial Revolution and had no representation. One hundred thirty-five new seats were created in all[60] and representation was given to the newly industrialized cities of Birmingham, Manchester, Leeds, Sheffield and new London Metropolitan districts.

The act also changed the entitlement to vote. The franchise was extended and standardized for men in the counties who were 40 shilling freeholders, £10 copyholders, holders of long-term leases over 60 years on land worth at least £10, and holders of leases of 20 to 60 years worth at least £50. The right to vote was also extended to tenants paying at least £50. This was an additional clause added to the bill and named The Chandos clause after the Tory Marquis of Chandos who introduced it. Freeholders in the boroughs were allowed to vote in the counties if they owned a freehold worth between 40 shillings and £10, or over £10 if occupied by a tenant.[61]

It is estimated that the Act increased the franchise from around 400,000 men to 650,000, but the majority of the population was still unable to vote and corruption was still widespread. In drafting the Reform Bill, Grey commented, "To cramp reform by pedantic adherence to existing rights would be to deceive expectation and bring on that revolution which is our object to

avert."[62] Grey believed, "The plan of reform ought to be of such scope and description as to satisfy all reasonable demands and remove all rational ground of complaint from the minds of the intelligent and independent portion of the community."[63] In effect, Grey and his government was ensuring that by giving the franchise to the new middle classes they would no longer side with the working classes, as the radical groups had done, and mass insurrection would be averted.

Unfortunately this was not to be. Taxes and the national debt were rising, and with little reform in the banking sector, about 63 banks crashed between 1836 and 1838. The crisis was fuelled by Britain having invested in America and President Jackson's refusal to re-charter the Bank of the United States.[64] In Britain, food prices continued to rise but wages fell, and there was no guarantee of employment. The gap between the rich and the poor widened and there was outrage that the 1832 Reform Act meant that the working classes would continue to be unrepresented by Parliament.

In 1838, a group who were to become known as the Chartists compiled a *People's Charter* based on six principles which had been agreed the previous year at the British Coffee House in London. The Charter's six principles included: the vote for every man aged 21 and over, and of sound mind and not a prisoner (eventually granted in 1918 and 1928[65]); a secret ballot (granted in 1872[66]); no property qualification for MPs (granted 1858[67]); MPs to be paid (granted 1911[68]); constituencies to represent an equal number of electors

Opposite: The House of Commons, *1833, by Sir George Hayter, oil on canvas, 1833–1843; NPG 54; National Portrait Gallery, London. Notes from the National Portrait Gallery catalog include the following: "This picture commemorates the passing of the Great Reform Act in 1832. It depicts the first session of the new House of Commons on 5 February 1833 held in St. Stephen's Chapel which was destroyed by fire in 1834. The largely Whig campaign for electoral reform had begun in the mid-eighteenth century and by 1832 it had proved unstoppable, following widespread agitation and economic distress. The Reform Act extended the vote to a larger number of men according to their rate-paying or property ownership. It also redistributed representation more fairly and new boroughs were created so that some new industrial centres had MPs for the first time. The picture includes some 375 figures and although Hayter abandoned the idea of depicting all 658 Members of the reformed Commons he maintained the relative proportions of the parties. In the foreground, he has grouped the leading statesmen from the Lords; [Charles] Grey (1764–1845), [William Lamb, Lord] Melbourne (1779–1848) and the Whigs on the left and [Arthur Wellesley, 1st Duke of] Wellington (1769–1852) and the Tories on the right. Painted without a commission it took Hayter ten years to complete and another fifteen to sell. Paradoxically, it was the Tories who finally agreed to purchase it, in 1858, for the recently founded National Portrait Gallery."*

Sir Francis Burdett is seen at the front of the painting, in the middle, the fourth on the left standing to the left of the gap; his collar is obscuring his chin. Joseph Hume is seated to the right of the painting, the second row down, the eleventh seated to the left, directly in front of the third pole. Daniel O'Connell is seated on the front row to the right of the painting, leaning forward. Sir Robert Peel is seated eight to the left of O'Connell, on the front row; he is wearing a beige waistcoat and has his legs crossed.

(granted 1884 and subsequent years[69]); and annual parliaments. The latter have never been put into practice. These were agreed by Daniel O'Connell, M.P., John Arthur Roebuck, M.P., John Temple Leader, M.P., Charles Hindley, M.P., Thomas Perronet Thompson, M.P., William Sharman Crawford, M.P., Henry Hetherington, John Cleave, James Watson, Richard Moore, William Lovett and Henry Vincent.[70] The signatories of the Charter very much represented the old radical views. One of these was William Lovett, who was Secretary of the London Working Men's Association, which he had helped to set up two years before and circulated the very popular *Poor Man's Guardian*. There is a view that the demands of the Chartists were too great, and like the Anti-Corn Law League, they should have focused on one aim at a time.[71]

The first Chartist Convention was held in 1839, and while members were careful not to break the law, there was certainly an element within the membership which advocated violence, particularly in the north of England. The Chartists were not as well organized as the Anti-Corn Law League, disagreement was rife and there was little support in Parliament for a movement which was perceived as working class. When O'Connell felt that progress would be slow in London, protests moved to Birmingham, but here riots broke out and when Lovett showed his support for the protesters, he was arrested. The focus returned to London, but between 1839 and 1840, over 500 Chartists were arrested, and many of the leading figures were imprisoned, including Lovett.[72]

A notice distributed in 1839 "To the People of Lambeth" by the Lambeth Political Union called the electoral system "a fraud and a mockery." The notice was signed by the Secretary, George Huggett, and continued, "every male person of full age, sane mind, and unconvicted of crime, ought to have a vote in the election of representatives in the House of Commons," and set out aims very similar to those agreed in the British Coffee House. The notice informed Lambeth residents that a public meeting would soon be called, but that the Council met every Thursday evening at 8.00 P.M. at the White Hart Inn, Kennington Cross.[73]

In 1839, supported by Benjamin Disraeli, the Commons voted to consider the Chartist petition, but the motion was defeated. Subsequently the Convention voted for a general strike, a *Sacred Month*, but this was defeated by its own members.[74] Conditions were simply not right for workers in the industrial areas to strike. Determined to continue the struggle, in November five thousand men led by John Frost, Zephaniah Williams and William Jones marched to Newport, in Wales, to release by force some supporters who were imprisoned in the local jail. Knowing of their intentions, the authorities were ready for the crowd and troops fired on them. Twenty-four of the marchers were killed, 125 were arrested and 21 of these were charged with high treason; the ringleaders were transported.

The struggle continued into the 1840s, and with Lovett's release from jail at the start of the decade, plans were made for another petition and another Convention. With over three million signatures on the petition this time, it was again overwhelmingly rejected by Parliament.[75] The petition also included complaints about lack of liberty, the police, the Poor Law, factory conditions and church taxes for nonconformists. The rejection caused uproar and it was decided in 1842, though it is not certain by whom, to call a series of strikes in Lancashire. These strikes became known as the Plug Plots, as striking workers pulled the plugs from the boilers holding water to drive the steam engines. The Duke of Wellington sent the troops in once again, and of the 1,500 or so activists arrested, 79 were found guilty and transported.[76] Unrest spread to Staffordshire, Yorkshire, Cheshire, Scotland and Wales, but the action was unsustainable and by the end of 1842 trade and pay increased following a good harvest.[77]

The Chartist movement began to fracture after 1842 as the different leaders and the various areas involved all had different, though equally important, aspects of the cause to fight for. Prime Minister Sir Robert Peel firmly believed that the answer to the social problems of the day was strong fiscal policy, and while the government looked at ways to improve working and social conditions, which placated the Chartist movement to some degree, the measures did little to ease conditions in the south, particularly in Lambeth.

From 1802 various acts were passed by Parliament as follows. The 1802 Health and Moral Apprentices Act was concerned with the working conditions of children in the cotton and wool mills. It advocated the ventilation and lime-washing of factory rooms twice a year, the supply of two outfits of clothing to children, and that children between the ages of nine and 13 years should work a maximum of eight hours; those between 14 and 18, 12 hours. Children under nine would not be allowed to work and had to go to schools provided by the factory owners; on Sundays there should be an hour's religious (Christian) teaching. Children's working hours would be 6 A.M. to 9 P.M. and not exceed 12 hours per day, and they should be instructed in reading, writing and arithmetic for the first four years of work. Male and female children were to sleep in different quarters with no more than two to a bed, and owners were to tend infectious diseases. While fines of £2 to £5 were the penalty for ignoring the new rules, these were rarely imposed and the new rules were not enforced. Further acts in 1819 and 1831 addressed child labor and the practice of night shifts.

The Factory Act of 1833, influenced by the investigative work of Sir Edwin Chadwick,[78] repeated and underlined much of what had been in the

1802 act as follows. Children aged 14 to 18 should not work more than 12 hours a day, and children aged nine to 13 should not work more than eight hours a day and have two hours of education; both age groups should have an hour for lunch. This Act stopped the employment of children under the age of nine in the textile industry and stopped night shifts for the under–18s. The most important aspect of the Act was the appointment of inspectors to make routine inspections of the factories.

The Factory Act of 1844 went further still, reducing the number of working hours for children aged nine to 13 to six, and extending conditions to women. Women were now no longer allowed to work for more than 12 hours a day during the week, nine hours on Sundays and were to have an hour-and-a-half for meals. Owners were to lime-wash walls every 14 months and surgeons (doctors) were to be employed to verify women's ages and to report on accidental deaths. The Act also demanded that records showing the enforcement of all these provisions be kept and machinery fenced in.

An additional Factory Act was passed in 1847, the so-called Ten Hour Bill, which again applied to textile mills and to women and child workers under 18 years of age, whose hours were limited by the bill to roughly ten hours a day.[79]

Many of the requirements contained in these Acts were restricted to the factories in the north of England, and it was not until much later in the century that the dangerous and unhealthy practices of factories such as those in Lambeth were finally eradicated.

The Public Health Act of 1848 was also a step forward in establishing the need to improve the living conditions of the working population. Campaigners for social reform were well aware that the ills of the working classes were caused in the most part by their living conditions. Sir Edwin Chadwick was one such reformer and, in 1832, Chadwick was appointed by the Royal Commission to investigate the workings of the Poor Laws, and in 1834 was appointed Secretary to the Poor Law Commissioners. His 1842 *Report on the Sanitary Condition of the Labouring Population of Great Britain* was the basis of the 1848 Act (see Chapter 2). The principles of the Act were to improve public health and to encourage the state and local authorities to take greater responsibility for public health. Following the passing of the Act, a Central Board of Health and regional boards (where the death rate was over 23 per 1,000) were established and responsibility for sanitation, water and *nuisances* (in Lambeth many of these were dung and dust heaps) was given to local authorities. The difficulties with the Act were that responsibility was still optional and London was not included. In addition, there was little money available for the setting up of the Boards and no Minister was appointed in Parliament to oversee matters.[80]

The Great Chartist meeting on Kennington Common, April 10, 1848; photograph by William Kilburn. The Royal Collection © 2009 Her Majesty Queen Elizabeth II.

In Lambeth, a Central Sanitary Commission and Sanitary Sub Committees were set up. There was genuine concern that cholera would return to the area, but the cleaning of the tenements and streets of Lambeth, and the provision of proper sanitation, would have been a vast undertaking and hugely expensive. It is little wonder that nothing very much was done before cholera broke out again in the summer of 1848.

That same year, on April 10, the last Chartist rally was held at Kennington Common in Lambeth. The rally was peaceful and it was intended that protestors would march from the common to the Houses of Parliament on the other side of the river to present another petition. Posters advertising the rally were headed, "Peace and Order is our motto!" The posters were addressed to "the working men of London" and read: "The Demonstration Committee ... consider it to be their duty to state that the grievances of us (the Working Classes) are deep and our demands just. We and our families are pining in misery, want and starvation! We demand a fair day's wages for a fair day's work! We are the slaves of capital — we demand protection to our labour. We are political serfs — we demand to be free ... it is for the good of all that we seek to remove the evils under which we groan."[81]

The Chartists decided that if this were rejected they would form a National Assembly and demand that Queen Victoria dissolve Parliament. Interestingly the Queen's signature appeared on the petition, but it had been faked, as had that of Sir Robert Peel. The government tried to ban the gathering and the Duke of Wellington organized the swearing in of 150,000 special constables, with the army on standby. Despite the ban, the meeting went ahead, just a few months before the first cholera cases began to appear in Lambeth. Estimates of the crowd size varied from 12,000 to 750,000, but the meeting was washed out by rain and the petition was taken to Parliament in a London cab. Chartism had had its day.

The radical societies and organizations like the Anti-Corn Law League and the Chartists planted a seed in the national consciousness. While some of their actions were extreme, they highlighted a need for political and social reform. Moreover, their struggle for rights and suffrage for all paved the way for a Socialist movement which would become an integral part of British politics.[82]

2

Public Health:
Common Diseases and Cholera

By the end of the eighteenth century, death rates in England and Wales fell. However, as rural workers began to move to the newly industrialized towns and centers, such as Lambeth, death rates in urban areas began to rise, and by the beginning of the nineteenth century, they were significantly higher than in the countryside.[1]

The death rate in urban areas rose because the living conditions for the working population were conducive to the spread of disease. In Lambeth, houses built on the low-lying marshy swampland were damp and poorly ventilated, packed tightly together. While there was some running water supplied by hand pumps in the streets away from the waterfront, the supply was sporadic. In the waterfront streets there was no water supply at all, and throughout the entire area there was no adequate system for the disposal of sewage or industrial and domestic waste products.

The situation in Lambeth was mirrored in other factory towns and urban areas in Britain. In Church Lane in the St. Giles area of London, in 1841 27 houses, averaging five rooms each, had housed 655, by 1847 this had risen to 1,095, an increase per house of about 24 to 40 people.[2] Workers paid dearly for living in such conditions. Rents in urban areas were higher than in the countryside and a study in Leeds by W.R. Rimmer showed that by the 1830s workers spent 10 to 20 percent of their wages on rent.[3] By 1842, when Sir Edwin Chadwick published his report into Britain's sanitary conditions, the situation had not changed.[4]

Tuberculosis was more prevalent in urban environments as it thrives best in the undernourished and in damp, unventilated living conditions. The disease was not widely understood in the nineteenth century and accepted as part of life, and in London deaths from tuberculosis peaked in the period from 1780 to 1830.[5]

In the countryside, the diseases which flourished in damp, dirty, overcrowded conditions were not so prevalent, but disease existed nonetheless. Cholera, diphtheria, dysentery, malaria, measles, scarlet fever, smallpox, syphilis, tuberculosis (also known as consumption or phthisis), typhoid fever, typhus, and whooping cough (also known as pertussis) all kept the population in check. However, in an age before antibiotics, streptococcal infections such as erysipelas ("A specific, acute inflammatory disease [of the dermis] caused by haemolytic streptococcus")[6] were also killers, as were infections caused by cuts, both accidental or from medical intervention, and those incurred in childbirth. Such was the ignorance of infectious disease at this time, a surgeon at St. Bartholomew's Hospital Medical School in London noted in his post mortem notes for December 1851 that his subject, Anne Davis, aged 40, had died of "debauchery."[7]

The statistician William Farr (1807–1883), the first Compiler of Abstracts for the General Register Office,[8] compiled statistics to compare the health of the population. In his *Report on the Mortality of Cholera in England 1848–49,* he compiled a considerable number of statistics to compare mortality. His figures for the weekly average deaths from 1844 to 1848 show that in London, the biggest killers were infectious diseases. The diseases causing the highest numbers of deaths (apart from cholera and diarrhea) were scarlatina, typhus, measles, whooping cough and smallpox. Additional causes of death in this period in London were tuberculosis, pneumonia and convulsions.

In his *First Annual Report of the Registrar-General* in 1839, Farr wrote of the City of London, "134 persons die daily in London: that the great majority are untimely deaths — children, fathers, mothers, in the prime of life; and that at least 38 die daily in excess of the rate of mortality which actually prevails in the immediate neighborhood. 38 persons are destroyed every day in London by local causes."[9] Farr compiled statistics for life expectancy. In his *Fifth Annual Report of the Registrar-General,* he published figures on the mortality of England and Wales for the year 1841, which covered males of "various classes engaged in various occupations." His figures showed that only 41.26 percent of the population could expect to live to the age of 18, and just over half of these (20.68 percent) could expect to live to the age of 49.[10]

By the writing of his *Tenth Annual Report* in 1847, Farr was firmly of the opinion that the only way forward to improve public health was parliamentary reform: "This disease-mist, arising from the breath of two millions of people.... Like an angel of death, it has hovered for centuries over London. But it may be driven away by legislation."[11]

Disease, most often culminating in death, was a constant in the life of everyone, rich or poor, but especially the latter. As yet there was no cure for any of the major diseases of the day, though a vaccine had been introduced for smallpox. For many, however, insufficient funds and lack of access to healthcare meant that they continued to die from smallpox. Such was the case of Lucy Osmotherly in Lambeth, whose death certificate records: "14th December 1848 at 11 Princes Street [Lambeth]. Lucy Charlotte Osmotherley. Female. 2 years and 11 months. Daughter of James Osmotherley, coal porter. Variola [smallpox] 2 weeks. Had not been vaccinated, certified."[12]

A popular insight into the suffering of the poor in Victorian England is the work of Charles Dickens (1812–1870). While Dickens was not the greatest supporter of sanitary reform, he openly criticized the new Poor Law in his descriptions of the workhouse, conditions in factories, and the lack of education for the poor. Dickens' novels were based in large part on real places and people, mainly in London and the Medway Towns in Kent. In the opening to *Great Expectations* (written from 1860 to 1861) Dickens described the rural graveyard, where the protagonist, Pip, contemplated the untimely deaths of his parents and siblings. According to local Medway historian Allan Cherry,[13] Dickens is almost certainly describing the 13 lozenge tombs in St. James' churchyard in the village of Cooling: "As I never saw my father or my mother ... my first fancies regarding what they were like, were unreasonably derived from their tombstones ... five little stone lozenges, each about a foot and a half long, which were arranged in a neat row beside their grave, and were sacred to the memory of five little brothers of mine — who gave up trying to get a living, exceedingly early in that universal struggle...."[14]

Cooling is situated next to Cliffe, on the northern edge of the Hoo Peninsula, jutting out into the Thames Estuary. Ten of these tombs belong to the Comport children and three to the Baker children, both well-known families in the area and none of whom lived for longer than five months in the late 1700s. According to Cherry, these children almost certainly died of malaria or "marsh fever," a killer in the Kent and Essex marshlands surrounding the Thames Estuary until the area was drained. Much of this in the Cliffe area was done by the farmer Henry Pye who came to the peninsula in the mid 1800s; the subsequent draining greatly increased the area of grazing farmland and helped to eradicate the fever.

Malaria had been common in Britain's marshland communities from the 1500s. Changes in living conditions, such as less overcrowding, and a trend to build houses with upstairs sleeping areas, meant that people slept away from the cattle and horses which mosquitoes are attracted to. The drainage of marshland meant that by the 1800s, malaria was in decline, moreover, quinine, widely considered to be an effective anti-malarial medicine, was also easier and cheaper to obtain. Other areas affected included the Fens, the Somerset Levels, the Severn Estuary and the Holderness of Yorkshire.[15]

In an article for Kent Archaeology, entitled *Cholera and Typhoid Fever in Kent*, Dr. Christopher Collins discussed the progression of waterborne diseases such as cholera and typhoid fever to the communities along the shores of the Thames Estuary. Not only did these communities receive effluent from the metropolis upstream, but they were also susceptible to discharge from boats and ships sailing in the river, from London and overseas. Collins noted that epidemics often originated in ports. At the port of Sheerness, situated on the Thames Estuary's Isle of Sheppey, yellow fever and the plague made early appearances in Britain's history.[16]

The first cholera pandemic erupted in India in 1817, but it is no coincidence that cholera did not spread to Europe until the 1820s, when travel became faster, more frequent and more common. The bacteria *Vibrio cholerae*, the causative organism of cholera, can survive for long periods in an estuarine environment, perhaps years. In a marine or estuarine environment, *Vibrio cholerae* "can be found as free swimming cells, attached to surfaces provided by plants, filamentous green algae, copepods, crustaceans, insects, and egg masses of chironomids [including midges and gnats]."[17] While it can travel distances in water, there is no evidence as yet that it can traverse whole oceans by itself or by its association with phytoplankton and zooplankton. The rapid spread of cholera by land was by human contact and through the pollution of estuarine environments by contaminated human waste; by sea, cholera was transported in the holds and bilges of boats and ships.

The first epidemic arrived in Britain at the northern port of Gateshead in 1831. By February 1832, cholera had reached London,[18] and by the end of the year the disease had claimed over 26,000 victims, an estimated 7,000 of which were in London.[19] From August 1 to September 7, 1833, a further outbreak in London claimed the lives of an additional 1,454.[20]

The arrival of cholera in Britain provoked great fear, not least because

A London Board of Health hunting for cholera, 1832. Wellcome Library, London.

the disease can kill with tremendous speed, and at a time when it was not understood how the pathogen was transmitted. The way in which it appeared to strike at random in predominantly poor areas caused tremendous anxiety.

In February 1832, the government introduced a Cholera Bill, "for the prevention, as far as may be possible, of the disease called the cholera, in England." The bill authorized "any three members of the Privy Council, of whom one must be a senior minister, to make orders for the prevention of contagion, the relief of the sick and the burial of the dead, and anyone violating these orders could be fined from one to five pounds."[21] These orders were sent to local Boards of Health and were to be financed from the parish poor rate, repaid subsequently by the county treasurer.[22]

The fear of cholera in the nineteenth century came about out of ignorance, indeed there were various theories as to how cholera spread:

animacular/miasmic-microscopic agents transported on the wind and
in bad odors;
fungoid — fungi in food and water;
telluric — poison exhaled by the earth;
electric — static electricity;
organic — lack of ozone.[23]

In 1848 and 1849 in London, the areas south of the river, and in particular Lambeth, were the worst affected. The population of these areas used water which had come directly from the River Thames. The waterfront area did not have water pumps, and residents took their water directly from the river by bucket. The areas which had a pumped water supply were no better off as the water companies derived their supply from the same source. The Thames and its tributaries, like the Effra at Lambeth, were open sewers and an ideal breeding ground for the *Vibrio cholerae* bacteria which cause cholera.

In 1855, Dr. Arthur Hill Hassall, working with Dr. John Snow (see Chapter 8) in their investigations on the causes of cholera, took some samples of Thames water for analysis. The quality of the water in the Thames differed little at this time to how it would have been in the 1840s. Hassall took samples from the river at the point where the Southwark and Vauxhall Water Company drew their supply, at the southern tip of Lambeth. The quality of this water would have been similar to that formerly used by the Lambeth Waterworks and to that taken by bucket by the waterfront residents. The water "reveal[ed] to the microscope not only swarms of infusorial life, but particles of undigested food referable to the discharge from human bowels ... cisterns supplied by the Southwark and Vauxhall Company were 'demonstrably contaminated with faecal matter.'"[24]

In 1852, and as discussed in Chapter 8, the Lambeth Waterworks moved to Thames Ditton and began taking their supply from an area of the river which was less brackish, and less polluted, though still not ideal: "Dr Hassall found 'organic productions dead and living, animal and vegetable in not inconsiderable numbers,' while a chemical analysis of it betrayed ... 'traces of nitric acid, enough ammonia to indicate an intermixture of sewage, and such proportions of organic matter as ought not to be insignificant to an educated community.'"[25]

Drs. Hassall and Snow were not able to determine if cholera bacteria were present in either sample. However, the more polluted water from the Southwark and Vauxhall Water Company would have been more favorable for sustaining the pathogen.

Cholera bacteria enter the human digestive system through the mouth. Bacteria may come from raw or cooked foods which have been washed or contaminated by tainted water (in fact cholera bacteria thrive more readily on cooked food where there is little competition from other bacteria which have been killed off by the cooking process), shellfish from the river, contaminated drinking water, or from unwashed hands. The bacteria can also be spread from surface to surface by rats, mice, flies and other flying insects. Research has shown that some people are more susceptible to cholera than others, and differences, such as blood group, play a part: those with blood group O are more susceptible.[26]

Cholera is most dangerous to those with a weakened immune system, and to pregnant women. In addition, the bacterium is sensitive to an acidic environment, so those with a low level of stomach acid are more prone to infection: high alcohol consumption and malnourishment both contribute to the under production of gastric acid. Lambeth's malnourished poor who supplemented their diet with alcohol were therefore extremely susceptible.

Reports vary, but the incubation period of *Vibrio cholerae* once ingested can be anything from a few hours to a few days and in a normal healthy individual the number of bacteria ingested to cause problems needs to be considerable (about 10^8 to 10^{10}).[27] *Vibrio cholerae* bacteria are rod shaped and have a single polar flagellum, and while their autochthonous environment is estuarine, they can grow anaerobically.[28]

Vibrio cholerae infect the jejunum and ileum in the small intestine, where there is little competition from other bacteria. This is also an alkaline environment due to the presence of bile salts. The bacteria have a single flagellum, or tail, which enable them to move more easily, and fine hair-like structures called *pili* on their bodies.[30] It is the pili which play a major part in the colonization process of the *Vibrio cholerae*. The pili allow the bacteria to adhere themselves to the microvilli in the lining of the intestine where they are able to multiply and secrete cholera toxin, a potent enterotoxin.[31] The cholera enterotoxin is a protein which is toxic to the cells of the intestinal wall and creates the formation of pores in the membranes of the intestinal cells. The cells die, breaking down the barrier between the lumen, or lining of the intestine, and the tissue which surrounds it.[32] This causes leakage of the interstitial fluid, the "hypersecretion of chloride and bicarbonate followed

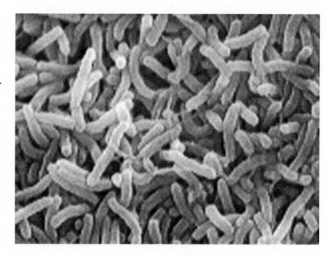

Scanning electron microscope image of Vibrio cholerae *bacteria (Dartmouth Electron Microscope Facility, Dartmouth College 29; Wikimedia Commons).*

by water, resulting in the characteristic isotonic voluminous stool."[33]

Research in 1996 by Matthew K. Waldor and John J. Mekalanos in the United States revealed that the process by which the cholera bacterium is infected by this virus is complex, but Waldor and Mekalanos showed that "the emergence of toxigenic *V. cholerae* involves horizontal gene transfer that may depend on in vivo gene expression."[34] In other words, it is the process of infection which can activate the pathogenic virus. Recent research has also shown that "the pilus is also of viral origin and therefore can be acquired from another [bacterio] phage infection. Thus a virulent cholera pathogen can be born from a totally avirulent strain."[35]

The stools of cholera patients resemble the white cloudy water which results from boiling rice as it contains particles of mucus and epithelial cells from the intestine lining. This excreted fluid, which spreads infection, can contain 108 viable vibrios per milliliter. As the secretion of chloride and bicarbonate increases, the cholera toxin inhibits the absorption of water and electrolytes, or salts, into the blood and rapid dehydration occurs.[36] Painless diarrhea is at first accompanied by violent vomiting. Vomiting precedes the dehydration phase and appears to be a direct result of the infection of the intestine by the bacteria.[37] The dehydration of cholera victims is caused by fluid being literally pumped through the intestinal cells from the blood and tissues.[38] In severe cases of cholera, "patients can purge a volume of stool in excess of their body weight in the course of the disease,"[39] around 10 to 12 liters of fluid a day.[40]

Severe dehydration is a characteristic of cholera and this manifests itself with an increase in pulse rate but a decrease in pulse volume, hypotension, an increase in the respiratory rate, severe thirst, a decrease in urine, and sunken wrinkled skin.[41] Plasma in the blood and interstitial fluid communicate freely and, as dehydration continues,[42] so the blood thickens and is unable to circulate properly around the body, depriving the organs of oxygen. It is this process which causes the characteristic blue color of the victims' skin, and in many cases cardiac arrest will also occur.

The bacterium *Vibrio cholerae* is endemic to the mouth of the River Ganges in India.[43] The first incidences of cholera in humans no doubt occurred before written documentation began, but there are accounts of a disease resembling cholera in ancient Sanskrit, Chinese and Greek texts, and it was reported by the Portuguese who visited India in the sixteenth century.[44]

The arrival of cholera on Britain's shores coincided with the Industrial Revolution, mechanization and the subsequent explosion in Britain's international trade. Refinements in the design of ships, including the development of steam power, diminished sailing times at sea and on rivers, and while this

The illustration shows the transformation of the appearance of a cholera victim and the characteristic color and sagging of the skin caused by severe dehydration. The annotation reads, "Giovane Viennese di 23 Anni. La med[esim]a un'ora appresso l'invasione del Cholera, e quattr'ore prima della morte." (A young woman of Vienna, aged 23 years. The same woman one hour after the onset of cholera, and four hours before death.) Wellcome Library, London.

enhanced trade, it also boosted travel and migration. Cholera was without doubt brought to Britain by sea, and the waters of the ports of Britain, such as Gateshead, Liverpool, Bristol and London, were an ideal environment for *Vibrio cholerae*, "an autochthonous inhabitant of brackish water and estuarine systems,"[45] whose "survival is enhanced in saline waters."[46]

Studies have shown that *Vibrio cholerae* is able to survive in aquatic and estuarine environments for long periods, probably years: "*V. cholerae* cells do not necessarily die when discharged into aquatic environments but instead remain viable and are capable of transforming into a culturable state if environmental conditions again become favourable."[47] Therefore, *Vibrio cholerae* could have easily survived in the bilges of ocean-going vessels, and was not solely transmitted from place to place by humans. The practice of emptying the bilges on arrival at port would, in many cases, have released the bacteria directly into an estuarine environment.

It is likely that *Vibrio cholerae* was transmitted across the globe from India by land and by sea aided by human migration. In his *Report on the Mortality of Cholera in England 1848–49,* the British epidemiologist and statistician William Farr (1807–1883) was convinced that cholera was spread by the wind. While he was wrong in thinking bad smells or *miasma* transmitted the disease, his theory contained an element of truth, as *Vibrio cholerae* crossed the oceans in ships with the wind in their sails.

Vibrio cholerae is the "type species of the genus *Vibrio*, which is the type genus of the family *Vibrionaceae*."[48] There are at least 139 serotypes for *Vibrio cholerae*. "The organism is classified by biochemical tests and is further subdivided into serogroups based on the somatic O antigen. The O antigen shows enormous serological diversity, with over 200 serogroups. Only the O1 and O139 serogroups cause epidemic and pandemic disease. Strains identified by biochemical tests as *V. cholerae* that do not agglutinate with O1 or O139 antisera are referred to as non-O1 non-O139 *V. cholerae*."[49]

In 1848 to 1849, the two strains of *Vibrio cholerae* which would have caused problems for the human population were *Vibrio cholerae* O1, which possesses the antigen O1, the enterotoxin described above, known as CT+[50], and a non-O1 strain which may still induce diarrhoea.[51] Up until recently it was thought that the "only reservoir of toxigenic *V. cholerae* O1 ... was the human intestine."[52] And, indeed, work by Waldor and Mekalanos does suggest that it is the infection process in the human gut which causes the activation of the pathogenic virus. However, the scientists Citarella and Colwell[53] made the discovery that the O1 and non-O1 strains are in fact a single species, and may live in a shared *aquatic* environment. This could account for the varying symptoms observed in London and Lambeth during the early stages of the 1848 outbreak, where cholera raged alongside severe diarrhea. It could also account for the seemingly random appearance of the disease. In 1848, observers noted that cases of cholera occurred among people living in the same area. It was presumed that these victims must have had some contact, when, in fact, they had merely been contaminated by a similarly-tainted water source. However, other cases which appeared in the capital did not appear to have been associated with these victims, or indeed with the same water source.

Dr. Edmund Parkes (1819–1876) observed and documented the early stages of the 1848–49 cholera epidemic and noticed some anomalies which he could not reconcile: "With regard to the generation of the poison [cholera] there is no doubt that in Horsleydown [Southwark, next to Lambeth], as well as Lambeth, Chelsea, and in many parts of London, some of those circumstances which we have termed 'local conditions of existence' existed in considerable intensity, and yet the cholera-poison did not develop itself in any commensurate degree. Was there not some essential condition wanting, whose deficiency prevented or nullified the effect which the other conditions would have had if conjoined with it? And if so, what was this condition?"[54]

It has always been thought that some areas of London were affected worse than others because of contaminated water supplies, and as discussed by Dr. John Snow (1813–1858) in his 1854 work, *On the Mode of Communication of Cholera* (see Chapter 8). This was indeed the case, however, it would appear from recent scientific research that there was, as Parkes rightly guessed, another factor at work. As discussed above, it has now been shown that strains of *Vibrio cholerae* can exist side-by-side, and it is likely that this is what was happening in the River Thames in 1848. Research has shown that the production of the pathogenic toxin CT+ on *Vibrio cholerae* is triggered by key influences: salinity, temperature and its association with phytoplanktons, or algae. Work by Tamplin and Colwell[55] "demonstrated that toxin production in microcosm cultures was related to salinity, demonstrating a salinity optimum between 2.0 and 2.5% for toxin production that was independent of cell concentration and toxin stability. A study reported by Miller et al[56] showed that cells do not lose enterotoxigenicity after long-term exposure (64 days) in microcosms under a variety of conditions, nor did a selection for either hyper- or hypotoxigenic mutants occur. However there is increased toxin production by toxigenic *V. cholerae* O1 when the organism is associated with *Rhizoclonium fontanum*, a green alga commonly found in natural water."[57]

This research was further observed by work at the Department of Tropical Hygiene at the London School of Hygiene and Tropical Medicine: "In the aquatic environment, the physiological state of *Vibrio cholerae* can be affected by various environmental conditions (e.g., sunlight, pH, temperature, competition with other bacteria for nutrients, etc.). The effect of these factors on the toxigenicity of *V. cholerae* was investigated. Toxin production by 5 toxigenic strains of *V. cholerae* incubated in laboratory microcosms containing *Rhizoclonium fontanum* was tested at different time intervals. The microcosms were exposed to sunlight, and the *V. cholerae* were in competition for nutrients with the resident bacterial flora of *R. fontanum*. Results of the study demonstrated an increase in toxin production by V. cholerae O1 during survival with *R. fontanum*."[58]

Recent work has also demonstrated that industrial effluent has a positive effect on the growth of certain algae. Samples taken by Dr. Arthur Hill Hassall , and as discussed above, revealed "swarms of infusorial life,"[59] and work undertaken in the last thirty years investigating modern outbreaks of cholera show that the condition of the water in the River Thames at Lambeth was probably perfect to produce the deadliest strain of *Vibrio cholerae*.

An article in 2000 by Tim Stephens for *Science Daily* reported the following:

> New research shows that a common type of marine algae may prefer urea, an organic nitrogen compound found in urine and agricultural and urban runoff, over inorganic fare such as ammonium and nitrate that occurs naturally in the ocean ... single-celled organisms, called dinoflagellates, can grow into potentially toxic blankets of algae commonly known as red tides. The new findings [are] published in the current issue of Aquatic Microbial Ecology ... research shows that urea represents an average of one-third of the total nitrogen uptake supporting growth of phytoplankton in regions where red tides can occur.... In some estuarine areas, such as Chesapeake Bay, urea can represent 60 percent of the nitrogen uptake at certain times of the year. Phytoplankton serve as the base of the marine food web, but unusually high levels of nutrients together with abundant sunlight can spur rapid growth, or blooms, of these single celled plants.[60]

Research published in the medical journal *The Lancet*, in 2004, showed that "*V. cholerae* can activate or inactivate a set of genes including those encoding colonization factors or toxins as an appropriate response."[61] The same article explains how pathogenic strains of *Vibrio cholerae* evolve in the environment:

> At the molecular level, the pathogenesis of cholera is a multifactorial process and involves several genes encoding virulence factors that aid the pathogen in its colonization, coordinated expression of virulence factors, and toxin action. In *V. cholerae*, the major virulence genes required for pathogenesis are in clusters and can apparently propagate laterally and disperse among different strains. Genetic analyses have revealed the presence of two important genetic elements that distinguish a pathogenic *V. cholerae* from an innocuous one. These are the previously called CTX [cholera toxin] genetic element, which is the genome of a lysogenic bacteriophage designated CTX Φ that carries the genes encoding cholera toxin, and the vibrio pathogenicity island

(VPI), which carries genes for the pilus colonization factor TCP [toxin coregulated pilus].[62]

The first step in the pathogenic evolution is the acquiring of the vibrio pathogenicity island (VPI), which most environmental strains of *Vibrio cholerae* do not have. Once the CTX Φ receptor has been acquired, the toxin coregulated pilus-positive strains can be infected by the virus, CTX Φ. "Experiments in animals have shown that the intestinal milieu is the site where strains can acquire these mobile elements efficiently. Thus, *V. cholerae* can be visualized as an autochthonous marine bacterium that colonizes and thrives in the human gut during phases of infection and spends the time between epidemics in its *original* habitat, the estuary."[63]

Further work by K. Eric Wommack and Rita R. Colwell shows how the environment of the *Vibrio cholerae* is important to this process:

> Viruses may be the most abundant organisms in natural waters, surpassing the number of bacteria by an order of magnitude ... enumeration of viruses in aquatic environments has demonstrated that the virioplankton are dynamic components of the plankton, changing dramatically in number with geographical location and season. The evidence to date suggests that virioplankton communities are composed principally of bacteriophages and, to a lesser extent, eukaryotic algal viruses. The influence of viral infection and lyses on bacterial and phytoplankton host communities was measurable after new methods were developed and prior knowledge of bacteriophage biology was incorporated into concepts of parasite and host community interactions. The new methods have yielded data showing that viral infection can have a significant impact on bacteria and unicellular algae populations and supporting the hypothesis that viruses play a significant role in microbial food webs. Besides predation limiting bacteria and phytoplankton populations, the specific nature of virus-host interaction raises the intriguing possibility that viral infection influences the structure and diversity of aquatic microbial communities.[64]

A report by the World Health Organization in 2002 supports the importance of the marine environment: "Chitinases and mucinases facilitate the attachment of *V. cholerae* to aquatic organisms, while algae surface films enhance the growth of the pathogen (Epstein, Ford and Colwell, 1993).... It has been suggested that *V. cholerae* can survive an inter-epidemic period and colonize the surfaces of algae, phytoplankton and water hyacinth (Islam, Alam and Neogi, 1992). In an epidemic area like the Ganges river delta, copepods favor survival of *V. cholerae* because of the organism's production of chitinase and ability to use chitin as a source of nutrients (Nalin, 1976)."[65]

At Lambeth, had there been huge blooms of brightly colored algae on the surface of the river, this would most certainly have been noted. However, there is considerable evidence that algae was on the surface and in abundance, in the form of a brown and greenish sludge. William Farr talks of the Thames giving off "vapours night and day,"[66] which may have had more to do with his conviction that cholera was spread spore-like within evaporating vapors, rather than an observation of algae photosynthesizing. However, he did note, when conducting experiments in the river, the instruments pulled from the water were covered with "a slimy adhesive mud."[67]

Other sources give further clues to the presence of algae. In Charles Dickens' novel, *Our Mutual Friend* (1864–65), the author described bodies floating in the river "allied to the bottom of the river rather than the surface, by reason of the slime and ooze with which it is covered."[68] A poem of 1837 called *To the River Thames* described the river thus:

> Blest ar the poor, the humble and the meek —
> But thou goest wallowing on, o'er weed and slime....[69]

Another poem, *Quoth Father Thames*, featured in *Punch* magazine in 1859, described:

> Steamers up-churning me,
> Quick-lime up-burning me-
> Never was river so ill-used as I.
> Sewage and slaughter-lvmpbs [sic]
> Kill off my water-nymphs,
> All between Teddington Lock and the Nore....
> Sewage-filled urn upon which I recline
> Sewage-crammed eyes and nose-
> ...Under my level, soaked green with my slime....[70]

Colwell et al.'s research established conclusively that the natural and preferred environment of *Vibrio cholerae* is brackish, estuarine water, and it is this environment which is essential to the bacterium's behavior. Estuarine environments are seasonable and therefore extremely variable. In this way the bacterium has learnt to be adaptable to "a wide range of salinity and temperature conditions."[71] Research by Tamplin et al. "reported attachment of *V. cholerae* O1 to zooplankton and phytoplankton from natural waters ... thus ... the existence of a viable but nonculturable state for *V. cholerae* O1 was indicated."[72] In addition, work by Colwell et al.[73] showed it was likely that in a nutrient deficient environment where salinity was high or where the temperature was too low, *Vibrio cholerae* could take on a "state of dormancy" but in which it was still viable, moreover the bacterium could remain in this state for years.[74]

One of the ways the dormant state is manifested is by the reduction in the size of the *Vibrio cholerae* and the alteration of its shape from bacillus (rod-like) to coccoid (ovoid).[75] This is called the "viable but nonculturable state," and further experimentation by Colwell et al. showed that when volunteers ingested nonculturable *Vibrio cholerae* cells, they developed diarrhea even when the gene which produces the cholera toxin had been removed. This is backed up by a more general observation made in the World Health Organization Report of 2002: "When present in the environment, *V. cholerae* may undergo a series of major physical and metabolic changes; while the altered cells are more difficult, or even impossible, to grow using conventional techniques, they have been shown to retain their virulence factors.... Laboratory studies have shown no loss of toxigenicity by *V. cholerae* O1 under conditions of low salinity, adverse pH, adverse water chemistry, low sodium, or long-term starvation, suggesting that toxin-producing ability is unlikely to be lost when the organism is exposed to environmental stress."[76]

The association of *Vibrio cholerae* with phytoplankton, the group to which algae belongs, is clearly essential, however, the bacterium's association with zooplankton, especially copepods, is also important, and recent research in the field of marine biology has investigated more closely the behavior of *Vibrio cholerae* in its natural environment: "It is not known if *V. cholerae* is a component of the normal commensal flora or a symbiont of a specific species in the plankton. Like many other vibrios, *V. cholerae* possesses chitinase and mucinase enzymes, which suggests that they are adapted to colonization of crustacean zooplankton."[77]

The purpose of chitinase is to dissolve chitin, a component of the exoskeletons of copepods, or zooplankton.[78] Chitin is an insoluble polymer and contains carbon and nitrogen, essential nutrients for marine microorganisms such as *Vibrio cholerae*. Scientists observing the progress of cholera outbreaks in recent years have noticed that they occur with an increase in phytoplankton and zooplankton blooms in estuarine and costal environments and further research has shown that *Vibrio cholerae* can "sense, attach to, and degrade natural chitin surfaces" in an aquatic environment.[79]

It is the attachment of *Vibrio cholerae* to chitin which makes the pathogen dangerous to humans who are well nourished and who produce normal levels of gastric acid, and as the work by Nalin et al. at the University of Maryland School of Medicine reveals: "Pandemic strains of *V. cholerae* of O-group 1 serotype might adsorb onto and multiply on contaminated chitinous fauna, including crabs, shrimp, or zooplankton. Adsorption appears to occur more readily at pH 6.2 than at 7.3 and may therefore be more likely to occur in estuaries than in ocean water. It is possible that chitin of previously cooked but recontaminated crabs or other crustacea, like the powdered crabshell used in these studies, could be a substrate for vibrio multiplication and might permit survival of stomach acid by *V. cholerae* on chitin particles ingested during a meal."[80]

Additional work by Wachsmuth, Blake and Olsvik showed: "*V. cholerae* O1 adheres to chitin, and survival of chitin-absorbed *V. Cholerae* in a dilute hydrochloric acid solution of approximately the same pH as human gastric acid is prolonged.... Chitin is also a component of crustacean shells and may protect adsorbed V. cholerae O1 from destruction by heat as well as by gastric acid."[81]

Vibrio cholerae will attach itself to plankton when it enters the non-culturable stage as part of its survival mechanism. It will remain in this state until copepods proliferate again, and in the case of the environment of the River Thames, when the weather warms and water temperature rises. Research has shown that the bacteria will also use this method of attachment to move to areas where there is increased sediment and where the bacteria can find higher concentrations of nutrients.[82]

While research continues on the behavior of *Vibrio cholerae* O1 it is clear from the above discussion that the River Thames at Lambeth was an ideal breeding ground for the pathogen, and by the hot summer of 1849, conditions were perfect. The warmth of the water, the sunshine, the salinity, the pH and the nutritional mixture of organic and industrial waste in the water were as good as that of a Petri dish in a laboratory.

More intriguing is whether the 1848 to 1849 outbreak, or indeed any outbreak after the original introduction of cholera to the British Isles in 1826, were separate incidents, or rather trigger years for a bacterium which had already adapted itself to the environment of the Thames, which, like the Ganges, had become a natural habitat. Cholera was at its most virulent during the summers of 1832, 1849, 1852 and 1866, years which were characterized by high pressure, high air and water temperatures and low rainfall; the latter months of such periods are often called *Indian Summers*. It is likely while successive strains of cholera were brought to Britain's shores from epidemic areas, a separate strain (or even strains) was already endemic in the River Thames. The observations of Dr. Edmund Parkes in 1849 should, perhaps, now be considered in a different light:

> The point being conceded that in nine localities ... the poison was not imported by any person ill of cholera arriving in the locality. Nor could it have been brought in by the clothes or baggage of any persons coming from infected districts in England.... There is no evidence either of any persons arriving from the Continent ... it is most probable they were connected with the shipping.... In Horsleydown [Southwark, next to Lambeth] ... the poison must have been imported ... it did not seem to propagate itself by contagion or otherwise.
>
> If therefore the poison was not brought to Lambeth ... by infected persons or non-infected persons or clothes, did it enter in some other way, or was it generated in these localities? It is not unreasonable to suppose that some

moving force, altogether independent of the bodies of men, may have driven particles of cholera-poison into these localities; for certainly there has been some power, which independent of human intercourse, and in opposition occasionally to winds, has driven this disease from the steppes of Tartary to the English shores.[83]

Today, there is a vaccine for cholera, prevention through education, and effective treatment. The current advice from the World Health Organization is as follows:

> Cholera is an easily treatable disease. The prompt administration of oral rehydration salts to replace lost fluids nearly always results in cure. In especially severe cases, intravenous administration of fluids may be required to save a patient's life.
>
> Outbreaks can be mitigated and case-fatality rates reduced through several other measures, many of which are suitable for community participation. Human behaviors related to personal hygiene and food preparation contribute greatly to the occurrence and severity of outbreaks.
>
> Health education aimed at behavior change is thus an important component of cholera prevention and control.[84]

Moreover, prevention rather than cure may be our only protection against *Vibrio cholerae*. The recent discovery that the pathogenic element of *V. cholerae* is viral is of concern: "It is also possible that multiple copies of the viral genome within the cholera pathogen can generate more virulent forms similar to the one causing the eighth pandemic. Another dangerous trend noticed in recent years in some clinical isolates of *V. cholerae* is the acquisition of resistance to common antibiotics, thus rendering them useless in controlling the pathogen."[85]

In the early nineteenth century, the treatment and cure of disease was still at an experimental stage. Some treatments were effective as they were the result of the experience of generations, while others were haphazard and based on a scant understanding of disease and almost no understanding whatsoever of its cause. A surgeon practicing in Dartford, Kent, in the 1820s noted in his report book that effective treatment for a variety of illnesses, including smallpox and venereal disease, were flannel waistcoats, beef broth and milk.[86]

In 1848 in his *On the Treatment of Asiatic Cholera*, Archibald Billing noted the most common medicine for cholera was as follows:

> Water half a pint
> Tartar emetic two grains
> Sulphate of magnesia half an ounce, mixed
> This dose is for an adult (15 years up) a table spoon every half hour; for a child of a year and a half or two years, a tea spoonful, for the intermediate years a proportionate dose.[87]

Billing noted, and the following is paraphrased from his writings, that the minute doses of neutral salt acted as a diuretic on the kidneys, and promoted the secretion of fluids which was halted when suffering from "true cholera." He continued that the saline coincided with the antimony (tartar emetic), the best of febrifuge medicines in counteracting the disease. Heat did not promote recovery and sufferers should "drink freely of cold water." Once the urgent symptoms were over, five grains of calomel should be taken, but only once vomiting had stopped. This helped the liver. A grain or more of bisulphate of quinine should be administered every fourth hour, and as long as the skin stayed dry and warmer than natural, half a dose of fever mixture with the quinine. Patients should be given a nutritious diet, at first milk with water, arrowroot, gruel given cold. Mustard was also beneficial to the nerves and counteracted the effects of the cholera poison. Billing concluded with his recipe for a substitute for the fever mixture:

Half pint water
Large tablespoon salt
Large tablespoon flour of mustard. Mixed. Doses as before.[88]

Billing's medicine included two key ingredients that would have helped cholera sufferers, water and salt, which would have combated the severe dehydration brought on by the effects of the bacterium's excreted enterotoxins. Sadly, as the causes of the disease were mired in confusion, fuelled by prejudice and snobbery within the medical hierarchy of the time, few would concede that the swiftest way to prevent cholera occurring in the first place would have been better sanitation and clean drinking water.

Even by 1854, when cholera appeared in London again, surgeons at St. Thomas' hospital were using the same mixture of medicines and treatments as Billing suggested, though they continued to experiment. Treatments included lead, opium, turpentine, carbon, lime juice, burnt coffee, soda water, hot air baths and ipecacuanha (a flowering plant with emetic properties).[89]

A popular medicine for cholera was calomel, which is also known as mercurous chloride, Hg_2Cl_2. The compound was added to water as a purgative, but is, in fact, toxic. Dr Manby, a surgeon in London in the 1830s, advocated calomel as the best medicine for cholera, and his recipe was as follows:

Calomel 1 grain
Ipecacuanha half a grain
Opium one qtr of a grain
All made into a pill to be taken every three hours till symptoms abated, which "they usually did" in 6 to 12 hrs.[90]

The 1854 notes of an unknown surgeon at St. Thomas' Hospital[91] included the case of James Kerr, aged 44, of Brighton, an unemployed printer, who during a trip to London, presumably looking for work, had fallen ill with cholera. The doctor made careful notes of his experimentation on the patient:

> 9 P.M. [patient] very much depressed, cold insensible and comatose, preparations were immediately made to inject the following solution into the vein of the right arm.
> Solution for injection
> Sodium Chloride: 60 parts
> Potassium chloride: 6 parts
> Sodium Phosphate: 3 parts
> Sodium Carbon: 20 parts
> 140 grains of the above composition dissolved in 40 ounces of distilled water, degree of solution 103½°
> 9.15 P.M. 3oz no effect
> 9.25 P.M. 3oz no effect on pulse but appears more easily roused
> 9.32 P.M. 3 oz no effect on pulse he speaks with more power
> 9.40 P.M. 3 oz no effect
> 9.46 P.M. 3 oz pulse now perceptible but exceedingly feeble and slow. He has relapsed again into a state of insensibility.
> 9.50 P.M. 3 oz no further effect
> 9.54 P.M. 3 oz no further effect
> 9.58 P.M. 3 oz no further effect
> 10.04 P.M. 3 oz pulse rather fuller
> 10.07 P.M. 3 oz pulse rather fuller
> 10.09 P.M. 3 oz pulse much fuller and he is more easily roused
> 10.12 P.M. 3 oz pulse slightly fuller
> 10.16 P.M. 3 oz perceptible improvement
> 10.18 P.M. 3 oz perceptible improvement
> 10.21 P.M. 3 oz pulse slightly improved
> 10.23 P.M. 3 oz does not seem to improve so much as he did
> 10.25 P.M. 3 oz not so well. Pulse not perceptible, cannot rouse him.
> Forty five ounces in all were injected so that barely 3 oz would be used each time.
> 10.30 P.M. he is now in a complete state of coma that the injection has not improved his condition although at one time he had slightly rallied under its influence.
> 12th August 9 A.M. He remained insensible right up to the period of his Death five minutes before one o'clock A.M. There was no positive evidence of his having passed urine from the time of his admission.

The surgeon commented on his patients' intake of fruit and vegetables and the quantity of alcohol they consumed, realizing that the undernourishment of the working classes played a role in their susceptibility to the disease. He noted that Ann Buckland, aged 46, was "more accustomed to gin than animal food."[92]

In September 1849, at the height of that epidemic, *The Times* published many articles which served to give advice on cholera. The following came from "A General Practitioner":

> I find that a very large number of persons who have never been accustomed to the use of alcoholic drinks, are now daily resorting to the frequent and immoderate use of brandy and other spirits, with the view, they say, of "keeping out the cholera;" while a few, who have been so accustomed, are now adopting total abstinence.... Now what are the direct effects of alcoholic stimulants on the mucous or digestive coats of the stomach, which is one of the principal seats of choleric disease? ... The best way to protect the system against ... choleraic, or any other poison, is to maintain the several organs and functions of the body ... as near as possible in a state of health....

The doctor went on to talk about medicines: "I give tonics, especially quinine and iron, with gentle stimulants and iron ... and a plentiful supply of beef tea."[93]

There was a growing awareness that educating the population as to the symptoms of cholera would be effective in promoting recovery from the disease. Mr. Dawes, a registrar in Lambeth, wrote in *The Times*, "At least half the cases I have registered were allowed to proceed unchecked until the most alarming and dangerous symptoms had manifested themselves.... People are so much accustomed to associate danger exclusively with pain, that the most fatal symptom, unaccompanied by pain, is neglected. They must ... be taught to look upon painless diarrhoea with the anxiety that people in the plague looked upon the swellings...."[94]

Pamphlets were circulated in Lambeth in September 1849, which may have been useful to those who could read:

> To the Inhabitants of Lambeth ... it mainly depends upon yourselves whether, if the cholera attack you, you escape with your life or not. Should you feel the slightest attack of diarrhea ... seek medical aid immediately, for ... when opposed at first the battle is won.... The cholera has four friends — dirt, drunkenness, slothfulness and fear. It hath also four great enemies — pure air, cleanliness, sobriety and courage ... keep yourself clean.... What you have to eat let it be of the best and nutritious kind ... a glass of pure water ... [and] do not forget to appeal to Him who watches over us all....[95]

For the poor of Lambeth the last piece of advice was probably the only one easily available to them. However, reports in *The Times* in September 1849 showed that house-to-house visitation helped keep cholera under control. From the evidence presented, it seems that catching the disease in the early stages prevented some deaths:

> The more early discovery and treatment of cholera, both in its premonitory and developed stages; the rescuing numbers of persons [sic] from the consequences of their own neglect, and the saving of many lives ... Dr. King, in

respect to Lambeth and Newington, reports that in the four days during which the visitation has been organized and in operation, the visitors have discovered and brought under immediate treatment 2,193 neglected cases of diarrhoea, and 67 cases on the verge of cholera; but that none of these, as far as has been ascertained, have passed into cholera. Dr. King further states that "the visitation has done good work, and far from refusing this kind of relief, the afflicted poor hail it as the greatest blessing that has yet befallen them in their calamity."[96]

By the 1850s, after repeated experimentation throughout the cholera epidemics, physicians began to realize which treatments were more effective than others, though they still did not fully understand why. As discussed above, the successful growth of *Vibrio cholerae* depends in part on the pH of its environment, and in 1852, John Parkin, in his *Statistical Report of the Epidemic in Jamaica*, noted the efficacy of carbonic acid gas "produced by the admixture of the bi-carbonate of soda and lime juice."[97]

From the end of the eighteenth century the new industrial towns and centers attracted migrants. The rapid building of densely packed tenements without proper sanitation for workers increased the incidence of disease and provoked a rise in urban mortality. The influx of workers from Ireland escaping from the famine created additional problems with the introduction of new strains of disease. It was clear to those working with the poor in the medical profession that something needed to be done to protect the population from the dangers of disease in the new urban areas. Some wanted radical reform, as discussed in Chapter 1, but many realized that the only way to improve conditions was to influence opinion with solid facts and thus create new legislation.

Sir Edwin Chadwick (1800–1890) was Assistant Commissioner and then Royal Commissioner to the Poor Law Enquiry in 1832 and 1833 respectively, looking at the working conditions of child factory workers.[98] He subsequently held the position of Secretary to the Poor Law Commission from 1834 to 1847 and Public Health Commissioner from 1848 to 1854. He "played a major part in the reform of factories, the police, and labour in early railway construction, as well as public health, water supply, burial ground and the relief of poverty."[99]

In July 1842, after three years of research and enquiries, Chadwick presented his *Report on the Sanitary Condition of the Labouring Population of Great Britain* to the House of Lords. The work had been put together by groups of local investigators and others who had been calling for sanitary reform for some time. However, Chadwick's findings were so controversial that the report was published in his name alone as the other Poor Law Commissioners were afraid to attach their names to the document. Chadwick was nevertheless adamant it was his work alone.[100]

The reform for public health did not attract popular support, as did the movements for the reform of factory conditions or the abolition of the slave trade. Moreover, sanitary reform would necessarily involve a good deal of expense and social upheaval. As M.W. Flinn observed in his 1965 *Introduction* to Chadwick's report, "The Whigs were landowners, and believed that the duties of government began with the safeguarding of the rights of property and in minimizing government expenditure; they were ... too closely concerned with ... balancing the budget and the preservation of law and order."[101] In addition, the working population did not have the vote and therefore had no effective representation in Parliament.[102]

The background to the publication of Chadwick's report began in 1834 when a group of doctors petitioned Parliament on the state of London's sewers and their adverse effect on health.[103] London's surgeons worked with the urban poor on a day-to-day basis. They understood the deprivation they suffered and how their living conditions were linked to the high incidence of disease. From the 1820s, a considerable number of surgeons practicing in the capital had trained at University College London and at the medical school at Edinburgh University in Scotland. It was the influence of Edinburgh which was to have a lasting effect on the progress of sanitary reform in London and the whole of England and Wales.

Formal teaching in the Theory and Practice of Medicine began at Edinburgh in 1720 under Alexander Monro, the first Chair of Anatomy. By 1726 a full School of Medicine was open to students and, of the 160 who graduated between 1726 and 1827, 50 were Scots, 46 were English, 36 were Irish, and the remainder were from North America, the West Indies and elsewhere. Many of these surgeons chose to practice in London.[104] Edinburgh quickly developed a good reputation for teaching, but its attraction was also due to the fact that it took those who were unable to apply to the Anglican universities, Oxford and Cambridge. As Druin Burch explains in his work on the life of the surgeon Sir Astley Cooper (1768–1841), at Edinburgh "dissenting religion went along with liberal thinking. With Nonconformist religion came non-conformist thought, and time and time again those who held novel views in religion drove forwards free thought in science. Edinburgh's openness to religious dissent and new ideas made it welcoming to foreign influences. Many of Edinburgh's own medical graduates went on to attend universities or hospitals in France and returned enlivened by Continental ideas."[105]

Following the Act of Union of 1707, Scotland experienced a less hostile relationship with England, and was able to develop its own trade. Trade with countries in Europe, such as France, and a strong belief in the importance of education, had a considerable impact on Scottish culture, and the second half of the eighteenth century has been dubbed the Scottish Enlightenment. The relationship with France was significant, and Scotland's considerable influence was noted by the French writer Voltaire (1694–1778), who said, "Nous nous tournons vers l'Écosse pour trouver toutes nos idées sur la civilisation."[106] We look to Scotland for all our ideas of civilization.

Edinburgh taught in a progressive manner, similar to the universities in Padua, Leiden and the Sorbonne in Paris.[107] M.W. Flinn, in his *Introduction* to Chadwick's report, and referring to an earlier work by David Roberts, summed up the influence of Edinburgh University:

> Three broad classes of social reformers appear to have emerged from Edinburgh University in the first half of the [nineteenth] century: first a group of aristocratic, mainly Whig politicians, which includes Lords Lansdowne, Russell, Brougham and Palmerston; second a group of civil servants, who as factory, health and educational inspectors, played major roles in the extension of public work in their respective spheres: they included Leonard Horner and James Stuart, factory inspectors; Gavin Milroy, Hector Gavin, and James Smith, health inspectors; and Peter Reid and J.D. Morrell, education inspectors; and third, a group of pre-eminent social reformers, including James Phillips Kay, Peter Gaskell, and doctors Percival and Farriar.[108]

Lord Palmerston (1784–1865), born Henry John Temple, was the third Viscount Palmerston, acquiring the title on his father's death in 1802. A Whig and Liberal politician, he served as Prime Minister from 1859 to 1865.[109] Palmerston had gone to Edinburgh to study under Dugald Stewart (1753–1828), professor of moral philosophy; Palmerston had also lodged with him. Stewart's lectures on Political Economy between 1800 and 1810 were particularly influential. While Stewart did not see himself as a radical, his effect on radical reformers was extensive.[110]

Another student influenced by Dugald Stewart was William Pulteney Alison (1790–1859), who went up to Edinburgh in 1803. He became professor of medicine and taught from 1820 to 1856. Alison had worked as Physician to the New Town Dispensary in Scotland and saw poverty at first hand, and it was from Alison that Chadwick drew on his experience in his sanitary report for the Scottish section. One of Alison's most noteworthy contributions to Chadwick's report was his belief that the miasma theory for the spread of disease was illogical. He could not understand how in the winter smells were not so bad and yet disease was still prevalent.[111]

The influence of Stewart and Alison spanned 70 years at Edinburgh and touched many of the great social and medical reformers of the late eighteenth and nineteenth centuries. The surgeon and anatomist Sir Astley Cooper studied at Edinburgh from 1787 and was undoubtedly influenced by the radical mood, though a trip to France tempered his revolutionary ideals. Cooper was more interested in the mysteries of the human body and gained inspiration from Alexander Monro's assistant, Andrew Fyfe.[112]

As a leading London surgeon, Cooper probably had more influence on sanitary reform than any of his peers at Edinburgh who preached revolution. His anatomical research pushed the boundaries of medicine and inspired many. Cooper had a long association with Guy's and St. Thomas' Hospitals in Southwark but split the two institutions in 1825 — out of anger that a senior post had not been given to his nephew — creating separate medical schools. In 1871 St. Thomas' Hospital moved to the Albert Embankment at Lambeth, and the two medical schools were not to be reunited until 1982.[113]

In 1834, the Poor Law Amendment Act "specifically authorized Justices of the Peace to order *outdoor* medical relief." In this way, salaried medical officers were appointed to almost every Poor Law Union in England and Wales, including that of Lambeth.[114] In addition, in 1835 the Municipal Corporations Act was introduced by Lord Grey's Whig government, continuing the work of the Reform Act of 1832. As this had reformed parliamentary constituencies, so the Municipal Corporations Act would reform local government.[115]

In 1838 some Poor Law Unions decided to spend money on improving sanitary conditions, in the belief that in the long term they would spend less on poor relief. The argument which ensued over whether the spending of this money was allowed under the existing law led to an inquiry being set up in London in 1838 to examine the relationship between living conditions and disease, the *Fourth Annual Report* of the Poor Law Commissioners. The report was put together by Chadwick, though other commissioners played a part. The report was accompanied by supplements written in 1838 and 1839 from three doctors, James Phillips Kay (1804–1877), Neil Arnott (1788–1874) and Thomas Southwood Smith (1788–1861). It was the first time qualified medical professionals had been commissioned by the government to comment on issues which might lead to legislation, and their role acknowledged the value their experience and expertise was accorded in the discussion of health reform.[116]

Dr. James Phillips Kay had trained at Edinburgh University, but it was his work in 1832 in the Manchester slums which enhanced his understanding of the reality of poverty and its association with disease; the study which followed, *The Moral and Physical Condition of the Working Classes* (1832), was extremely influential in the cause for sanitary reform.[117]

Kay had been Assistant Poor Law Commissioner in East Anglia and it was on his suggestion that in the mid 1830s around 4,000 people were moved out of the area to work in the industrial north.[118] Kay had good reason to do this, as it provided unemployed rural workers with new opportunities in the wool and cotton mills of Yorkshire, Lancashire and Cheshire. However, in some cases families were split up, as those who were too young or too old to work were left behind.[119]

Kay's solution to poverty was education, but in East Anglia this met with financial difficulties and he moved to the Central Commission to examine poverty in London. His first investigation began in 1837 with the weavers in Spitalfields and then (with Dr. Neil Arnott) he looked at the causes of fever in London. In 1839 Kay became Secretary to the Privy Council's Committee on Education.[120]

Dr. Neil Arnott was a friend of the social reformer Jeremy Bentham (1748–1832) and the philosopher and economist John Stuart Mill (1806–1873), and it was through their acquaintance that he met James Kay and Thomas Southwood Smith. Arnott had studied at Aberdeen University in Scotland and had been a ship's surgeon for the East India Company; he was also Edwin Chadwick's family doctor. In 1838 he worked at the Poor Law Commission and later wrote two papers on poverty in Scotland for Chadwick's sanitary report. Later, in 1843, Arnott became a member of the Health of Towns Commission.[121]

Dr. Thomas Southwood Smith was probably the main contributor to the cause of sanitary reform, and he too studied medicine at Edinburgh University, graduating in 1816. In 1824 Southwood Smith was appointed physician at the London Fever Hospital, which gave him an excellent grounding in understanding the relationship between poverty and disease. He was also a friend of Jeremy Bentham, and, like Dr. Astley Cooper, understood the importance of anatomical research to further medical knowledge. When Bentham died in 1832, he requested his body be dissected, and Southwood Smith performed the public dissection. (Bentham's preserved body is still on display at University College London, though his head was lost in a student prank and had to be replaced with a replica.)

Southwood Smith began writing papers on public health in 1825 and, in 1838, was invited to take part in the Poor Law Commission's preliminary inquiries on disease and the lack of sanitation in London's East End (1838–39). From 1848 to 1854, Southwood Smith worked with Chadwick at the Central Board of Health.[122] Chadwick's inquiry into the sanitary conditions of the working classes was preceded, and influenced, by the report initiated in 1838 by the Poor Law Commission and undertaken by Drs. Kay, Arnott and Southwood Smith. Their report linked disease directly to the dreadful living conditions of the working population.[123]

The issue was debated in the House of Lords in May 1838, but no action was taken. Then, in June, Chadwick wrote to Lord John Russell asking him to consider an act to regulate the building of houses for the poor. The following year, when Southwood Smith's supplementary report was published,

Lord Blomfield, the Bishop of London, asked the House of Lords for an inquiry by the Poor Law Commission into the sanitary conditions of the laboring classes.[124]

The inquiry was requested by the House of Lords and not the House of Commons. The call for sanitary reform was just one voice bombarding successive governments of the time who were grappling with a myriad of problems thrown up by the new demands of Empire and the industrial age. When Chadwick was released from the Poor Law Commission and put in charge of the inquiry he knew that in order for his voice to be heard, his report needed to contain evidence which was both accurate and comprehensive.

Chadwick began his preparation for his report on sanitary conditions in 1839. He was well aware that many of the problems in the industrial towns and centers like Lambeth could only be solved by galvanizing the central and local government into spending money and by introducing legislation controlling building practices.[125]

Nassau Senior (1790–1864) was co-author with Chadwick of the New Poor Law, and a member of the handloom Weavers Commission of 1837. In his 1841 *Report of the Commissioners on the Condition of the Hand-Loom Weavers,* he commented:

> What other result can be expected, when any man who can purchase or hire a plot of ground is allowed to cover it with such buildings as he may think fit, where there is no power to enforce drainage or sewerage, or to regulate the width of streets, or to prevent houses from being packed back to back, and separated in front by mere alleys and courts, or their being filled with as many inmates as their walls can contain, or the accumulation within and without, of all the impurities which arise in a crowded population? ... with all our reverence for the principle of non-interference, we cannot doubt that in this matter it has been pushed too far. We believe that both ground landlord and the speculating builder ought to be compelled by law, though it should cost them a percentage of their rent and profit, to take measures which shall prevent the towns which they create from being the centers of disease.[126]

However, Chadwick was not popular. His earlier work on the Poor Law and its draconian measures, particularly the introduction of the workhouse, had not gone down well, yet it would seem Chadwick had never intended workhouses to become types of prisons, and was particularly concerned for the welfare of children.[127] His forceful way did not help either, and clashes of interests and personalities meant that he was ordered to abandon his work on the report in 1841. However, after the election of Sir Robert Peel's Conservative government, the new Home Secretary, Sir James Graham (1792–1846), eventually conceded that Chadwick should continue and ordered the report to be completed by February, 1842.[128]

Chadwick prepared the report with his usual systematic approach. The report looked at specific problem areas and gave documented evidence from specific examples. It covered England, Wales and Scotland, though gathering information in the latter was problematic as the Poor Law did not extend to Scotland and neither did civil registration, which had been introduced in England and Wales in 1837. Chadwick gathered information by extensive reading and by first-hand investigation. He wrote to individual Assistant Poor Law commissioners (who in turn acquired their information from Poor Law medical officers), local relieving officers, clerks to Boards of Guardians, guardians, and learned and distinguished figures such as William Farr, William Alison at Edinburgh University, and the economist and statistician Charles Babbage.[129]

When the Report was completed, one of the three commissioners refused to publish it. Chadwick would not modify its controversial content and it was agreed to have it published in his own name on July 9, 1842. However, Chadwick had a problem disseminating his ideas. As the report had been prepared for the House of Lords, only a limited number would be printed and its distribution would be restricted. Just as he had done with the Poor Law Report in 1834, Chadwick ordered a separate publication. This was in quarto form and much easier to read than the bulky parliamentary version. Thousands were printed, reports varying from 10,000 to 100,000, and Chadwick also advertized it in *The Times*, the *Morning Chronicle* and the influential *Quarterly Review*.[130]

Each Board of Guardians was sent a copy of Chadwick's report, including Lambeth's, and the report must have made a significant impact as the Lambeth District Sanitary Reports of 1849 follow similar arguments to Chadwick's. Chadwick also tried to rally the support of individuals. He sent a copy to Henry Austin (1812–1861), who had married Charles Dickens' sister Letitia. Henry Austin was a campaigner for health reform and established the Health of Towns Association in 1844, becoming Honorary Secretary. He later became Consulting Engineer for the Metropolitan Commission of Sewers (see Chapter 4). Austin sent the report to Dickens, but Dickens' views on Chadwick were already biased, as is illustrated in his brutal portrayal of the workhouse in his 1838 novel, *Oliver Twist*.[131]

Dickens' response in his *American Notes* of 1842 was not overly enthusiastic: "Much of the disease which does prevail might be avoided if a few common precautions were observed." Though he did add, "There is no local legislature in America which may not study Mr. Chadwick's excellent report on the Sanitary Condition of our Labouring Classes with immense advantage."[132] In the end, however, he did become a supporter of Chadwick's ideas for sanitary reform.[133]

Chadwick's *Report on The Sanitary Condition of the Labouring Population of Great Britain* covered the following topics, preceded by a Summary:

1. General Condition of the Residences of the Labouring Classes where Disease is found to be most Prevalent
2. Public Arrangements external to the Residences by which the Sanitary Condition of the Labouring Population is affected
    i. Town drainage of streets and houses
    ii. Street and road cleansing: road pavements
    iii. Supplies of water
    iv. Sanitary effect of land drainage
3. Circumstances Chiefly in the Internal Economy and Bad Ventilation of Places of Work; Workmen's Lodging-Houses, Dwellings and the Domestic Habits Affecting the Health of the Labouring Classes
    i. Bad ventilation and overcrowding of private houses
    ii. The want of separate apartments, and overcrowding of private dwellings
    iii. Domestic mismanagement, a predisposing cause of disease
    iv. Contrast in the economy of families
4. Comparative Chances of Life in Different Classes of the Community
5. Pecuniary Burdens Created by the Neglect of Sanitary Measures
6. Evidence of the Effects of Preventative Measures in Raising the Standard of Health and the Chances of Life
    i. Costs to tenants and owners of the public measures for drainage, cleansing, and the supplies of water, as compared with the cost of sickness
    ii. Employers' influence on the health of workpeople by means of improved habitations
    iii. The employers' influence on the sobriety and heath of workpeople by modes of payment which do not lead to temptations and intemperance
    iv. Employers' influence on the health of workpeople by the promotion of personal cleanliness
    v. Employers' influence on the health of workpeople by the ventilation of places of work, and the prevention of noxious fumes, dust, etc.
    vi. Employers' means of influencing the condition of the working population by regard to respectability in dress
    vii. Employers' or owners' influence in the improvement of habitations and sanitary arrangements for the protection of the labouring classes in the rural districts
    viii. Effects of public walks and gardens on the health and morals of the lower classes of the population
7. Recognised Principles of Legislation and State of the Existing Law for the Protection of the Public Health
    i. General state of the law for the protection of public health
    ii. State of the special authorities for reclaiming the execution of the laws for the protection of public health

       iii. State of the local executive authorities for the erection and mainte-
           nance of drains and other works for the protection of public health
       iv. Boards of health, or public officers for the prevention of disease
    8. Common Lodging-Houses
    9. Recapitulation of Conclusions[134]

The various discussions of the report are easily grasped by the titles of each chapter and sub-chapter. However, the main aim of the report was to establish a correlation between insanitary living conditions and disease amongst the working poor; reference was also made to high mortality rates and low expectation of life. The conditions Chadwick described of towns all over Britain were not dissimilar to those experienced by the Sub Committees in their investigations in Lambeth (see Chapter 6), with open sewers, overflowing cesspits and streets strewn with rubbish and excrement. As in Lambeth, the supply of running water was also a problem. In Chapter 6 of his report Chadwick noted that many jails had no running water or sanitation. With regard to the supply of water to private dwellings, he noted that in Manchester property changed hands so regularly there was little incentive for landlords to spend the considerable sums necessary to provide tenants in urban areas with running water and sanitation. For this reason Chadwick advocated a loan scheme to facilitate the process. Indeed, it was the financial cost which was one of the greatest obstacles to sanitary reform, despite the long-term cost of the poor's ill health to the economy. Chadwick stressed employers' responsibility towards their workers, both in maintaining a healthy workplace and by setting a good example morally.

Chadwick was also interested in sewage disposal, though in 1842 he was not aware of the role sewage played in the spread of cholera. He did, however, understand that in the urban areas of Britain, the accumulation of sewage was a serious problem, believing the smells emanating from rotting matter of all types to be the cause of disease and responsible for its spread. Chadwick's solution was to sell untreated sewage to farmers for fertilizer. It is strange that he should have persisted in this view as the practice had been condemned in Scotland precisely because of the dreadful stench, indeed it was the reason why Queen Victoria refused to stay at Holyrood Castle in 1842.[135]

Chadwick advocated "the engagement of properly qualified, professional men in all public employment in the field of public health.... Only the highest professional standards ... were good enough for the service of the public."[136] But perhaps most significantly, Chadwick recommended that sewage should be removed from dwellings "suspended in water in glazed, circular-bored drains."[137] The existing drains and sewers in London were brick-built,[138] much in the style the Romans had used. The difficulty with this design, as discussed in Chapter 4 with regard to the sewers at the new Houses of Parliament, is that they did not facilitate the easy passage of waste and fluids and often became blocked.

As Chadwick's report was published for the House of Lords in July, at the end of the parliamentary year, it was unlikely to have an immediate impact or develop into prompt legislation. However, in 1843, Sir Robert Peel's government appointed a Royal Commission on the Health of Towns under the Duke of Buccleuch, which would also consider the evidence in Chadwick's report. Members of the commission included Dr. Neil Arnott, Dr. Thomas Southwood Smith, James Smith of Deanston (a textile industrialist and agricultural engineer), Llyon Playfair (a Scottish chemist), the engineers Captain Denison and Robert Stephenson, and Robert A. Slaney, M.P.[139]

Two reports were published, one in 1844, heavily influenced by Chadwick, and a final report in 1845. A bill was introduced, but came under heavy criticism from the Health of Towns Association. The Association was led by Lord Ashley, Lord Normanby and Dr. Thomas Southwood Smith, who had also founded the association in London in 1844.[140] Southwood Smith organized public meetings where speakers included the Association's leaders and members of the medical profession, and the dissemination of books and pamphlets. Chadwick did not get involved, perhaps because he was not a good public speaker, and perhaps because of his lack of popularity.[141] Chadwick was also busy working on a report for urban burials, which Sir James Graham had asked him to write in 1843 as an additional supplement to the sanitary report.[142] The Health of Towns Association was a poor cousin to the Anti–Corn Law League,[143] which was well organized and well financed (see Chapter 1) and with which it vied for government attention.

The 1844 Metropolitan Buildings Act also had little effect on the reform of sanitation. The Act required all new buildings to be connected to a common sewer, as long as this was within 30 feet of the dwelling. It also specified how drains should be built. However, the law could not be implemented on existing buildings[144] and even the 1846 Nuisances Removal and Diseases Prevention Act (one of a series of Acts which became known as Cholera Bills), which was supposed to apply to existing buildings, did little to help the existing situation in areas such as Lambeth.

In 1847 Parliament passed a new bill, the Town Improvement Clauses Act. The Act "set out clauses which local authorities could incorporate into their own legislation and, as such clauses had already been approved, opposition to them was unlikely when new Bills containing them were introduced into Parliament."[145] In the same year Lord Morpeth (1802–1864), formerly known as George Howard, tried to introduce a Public Health Bill, but it was thrown out of Parliament. However, cholera had begun to rage again in Asia and Europe and Lord John Russell's Whig government feared it would only be a matter of time before it reached Britain's shores. The threat of a new epidemic and further agitation from Chadwick and Southwood Smith meant that Chadwick was dismissed from the Poor Law Commission and appointed Royal Commissioner on London Sanitation, and Metropolitan Commissioner of Sewers to the Royal Commission on London Sanitation, or the Metropolitan Sanitary Commission. The Royal Commission began its work in September 1847, and presented its findings in 1848. This *First Report* was presented to Lord Robert Grosvenor and was prepared by Edwin Chadwick, Dr. Thomas Southwood Smith, Richard Owen (Hunterian professor at the College of Surgeons), and Richard Lambert Jones. It revealed an appalling situation and considerable inefficiency and corruption in the capital. Evidence for the *First Report* was given by the following:

> R. Bowie, Esq., Surgeon, east Smithfield (1st and 2nd parts)
> R.L. Hooper, Esq., Surgeon, Southwark
> Dr. Murdoch, Rotherhithe
> M.F. Wagstaffe, Esq., Surgeon, Lambeth
> T.R. Leadam, Esq., Surgeon, Southwark
> William Simpson, Esq., Surgeon, Bloomsbury
> J. French, Esq., Surgeon, St. James'
> Edward Doubleday, Esq., Surgeon, St. Saviour's
> Thomas Taylor, Esq., Surgeon, Bethnal Green
> Dr. John Wright, Westminster
> L.C. Hertslet, Esq., Clerk to the Court of Sewers for Westminster and part of Middlesex
> Mr. J. Phillips, Surveyor to the Westminster Court of Sewers
> Captain Bague, R.N., Chairman of the Westminster Court of Sewers
> Sir George Phillips, Bar., M.P.
> Mr. G. Wilson
> David Henry Stable, Esq., Clerk to the Holborn and Findsbury Commission of Sewers, and John Roe, Esq., Surveyor
> Beriah Drew, Esq., Clerk to the Surrey and Kent Commission of Sewers
> Joseph Gwilt, Esq., Surveyor to the Lambeth District of the Surrey and Kent Commission of Sewers
> Mr. Edward I'Anson, Surveyor to the Southwark Division of the Surrey and Kent Commission of Sewers
> Mr. J. Newman, Surveyor to the Rotherhithe District of the Surrey and Kent Commission of Sewers
> Henry Austin, Esq., C.E.
> Edward Cresy, Esq., Architect

W. Ranger, Esq., C.E.

J. Roe, Esq. (3rd part)

The Rev. Morgan Cowie, M.A.

Mr. Alderman Musgrove, Chairman, and J.W. Unwin, Esq., Clerk, the Tower Hamlets Commission of Sewers

Mr. J. Beek, Surveyor to the Tower Hamlets Commission of Sewers

William Baker Jr., Esq., Clerk to the Poplar Marsh Commission of Sewers

C.A. Smith, Esq., Clerk to the Greenwich Commission of Sewers

Lieut. Col. Hall, R.E.

Captain W. Yolland, R.E.

The Rev. John Garwood

J. Billing, Esq., Architect[146]

This *First Report* makes no direct mention of the information compiled by the various Sub Committees set up in 1848 under the Lambeth Central Sanitary Committee, however, it is likely that the information in those reports was used as evidence. The reports of the Sub Committees followed a similar pattern to Chadwick's earlier sanitary report and commented on the living conditions of Lambeth's poor, including the structure of the housing, the low-lying nature of the habitation in relation to the River Thames, the sanitation, the water supply, the drainage, the state of paving and roads, and the *nuisances*, dust heaps and general rubbish (including human excrement) which had accumulated in the courtyards and roads. The Lambeth District Sanitary Reports are discussed in detail in Chapter 6.

Verbal evidence given to the Royal Commission by Mr. Wagstaffe, a surgeon in Lambeth, painted a picture quite different from reality and that depicted in the District Sanitary Reports. When describing the lack of drainage into sewers from houses, Wagstaffe answered, "Every person is, and always has been, permitted to drain into the sewer, on application to the Commissioners. It was only in the Act passed this year that we got power to take care that should be done." The questioner asked if this had been done. "They are in the course of exercise. At this moment I am engaged in making out a long list for putting the act in force in that respect."[147]

Perhaps Wagstaffe was making a list, but the majority of houses in Lambeth were not immediately connected to the main sewers, and certainly for the houses along the Lambeth waterfront, this was never to be the case.

Wagstaffe also explained how there was a rota for cleaning out the sewers and that this was done about every nine months. The filth dredged out of the sewers and ditches was left on the side of the road and then cleared away. When queried about whether this was also the practice in heavily populated areas, and if indeed the mounds of filth were cleared away, Wagstaffe said there would always be exceptions to the rule. A discussion concerning the work necessary to provide drainage and sanitation to Lambeth resulted in Wagstaffe's admission that they would have to borrow money to do so. It was the cost of providing sanitation for the area which made the proposed works prohibitive.

With the exception of the City of London, six Commissions of Sewers were subsequently abolished, including the one for Lambeth.[148] The Metropolitan Commission of Sewers employed 23 members, replacing the positions of around six or seven hundred Commissioners. The members included Lord Ebrington, Joseph Hume, R.A. Slaney M.P., Dr. Neil Arnott, Dr. Thomas Southwood Smith, Professor Richard Owen, Sir James Clark (physician to Queen Victoria), Sir Henry de la Beche, the Rev. W. Stone, the Dean of Westminster, Sir Edward Buxton and John Bullar (both philanthropists), John Walter III (the proprietor of *The Times*), Lord Ashley, Lord Morpeth and Edwin Chadwick himself.[149] The new authority which emerged, the Metropolitan Commission of Sewers, appointed Joseph Bazalgette as Assistant Surveyor[150]; the authority was a forerunner of the Metropolitan Board of Works.[151]

At first the City of London was not to be included in the Metropolitan Commission of Sewers Bill, the legislation for which the investigation was making its inquiries, but following publication of the *First Report*, Chadwick realized it would be advantageous for London as a whole for the City to be included. The City of London was not happy to be included under a central power, but Lord Morpeth supported the benefits of Chadwick's proposal. The Health of Towns Association also became involved, and in the end Morpeth — and the City's own representative in the House, Lord Russell, the Prime Minister — insisted the City be included in the Consolidated Metropolitan Commission of Sewers. The City continued to protest and in the end two Bills went through Parliament, the City being covered by its own City Sewers Bill.

Lord Morpeth had hoped that a single body would oversee drainage, water, cleansing and paving, but this was not to be until 1854. Until then the General Board of Health and the Metropolitan Commission of Sewers existed separately. Chadwick had also wanted to see greater control for burials and the water companies brought under tighter control, particularly the Lambeth Waterworks Company, which was trying to expand and yet still supplying poor quality water.[152]

One of the members of the Sub Committees which undertook The Lambeth District Sanitary Reports in January 1848 commented on how the abolition of the Commissioners of Sewers was a move in the right direction:

"...now fortunately abolished ... who during so long a succession of years abstracted large sums of money from the pockets of the people. Neither ought we to be much surprised ... when we learn from ... the Metropolitan Commissioners of Sewers...."[153]

A report in *The Times* in 1852 commented on how "Formerly the sewers were managed by a number of local commissioners, whose surveyors were paid by a percentage upon the works they proposed, and these gentlemen, in order to enrich themselves, proposed ... works to the amount of £100,000.... It was found upon enquiry that the amount of works necessary did not exceed £10,000."[154]

The *First Report* of the Metropolitan Sanitary Commission of 1848 confirmed that the Commissioners in Lambeth (Joseph Gwilt, Edward I'Anson and Joseph Newman) earned £50 per year and did indeed receive a commission for new work done.[155] It is doubtful, however, that much new work was undertaken, as successive reports on the state of Lambeth's sewers would indicate that very little was ever done to alleviate the poor service in the area.

By 1848, Chadwick was firmly convinced that insanitary living conditions were inextricably linked to the development and spread of cholera, although the prevalent view in the *First* and *Second Reports* of the Metropolitan Sanitary Commission was that the disease was contagious. Chadwick felt that the cleansing of areas like Lambeth would prevent the spread of cholera, but Sir William Pym, Superintendent of Quarantine at the Privy Council Office, had other ideas, based on his own conviction that cholera was a contagious disease, and as Chadwick related: "Sir William Pym has been over to me to urge remonstrances against appointing these Boards [to cleanse and remove *nuisances*] on account of the work it will occasion."[156]

In order to resolve the difference of opinion between Pym and Chadwick on how to avoid a full-blown resurgence of cholera, on July 10, 1848, Lord Morpeth moved to introduce a Cholera Bill. Chadwick still persisted with insisting that his way of dealing with the matter be adhered to, and eventually Lord Morpeth convinced Lord Lansdowne, the President of the Privy Council, to transfer responsibility for cholera to the General Board of Health. On August 7, 1848, the Bill, known as the Nuisances Removal Act, was passed, replacing the Act of the same name of 1846 and revising the power of local authorities to deal with nuisances; it also gave responsibility for cholera to the Board. Unfortunately the Act was badly thought through, creating ambiguity as to who exactly was responsible for the removal of nuisances:

> Cesspools may be emptied: but stinking dust heaps are left, because the scavenger removed them when it suits his convenience. The cesspools may be cleansed and the dust removed but heaps of old dung are left which is neither the business of the dust contractor, nor of the sewers men to remove. By

a fortunate concurrence the night soil, the coal ashes and the dung may be removed and the court would smell sweet but for some dead cats, or a dead dog, or fish garbage which the dustmen and the sewer men under some contracts declare it is not *their place* to remove. The Inspector of Nuisances is sent for and he says it is not his place to do it, he has no allowance for paying anybody to take it away: the overseer won't allow it and [the] overseer says he would not mind but the Poor Law commissioners won't allow it. The Inspector of Nuisances says his place is to prosecute the parties who left the animals there — if he could only find them.[157]

The General Board of Health had no power to enforce the legislation, and the plain fact was that the Poor Law guardians did everything they could to avoid spending money.[158] With the threat of a new cholera epidemic imminent, on August 31, 1848, The Public Health Act was finally passed, though it did not include many of the recommendations of Chadwick's sanitary report, such as national sanitary, sewerage or public health commissions. However, it did establish a Central Board of Health and local boards of health in England and Wales, but not in London and only where the death rate exceeded 23 per 1,000; elsewhere they could be established by petition from not less than one-tenth of rate payers. The boards of health were not obliged to appoint medical officers but were permitted to do so if they wished. They had responsibility, but were not obliged, for water supplies and drainage, the sewers, the cleaning of streets, the removal of nuisances and the regulation of slaughterhouses. However, all new houses had to be built with provision for sewage disposal. The Act was to be extended to Scotland but this proved to be impossible as without the civil registration of deaths, rates could not be ascertained, moreover, the Scots were not content to submit to rule from London. William Alison also expressed his doubts in the legislation and a bill was not introduced in Scotland until 1867.[159]

Chadwick resigned from the Metropolitan Commission of Sewers in 1849 but continued in his role as Commissioner to the new Central Board of Health, established in 1848, working alongside Dr. Thomas Southwood Smith (Medical Commissioner) and Lord Ashley. The Board existed until 1854 when public health was passed to a new committee led by Sir John Simon (1816–1904),[160] who in 1848 had been appointed first medical officer of health for the City of London.[161] Chadwick was knighted in 1889.

3

Migration

London has always attracted migrants as it is there that many of them think they will make their fortune — like the rags-to-riches story of Lord Mayor, Dick Whittington, who came to London believing the streets were paved with gold. The Industrial Revolution in Britain served as a catalyst for economic migration, and many migrants left the countryside to find work, and in some cases their fortune, in industrial centers such as Lambeth. In almost every case of relocation from a rural to an industrialized working environment, migrants moved to improve their economic status and, like Dick Whittington, many also harbored a desire for social mobility.[1]

The capital city of the United Kingdom, London is one of the oldest and busiest cities in the world. Its position in the moderately temperate southeast corner of England, close to the mouth of the River Thames, made it a pleasant, well protected place to live, work and trade. The Romans founded a settlement, which they named Londinium, on the north bank of the Thames, on the site of today's City of London, after their arrival in Britain in 43 A.D. Today's infrastructure still mirrors much of what the Romans established, but especially the ancient trackways they adopted and developed, many of which inevitably lead to the crossing points of the River Thames. A 60-foot-long Roman flat bottomed boat was found in 1910 during building on the south bank of the river, just to the north of Westminster Bridge by Lambeth. Coins found in the remains dated the boat to around 300 A.D. and further work has suggested it was a ferryboat.[2] Until the eighteenth century, ferries were the only way to cross the river, because up to 1729[3] the only bridge crossing the Thames was London Bridge.

The Romans understood the value of good transportation. By land and by sea they were successful travelers and skilled at moving their marching army swiftly from one place to the next, expanding their empire. In Britain, the Roman infrastructure caused a significant change to the landscape as the Romans engineered roads, often straighter, and in places more direct, than the ancient trackways they had set out to follow. Settlements developed around the roads which connected the main Roman cities and the capital. In London settlements sprung up around the river crossing points and the area around the City and the Tower of London swiftly developed, transforming London into a major international center for commerce and trade.

Watling Street linked Dover (*Dubris*) to Canterbury (*Durovernum*) and to London, where it crossed the river close to Lambeth at Southwark over a bridge to the east of the modern London Bridge. Watling Street gave access to the Roman city and then continued north to St. Albans (*Verulamium*), in Hertfordshire, and Wroxeter (*Viroconium Cornoviorum*), in Shropshire. Stane, or Stone, Street started on the southwest side of modern London Bridge and followed the route of today's Borough High Street on the eastern edge of Lambeth, linking London to Chichester (*Noviomagus Regnorum*), in West Sussex, across the North and South Downs. It is possible that there was an extension of Stane Street across the Lambeth Marshes to Stangate[4] on the southern shore of the Thames, close to today's St. Thomas' Hospital, and very near to where the Roman ferryboat was discovered in 1910. While boats would have crossed the Thames at this point, there is as yet no archaeological evidence for formal bridging. Pre-Roman remains of an ancient causeway-type structure have been found on the southern shore further up river at Nine Elms, Vauxhall, the southern tip of the Lambeth waterfront.[5] The Roman road Portway linked a river crossing at Pontes, modern-day Staines, in West London, to the towns of Silchester (*Calleua Atrebatum*), in Hampshire, and Dorchester (*Durnovaria*), on the Dorset coast. Ermine Street started at London's Bishopsgate, north of the Thames, and the route, with some extensions, linked London to Leicester (*Ratae Corieltauorum*), Lincoln (*Lindum*), Doncaster (*Danum*), in Yorkshire, and York (*Eburacum*).[6]

Until the eighteenth century most people in Britain traveled on foot, the more affluent on horseback or by carriage. The famous diarist Samuel Pepys (1633–1703) mentions departing on journeys from London by coach from Lambeth many times. In Chaucer's *Canterbury Tales*, written in the last quarter of the fourteenth century, the pilgrims in the story met at an inn in Southwark, and set off by foot and by horse down Roman Watling Street to Canterbury:

> And specially, from every shire's end
> Of England, down to Canterbury they wend
> To seek the holy blissful martyr, quick
> To give his help to them when they were sick.
> It happened in that season that one day
> In Southwark, at *The Tabard,* as I lay
> Ready to go on pilgrimage and start
> For Canterbury....[7]

The Romans had built Watling Street to link London to Rochester, Canterbury and the port of Dover. By the fourteenth century, the route was well established, latterly trodden by pilgrims en route to Canterbury Cathedral, where the Catholic saint and martyr Thomas Becket had been murdered in

1170 by followers of King Henry II. Today, stretches of Watling Street are still known as The Pilgrims' Way.

Southwark butts onto Lambeth and was well known from medieval times as a centre for inns, bearbaiting and entertainment of all sorts. Shakespeare's association with the place is well known, but Chaucer also knew the extended area well: "Kennington lies south-east of Vauxhall and Lambeth.... The old manor-house is supposed to have stood a little east of the Wandsworth Road. The manor became royal property towards the end of the 14th century. Geoffrey Chaucer was made clerk of the works there in 1389, for which with several other charges he received 2*s.* a day."[8]

Even in the eighteenth century with the dawn of stagecoach travel, walking was the only affordable option for most people. In Charles Dickens' 1850 work, *David Copperfield,* his protagonist of the same name flees from London to Dover. Unable to afford any other means of transport, the young boy decides to walk, starting his journey on a Saturday night and joining Watling Street at Greenwich, a short distance to the southeast of Lambeth and Southwark. It took David several days to walk from London to Dover, but in those days walking such long distances was not unusual. "For anything I know, I may have had some wild idea of running all the way to Dover ... and started for Greenwich ... I came to a stop in the Kent Road ... I got, that Sunday, through three-and-twenty miles on the straight road, though not very easily.... I see myself, as evening closes in, coming over the bridge at Rochester."[9]

Another famous protagonist of Dickens is *Oliver Twist,* who, in the 1838 novel of the same name, walked to London to seek his fortune:

> Oliver reached the stile at which the by-path terminated; and once more gained the high-road.... The stone by which he was seated, bore, in large characters, an intimation that it was just seventy miles from that spot to London. The name awakened a new train of ideas in the boy's mind. London!— that great large place! ... no lad of spirit need want in London; and that there were ways of living in that vast city, which those who had been bred up in country parts had no idea of. It was the very place for a homeless boy....
>
> Oliver walked twenty miles that day; and all that time tasted nothing but the crust of dry bread, and a few draughts of water, which he begged at the cottage-doors by the roadside. When the night came, he turned into a meadow; and, creeping close under a hay-rick, determined to lie there, till morning ... when he set forward on his journey next morning, he could hardly crawl along.
>
> He waited at the bottom of a steep hill till a stage-coach came up, and then begged of the outside passengers; but there were very few who took any notice of him....
>
> In fact, if it had not been for a good-hearted turnpike-man, and a benevolent old lady, Oliver's troubles would have been shortened by the very same process which had put an end to his mother's....

> Early on the seventh morning after he had left his native place, Oliver
> limped slowly into the little town of Barnet [northwest London].

Many migrants would have arrived in Lambeth in the same manner as young Oliver Twist.

In the eighteenth century, and with the start of industrialization, it was realized, for the first time since the Roman period, that a good and efficient road system was important to Britain's development. Thomas Telford (1757–1834) devised a way of re-surfacing roads which was similar to that used by the Romans, using layers of different sized stones and ensuring that surfaces had a camber to allow for drainage.[10]

The Turnpike Trusts were set up by Act of Parliament in Great Britain in the 1700s, the first being passed in 1707.[11] The trusts were private organizations whose members were made up of local landowners and businessmen, transferring responsibility from the local parishes. Legislation was necessary to resolve the terrible state of Britain's roads and throughout the eighteenth century, gates, toll bars and toll houses were set up in towns and villages all over the country to charge road users; funds were intended for the upkeep of the highway.[12]

Telford's methods were expensive and not as widely adopted as those of John Loudon McAdam (1756–1836) whose system for road building was less complicated, incorporating fewer layers of stone, still laid with a camber for drainage, but with a top layer of crushed stone and gravel. The new macadam roads and a gradual improvement in the building of coaches meant that the length of long distance journeys were reduced by several days.[13]

Lambeth was directly affected by the trusts which maintained and improved Kennington Park Road (now called Brixton Road), part of Roman Stane Street, and Clapham Road (now called Brixton Hill), which improved access from the southern counties of England to Lambeth and the river. The trusts started the steady process of opening up the south bank of the River Thames and by the second decade of the nineteenth century, the old fields and enclosures of the Lambeth estates had been linked by a network of roads which still exist today. Much of this work was done by the Lambeth Manor Enclosure Commissioners, who were able to define and formalize the boundaries of common land with the Enclosure Acts of the early 1800s (see Chapter 1).[14]

Lambeth's development was further accelerated with the building of Westminster Bridge in 1750, Blackfriars Bridge in 1769, Vauxhall Bridge in 1816 and Waterloo Bridge in 1817.[15] However, it must be recognized that while the roads were improved, they were most certainly not up to today's standards. Travel by stagecoach was uncomfortable and robbery was common, moreover, the coaches were expensive and therefore out of reach of the aver-

Circa 1840, a stagecoach leaves the Coach and Horses inn, Strood Hill, Strood, Kent, progressing east down Watling Street towards Rochester Bridge and the North Downs. Print from an engraving entitled "Rochester." The Medway Archives and Local Studies Centre, Couchman Collection; [cf. p.19] c.1840 p.20 (L). Reproduced by kind permission of the Director of Regeneration, Community and Culture.

age worker. The fare from London to Edinburgh, for example, would have cost the equivalent of several months' wages.[16] While stagecoaches may not have revolutionized travel for the average person, they did change communication. Mail coaches were introduced in 1784 and these were able to bring news from London to every part of the country, perhaps including the information that there were jobs to be had in Lambeth.[17] Coaching became an industry in itself, with inns being established at points along the main thoroughfares where travelers and horses could rest and be fed and watered. Stables and blacksmiths benefitted, as did the makers of the coaches themselves.

The illustration shows a stagecoach leaving Strood in Kent in around 1840, though this is going east along Watling Street in the direction of Canterbury or Dover. The proximity of Kent to London meant that migration to London was relatively easy. The *Pigot's Directory* of 1832 to 1834 shows that travel was frequent from Rochester by coach, van (passengers and goods) and "carriers." Travel to London by water was also common. The River Medway flows into the Thames Estuary, which in turn flows past much of the North Kent Coast till it joins the North Sea. The Thames and Medway Canal, which opened in 1824, made journeys even faster. Deep enough for sailing barges, it linked the Medway at Strood to the Thames at Gravesend, cutting through the Hoo Peninsula. While the link boosted trade temporarily, and livened up trade — and even the marriage prospects — of villagers on the peninsula, technical problems and the slowness of the locks meant that enthusiasm for the new canal was short lived, and by 1846 the canal was filled in by the South Eastern Railway.[18]

The most common boats plying the Thames and the Medway at this time were spritsail barges, hoys (a type of barge), and steam packets. Pigot's advertizes "conveyance by water" from Strood on James Thomas' hoys by the Thames and Medway Canal every Wednesday and Saturday. In *Wright's Topography of Rochester*, records show that Feeland's hoys went from Rochester to London once a week, and Crockford's and Joslin's hoys also went from Chatham to London, each once a week.[19]

In the early years of the Industrial Revolution, migration was inhibited by The Laws of Settlement of 1662, whereby parishes were financially responsible for their population. Should someone arrive from the outside, parishes were reluctant to take responsibility, and travelers were often *removed*. Naturally there were exceptions, and the law generally applied to those without the means to set up independently in a new parish:

> First, anyone able to rent a tenement for £10 per annum was exempt from its provisions and, second, anyone who did not meet this criterion had to reside in a parish for forty days without objection if they were to gain a *settlement*. A settlement would entitle migrants to poor relief in the parish in which they

Barges similar to those which would have sailed the Thames and Medway in the nineteenth century taking part in the 100th Medway Barge Match in May 2008. Photograph by Elaine Gardner, first published in the August 2008 edition of The Clock Tower, *the journal of The Friends of Medway Archives and Local Studies Centre.*

lived. In addition, there were other routes for men and women to gain a settlement; for example, by being bound to an indentured apprenticeship ... by being hired into service for a year and fulfilling that time, and, for a woman, by marriage. However, these provisions were all conceived as exceptions to the basic rule. The fundamental purpose of the law was to prevent poor migrants from acquiring a settlement and to sanction their removal.[20]

By the early years of the nineteenth century, factory owners were finding that the existing poor laws were stifling their ability to attract unskilled workers, as parishes were usually small areas of jurisdiction. The Poor Law Amendment Act of 1834 created a Poor Law Commission in England and Wales whereby responsibility for the poor was moved from the parish to the Poor Law Union, which tended to cover a larger geographical area. These were controlled by a Board of Guardians from the well-to-do of the locality, including the church and business. Then in 1846, Sir James Graham (1792–1861), the then Home Secretary, introduced The Poor Removal Act which meant that Poor Law Unions could not remove any resident residing in a parish for a minimum of five years who had not yet gained settlement.

Lambeth's rapid development as an industrial centre (see Chapter 5) meant that businesses were in constant need of skilled and unskilled workers. The variety of businesses in Lambeth, including distilling, pottery, boat building, bone crushing, and candle manufacturing, to name but a few, meant that every type of skill was required, though the need for laborers was probably the greatest. The need for unskilled labor was particularly attractive to agricultural workers who had no particular skill to offer. Lambeth was unique at the beginning of the nineteenth century in having a highly developed communications network of roads, rivers, canals and railways linking it to the rest of the country. The number of people coming in and out of Lambeth on a daily basis would have enhanced verbal communication and enabled those living farther afield to know of the job opportunities available. For example, James Osmotherly, living on the Hoo Peninsula, would no doubt have heard of the need for laborers from someone traveling on a hoy or barge, and he himself may even have travelled to Lambeth down the Thames.

Despite a relaxation in the rules covering interparish migration, people still tended to move shorter rather than longer distances to start a new job, though London's reputation for having streets *paved with gold* had a tendency to attract workers from farther afield and from abroad. Apprentices also traveled greater distances to work, the terms of which were often set up through business or family connections. Traveling a long distance to a secure job with accommodation was very different from arriving in London with no job and nowhere to stay, especially if you had very little money. Unskilled workers therefore tended to be employed locally, or from not very far afield. A worker's reputation and loyalty were also important and to rebuild one's reputation in a new area would have been risky.[21]

Statistics compiled by Pooley and Turnbull in their study on migration and mobility show that migration for the period 1750 to 1879 was on the whole over shorter distances and by younger male workers with their immediate family. Whether males journeyed first and families joined later is unclear. However, a move to an industrialized centre such as Lambeth would have been undertaken not just for the benefit of the father but also for male sons, in the expectation that they would later be able to take up apprenticeships. This data was compiled from "16,091 life histories provided by family historians."[22]

Migration, 1750–1879[23]

Distance	Semi-Skilled Industrial	Unskilled Industrial	Agricultural Laborer
5–9.9 kms (3–6 miles)	10.1	12.2	20.1
10–19.9 kms (6–12 miles)	13.5	15.6	16.1
20–49.9 kms (12–31 miles)	21.3	16.0	14.8
50–99.9 kms (31–62 miles)	14.9	11.8	6.8
Age			
< 20	17.5	15.9	26.8
20–39	64.8	67.3	55.8
40–59	16.6	14.4	15.0
Marital Status			
Single	37.4	35.7	42.5
Married	61.2	62.9	56.1
Companions			
Nuclear family	61.6	62.1	54.2
Position in Family			
Male head	80.7	83.7	83.6

The flow of people into Lambeth was rapid as the area developed. Figures compiled from census parish tables show that Lambeth's population grew from 34,135 in 1801 to 131,131 in 1841, a rise of 96,996 in just 30 years.[24] It must have been almost impossible for the authorities to keep track of who was coming in and out of the parish, moreover, a comparison of the 1841 and 1851 Censuses shows that residence was not permanent and workers would move from one place of rented accommodation to another.

Permanent residence in the parish may be reflected in the register of births, marriages and deaths, indicating an affiliation to the parish church. Moreover, a comparison of successive census records also indicates the number of generations born in the parish, again, reflecting permanent settlement within the area.

A comparison of the 1841 and 1851 Censuses for Lambeth[25] shows that in 1841 97,799 people were counted in Lambeth, and this increased to 141,060 by 1851, an increase of 43,261, or just over 44.2 percent. The real figure for this is probably slightly higher as the cramped living conditions in Lambeth, and the nature of shift work in factories, would have made it difficult for the enumerators to count numbers accurately.

The census figures confirm the work of Pooley and Turnbull, that migration to the industrial centers was over shorter distances. In the 1841 Census, information on birth was compiled on the basis of whether an individual was born in the same county of residence. So, in the case of Lambeth, of the 97,799 counted, 45,434 were born in the county of Surrey, which included Lambeth. 52,365 were not born in Lambeth. The 1851 Census gives a more detailed picture, though it naturally excludes those who migrated to Lambeth in the period from 1841 to 1851 and who subsequently died in the cholera epidemic of 1848 to 1849.

The 1851 Census shows that roughly 25.8 percent of the population was born in Lambeth. At this time, London parishes were still included within the old county boundaries. Around 15 percent of Lambeth's population was born in Middlesex, which included, to name but a few, St. Pancras, Whitechapel, Pimlico and Marylebone, all areas within a few miles of Lambeth. In addition to this, 11.5 percent were born in Surrey, the county which included Lambeth, so it is fair to deduce that about 38 percent of the population were born in the area around Lambeth and had not traveled far to live in the parish in 1851.

The highest proportion of migration to Lambeth came from Kent (4.3 percent), which is not surprising considering the historic connections between Lambeth and that county, and their proximity to each other, as discussed above. Other large migration groups came from the counties of Essex (around 2 percent), Suffolk (around 1.2 percent) and Norfolk (around 1 percent). These figures may well indicate that migration to Lambeth occurred in those places where raw materials for Lambeth's industries were being sourced. By the 1840s, the manufacture of pottery was well established in Lambeth and, by the 1850s, Doulton had established itself as one of the parish's biggest employers. Up until 1846, the manufacture of tin-glazed pottery required clay with a high calcite content, and this was brought from Boyton in Suffolk, Winterton and Yarmouth in Norfolk and Aylesford in Kent.[26] It is perhaps also significant that the boats carrying goods, particularly the spritsail barges, were also mostly made in the Medway Towns of Kent.

The manufacture of tin-glazed ware shifted to Staffordshire by 1851. Many of the migrants who had come to Lambeth to work at the potteries would no doubt have remained and continued to work on the production of salt-glazed stoneware, which expanded considerably when John Doulton realized that it could be used for industrial purposes.[27] Salt-glazed stoneware required Dorset clay, which is only found in Dorset, Devon and Cornwall. This and other raw materials, such as sand and stone, were brought to Lambeth by sea on the spritsail barges, the workhorses of the Thames.[28]

By 1851, there were only 629 people living in Lambeth who had been born in Dorset,[29] which may confirm Pooley and Turnbull's findings that people were more reluctant to migrate large distances. However, 2,013 (around 1.4 percent) came from Devon and 642 (a little less than 0.5 percent) from Cornwall. Both counties are farther from Lambeth than Dorset, so there are clearly other factors at work affecting migration, one of which may have been the abundance, or lack, of work in migrants' home counties. Nevertheless, the migration of workers from areas where raw supplies were being sourced indicates how communication was an important catalyst for migration.

The building of the railway would also have had an impact on migration to Lambeth, though travel by rail was still expensive in the 1840s. The London and South Western Railway opened the first stretch of railway in 1838 to link London to the port of Southampton, in Hampshire.[30] Then, in 1834, The London and Southampton Railway Company's Act enabled the building of a branch line from Southampton to Portsmouth, which opened up the Gosport peninsula, just across the water from which lies the Isle of Wight,[31] which was already easily accessible by steamship.[32] In 1841, the first locomotive made the journey between Nine Elms and Gosport, and just a few years later, in 1848, an additional branch line was built from Nine Elms to the new Waterloo Station.[33] Thus, by the end of the 1840s, Lambeth, and London, was within much easier reach for those living to the south and even across the Solent on the Isle of Wight. Indeed, in 1851 the number of people living in Lambeth who were born in Hampshire numbered 2,210, almost 1.6 percent of the population, and an additional 138 (almost 0.1 percent) were born on the Isle of Wight.

The 1841 Census shows that 2,481 Irish were residing in Lambeth, around 2.5 percent of the population, and by 1851 this had grown to 4,303, or around 3 percent. Irish migration was caused by several factors, though the best known was the Great Famine, which began in 1845 with the first failure of the potato crop, caused by the fungal disease *phytophthera infestans*.[34] The population of Ireland had experienced rapid growth by the latter half of the eighteenth century and the country had also experienced famines in 1800 to 1801 and 1817 to 1819.[35] While the Napoleonic Wars and the buoying of prices by the Corn Laws had supported Irish agriculture, the country fell into depression once the wars ended and financial support was removed by the government at Westminster. In the period 1841 to 1850, 14.6 percent of the population emigrated, 9.5 percent of that figure to the United States. It is estimated that from 1780 to 1845 630,000 Irish migrated to Britain, and a proportion of these migrants settled in Lambeth.[36]

In the 1848 Lambeth District Sanitary Report of the area around Lower Marsh, local surgeon Mr. J. Sewell made particular reference to the Irish inhabitants:

> The houses in these streets are occupied by the poorest class of society, in most cases by one family in each room. This was particularly instanced in Frances Street which is occupied chiefly by Irish families. In the house no. 28 in that street there are seven rooms, occupied by seven families amounting to no less than 13 adults and 24 children and the Subcommittee were informed that all the houses in that street are similarly tenanted. The cesspools are generally very full and the drainage bad in this district — the privies in many instances full or nearly so and producing always a stench which in wet and sultry weather is almost insupportable and very injurious to the health and comfort of the poor inhabitants.
>
> The Subcommittee find that many of the inhabitants of this District keep pigs producing very great nuisance. A man in Gloucester Street has 10 pigs in his cellar and on opening the front door the stench was dreadful, the neighbors generally who do not keep pigs complain of the nuisance of those who do.[37]

The migrant Irish community in Lambeth were no different to others living in filthy, insanitary conditions. However, many of them found it hard to adapt their rural ways to confined urban living, and certainly their keeping of pigs in cellars did not contribute to a healthy lifestyle. While the Act of Union in 1800 had united Ireland with Great Britain, there was still hostility towards Roman Catholics. The Irish were perceived as the least able to adapt to the restraints of living in towns and to keep their neighborhoods clean. In addition, their reputation was not enhanced by the possibility they had brought typhus to Britain, which resulted in an epidemic in the years 1817 to 1818.[38]

In 1836 the Irish Poor Inquiry reiterated this view: "The Irish in Birmingham are the very pests of Society ... they generate contagion ... from the filthy conditions of their bedding, the want of the commonest articles of furniture, the uncleanly habits of the inmates themselves, and the numbers which, without distinction of age or sex, are closely crowded together, are frequently the means of generating and communicating infectious disease."[39]

The rapid influx of migrant workers into Lambeth was detrimental to living conditions. Workers needed to live near their place of work, and for every factory worker there was a support network of many others, including publicans, grocers, butchers and shopkeepers. However, as the population of London increased, the infrastructure remained the same, forcing families to live in single rooms without sanitation and running water. The network of courtyards and streets which wrapped themselves around the Lambeth factories were not paved with gold but were piled high with refuse of every sort, including sewage, which seeped from the cesspools and ditches. These areas were flooded regularly by the River Thames, which was itself an open sewer. Life in Lambeth in the 1840s was comparable to that which one sees today in the shanty towns of Third World countries, where families are jammed together with no thought for comfort or sanitation. In such countries it is well known that the combination of these conditions and monsoon rains will bring flooding and the threat of cholera, and this danger was well understood in Lambeth, though the part water played in the process was still not understood.

4

The Development of Lambeth

Since its founding, London has grown both in size and population, but growth was particularly rapid throughout the late eighteenth and nineteenth centuries, mainly due to the industrialization of Britain. Lambeth became the industrial hub of London, and its development depended entirely on its geographical position on the low, south bank on a bend of the River Thames. The Thames was essential for the transportation of people and materials, as was the network of roads leading to ancient river crossing points, such as the Horse Ferry, which was replaced by the first Lambeth Bridge in 1862.

Lambeth was the ideal place to set up a polluting factory, far from the established business and residential areas of London. Here land was cheaper and the parish was unaffected by the rules and regulations of the City of London and the Guilds. The Thames provided an unending supply of water for the new steam-powered engines, and the low-lying marshland, originally two islands named Water Lambeth and Lambeth Marsh, made for easy drainage.[1]

However, as Lambeth and London grew, the waste products of their populations and industries had only one place to go. By the 1840s, London's main source of water, The River Thames and tributaries like the Effra, which emptied just upstream of Vauxhall Bridge, had become open sewers which regularly flooded low-lying areas such as Lambeth. The authorities knew that it would only be a matter of time before cholera returned.

In February 1848, Mr. J. Sewell, reporting back to the Central Sanitary Committee of the Parish of Lambeth commented on the state of St. Thomas' Division, which included the area around Waterloo Road and Westminster Bridge Road: "From the open ditches, bad drainage, filthy state of the streets, and want of cleanliness in the houses of the poor generally, the Subcommittees fear that should it please God to visit London with that awful scourge, the Cholera, the state of St. Thomas' District would augment the spread of that disease to an alarming extent to more healthy localities."[2]

From the start of the nineteenth century to the end of the 1840s, intense development and industrialization attracted migrants and caused the population of Lambeth to rise to almost 100,000, though statistics vary from source to source. John Snow, in his *On the Mode of Communication of Cholera*, cites the 1849 population as 134,768, but he includes Southwark and Vauxhall in this figure. For the same period, William Farr, in his *Report on the Mortality*

The horse ferry in 1840 at high tide; Lambeth Palace is in the background. Reproduced by kind permission of Lambeth Archives department.

of Cholera in England 1848–49, calculates the population of Lambeth at 115,888, which includes the districts Waterloo Road 1st and 2nd, Church 1st and 2nd, Kennington 1st and 2nd, Brixton and Norwood. However, current official figures compiled from census parish tables show that Lambeth's population grew from 34,135 in 1801 to 131,131 in 1841, a rise of 96,996 in just 30 years.[3]

H.E. Malden, writing in 1912 in the *Victoria County History, A History of the County of Surrey: Volume 4,* noted: "In the last 150 years Lambeth and Vauxhall have been transformed from rural suburbs into a part of London itself. Between 1801 and 1831 the population was more than trebled, and ten years later had increased from 87,856 to 105,883. At the beginning of the 17th century the arable land amounted to 1,261 acres and the pasture to 1,026 acres; garden ground was then 37 acres, wood 150, and common land was supposed to be 330 acres. About 1809, 1,271 acres represented the sites of buildings and roads; arable land was then only 540 acres, gardens, private and public, amounted to 830, and common land to 280 acres. The last was enclosed by an Act of 1822. The common fields were enclosed by an Act of 1806."[4]

In his *The Criminal Prisons of London* of 1862, Henry Mayhew, with his associate John Binney, described Lambeth on their approach by boat to Millbank Penitentiary, which was situated on the shore directly opposite:

The yellow-gray stone turret of Lambeth church, close beside the Archbishop's palace, warns us that we are approaching the stenches which have made Lambeth more celebrated than the very dirtiest of German towns. During six days in the week the effluvium from the bone-crushing establishments is truly nauseating; but on Fridays, when the operation of glazing is performed at the potteries, the united exhalation from the south bank produces suffocation, in addition to sickness — the combined odors resembling what might be expected to arise from the putrefaction of an entire Isle of Dogs. The banks at the side of the river are lined with distilleries, gas works and all sorts of factories requiring chimneys of preternatural dimensions. Potteries, with kilns showing just above the roofs, are succeeded by whiting-racks, with the white lumps shining through the long, pitchy black bars; and huge tubs of gasometers lie at the feet of the lofty gasometers. Everything is, in fact, on a gigantic scale, even to the newly-whitewashed factory inscribed "Ford's Waterproofing Company," which, with a rude attempt at inverted commas, is declared to be "limited."

On the opposite shore we see Chadwick's paving-yard, which is represented in the river by several lines of barges, heavily laden with macadamized granite; the banks being covered with paving stones, which are heaped one upon the other like loaves of bread.

Ahead is Vauxhall bridge, with its open iron work at the side of the arches, and at its foot, at the back of the dismal Horseferry Road, lies the Millbank prison.[5]

Lambeth was first mentioned in 1042 in connection with the wedding feast of Dane Tofi the Proud to Gytha, daughter of Osgood Clapa the Theyne, at which died the last Viking King of England, Harthacanute.[6] The church of St. Mary-at-Lambeth, cited in the Domesday Book of 1085, is situated next to the redbrick Lambeth Palace, the residence of the Archbishops of Canterbury since the thirteenth century. The archbishops had first started using a chapel at Lambeth, owned by the Diocese of Rochester, in the twelfth century. This was to ease tension between themselves and the church at York, but also to appease the Benedictine order in Canterbury who saw the archbishops as a threat to the rule of Rome.[7]

In the summer of 1189, the Bishop of Rochester was persuaded to swap Lambeth Palace for the manor and church of Darenth, in Kent, and the chapel of Helles, St. Margaret Hills, also in Darenth.[8] However, pressure from the Pope, concerned that the archbishops were building a powerbase far too close to Westminster, meant that Lambeth was to become merely a residential site.[9] Today, these distinctive buildings are the only ancient buildings still standing on this section of the south bank of the River Thames.

In Tudor times, Lambeth's biggest industry was boat building, and King Henry VIII had a barge house in the area. This section of river was also a favorite for sailing and grand displays like fireworks.[10] Lambeth's position as a backwater — yet conveniently close to Westminster Palace, being directly across the river — was most useful in 1605 to the members of the Gunpowder Plot. Robert Catesby rented a house in Upper Fore Street, Lambeth, where he stored the barrels of gunpowder intended to blow up King James I of England, VI of Scotland.[11]

The industrial development of Lambeth started as early as the 1630s when brewers in Westminster were prosecuted by Archbishop Laud for burning coal and polluting property belonging to the Church of England. Lambeth was considered an ideal place to open a factory where not only would the coal fumes not bother local residents (and there were few, thanks to the marshy environment), but to where coal could be easily delivered by boat. The production of glass at Vauxhall was assured in 1635 when Sir Robert Mansell devised a new way to manufacture glass using coal-fired ovens and secured the supply of sea-coal from Newcastle to London. While the use of coal was still not popular, and Sir Robert's monopoly was ended by Parliament in 1642, Lambeth's role as the industrial centre of London was established.[12]

Until the end of the eighteenth century, Lambeth, with its ecclesiastical connections to Canterbury and the Diocese of Rochester, had been mostly rural in character. Lambeth had been home to fishermen, boat builders, farmers, market gardeners, nurserymen and botanists, like the Tradescant family

"The Thames near Vauxhall Bridge." The view from Millbank shows the early industrial development of Lambeth. City of Westminster Archives Centre.

and William Curtis. However, by the turn of the century, Curtis was forced to move his botanical garden to Fulham, commenting, "I had long observed with regret that I had an enemy to contend with in Lambeth Marsh, which neither time, nor ingenuity, nor industry could vanquish; and that was the smoke of London which, except when the wind blew from the South, constantly enveloped my plants."[13]

The building on virgin land of large residential buildings began in Lambeth in 1776 when an Act of Parliament enabled William Clayton, a lessee of land owned by the Duchy of Cornwall, to grant building leases.[14] By 1794, the land and old great houses at Lambeth were being divided up and sold on at a rapid pace, as this advertisement shows:

> Copyhold and leasehold estate, eligibly situated On the Bank of the River Thames, at the Extremity of Lambeth, And communicating into Prince's street; comprising the EXTENSIVE PREMISES lately belonging to The English Copper Company: which will be sold at auction by Messrs. Skinner and Dyke on Wednesday the 2nd April 1794, at Twelve o'Clock [sic] at Garraway's Coffee-House, 'Change Alley, Cornhill in one lot.
>
> Consisting of A capital working house next to the Thames, Ware-house, various Out-buildings, and a large yard with the Right of Mooring Craft to Low Water Mark, and the Privilege of Shipping Goods; a convenient Dwelling House and Offices.
>
> Also 3 messuages, let to tenants at will at £12 12 0 [twelve pounds and twelve shillings] p.a. And Two in Hand, yearly value   <u>£12 00 0</u>
>   £24 12 0
>
> The Estate is exceedingly compact and very suitable for a Distillery, Brewery, Iron Foundry or any Business where much room is wanted and Water Carriage Required. The copyhold part is held under the Prince of Wales Manor of Kennington [Duchy of Cornwall], subject to an annual quit rent of 2s 4d [two shillings and four pence, about 11p] and a customary fine on death or alienation.[15]

By 1807, the Archbishop of Canterbury was also allowed to grant leases in Lambeth Wick Manor and Lambeth Manor, and so the division of land continued.[16] The Duchy of Cornwall had leased land to brothers Thomas and John Letts for their timber yards. In 1824, the Letts brothers began to sublet land for building on Prince's Meadows between Blackfriars and Waterloo Bridges.[17] In 1832, the Letts brothers leased land between Fore Street and Princes Street for use as a distillery premises, and by 1846, this land had been bought up by the London Gas Light Company.[18]

The distilleries in Lambeth, manufacturing both vinegar and gin, drew in a large workforce. Between 1767 and 1777 Sir Joseph Mawbey set up a gin distillery, Pratt and Mawbey's, in Vauxhall, at the southern tip of the Lambeth foreshore on the site of Copt Hall, and on land leased from the Dean and Chapter of Canterbury.[19] Mawbey joined forces with his uncle, Joseph Pratt, who had been running a gin distillery in Vauxhall.[20]

The site had formerly been used to manufacture glass. Founded by the Venetian artist Rossetti in the 1670s, the company had achieved great success with their blown plate glass, even outselling Venetian imports. The firm was later known by the name of Dawson, Bowles and Company,[21] but by 1785 the once prosperous company had closed, its owners having refused to invest in new technology.[22] The glass industry is still remembered in Lambeth, commemorated in the name of the street near where the factory once stood: Glasshouse Street, later called Glasshouse Walk.

Distilleries and breweries often kept pigs near the premises which would eat the organic waste products of the distilling process. In turn these pigs could then be sold on to local butchers creating additional profit for the business; Mawbey sold his pigs to the Royal Navy.[23] Mawbey's distillery was later taken over by Sir Robert Burnett to produce vinegar.[24] Mark Beaufoy (1718–1782), a Quaker from the well-known family in Evesham, acquired Cuper's gardens in 1763. The gardens had once been a popular local "pleasure ground" or public park, and Beaufoy used the wood from its buildings to build a vinegar distillery. Following the early death of his malster father, John, Mark Beaufoy was apprenticed at a distillery in Bristol. Family legend has it that Hogarth's illustrations of gin drinking in London made such an impression on him that he decided to distil vinegar rather than gin,[25] however, it is likely that his Quaker beliefs also played a part. Beaufoy transformed Cuper's Bridge into a successful works, using its river frontage for the loading and unloading of goods. He had a canny business mind and, as Mawbey sold his pigs to the navy, so Beaufoy ensured that his vinegar was used for pickling and cleaning onboard the Admiralty's ships. The building of the new Strand Bridge, later Waterloo Bridge, forced Beaufoy to move to South Lambeth Road in 1810.[26]

Lambeth Palace also fell victim to the steady transformation of the parish, and in 1828 the architect Edward Blore was invited by then Archbishop Howley to renovate and repair the ancient building. Blore commented that its condition was "miserably deficient as the residence of so distinguished a person as the Archbishop of Canterbury."[27] As a result, he went on to build a gothic style residential wing, The Blore Building, in Bath stone, which was completed in 1833 and is still in use today.

The writer and artist William Blake (1757–1827) lived at Lambeth, at 13 Hercules Buildings, from 1790 to 1800. His time at Lambeth was a productive one, and Lambeth was most certainly an influence on his work, though Lambeth historian Hannah Renier believes that the growing industrialization of Lambeth forced Blake to leave Lambeth for good. His poem *Milton* contains the famous words of the hymn *Jerusalem* and a reference to "dark satanic mills." Much discussion surrounds the true meaning of this passage, but there is a theory that Blake is referring to the factories of Lambeth, and in particular the Albion Flour Mills which were situated to the northeast of Fore Street, near Blackfriars Bridge. Rural Lambeth and this stretch of the River Thames had been a popular site for millers, and the mill for Westminster Abbey (from where the name Millbank comes) was situated on the opposite bank.

The Albion Flour Mills were built in 1769 by Matthew Boulton (1728–1809) and James Watt (1736–1819), two of the great names of the Industrial Revolution and the pioneers and perfecters of steam technology. The machinery at the Albion mills was designed by the Scottish engineer John Rennie (1761–1821), who had been educated at Edinburgh University. Steam power had transformed industrial processes and the Albion Flour Mills benefited from this new technology, churning out around 6,000 bushels of flour a week. However, in March 1791, the factory was destroyed by fire, perhaps no accident, as there was already opposition by workers' groups, perhaps Luddites, to new machinery which made traditional methods — and workers — redundant. The burnt-out factory was not pulled down until 1809.[28]

Thus Lambeth transformed from London's rural backwater to an industrial hub. Parts of the marshland were drained, the large vacated houses of the market gardeners, botanists and artists were swiftly taken over, farmland was built on and the river bank trussed up by a succession of wharves. Boat building continued here, as did the association with the royal family. In 1848, Searle's at Stangate Street were boat builders to the Prince of Wales (later King Edward VII) and in this year they completed a 20-foot skiff, a type of boat resembling a gondola, "used by gentlemen on the Thames."[29]

The owners of Lambeth's new factories were swift to adopt the ideas of the Industrial Revolution. Britain's growing population fueled the need for manufactured goods and the Napoleonic Wars (which ended with France's defeat at Waterloo on June 18, 1815) gave a much-needed boost. In his *History of the County of Surrey* of 1831, Thomas Allen states that there were at least two shot factories operating on and near the Lambeth waterfront, producing lead shot and musket balls.[30] The most famous of the shot towers was probably that of Thomas Maltby and Co., built in 1826. It was still standing in 1951 during The Festival of Britain, right by the Festival's Royal Festival Hall, which was built on the site of the Lion Brewery and the old Lambeth Waterworks.[31]

Steam power was a further catalyst to development. The first steam powered printing press had been opened in London by Applegarth and Cowper in 1819, on a site in Lambeth leased from Thomas and John Letts. The firm was taken over in 1825 by William Clowes and Son, who later moved to a site between Upper Ground and Stamford Street near Blackfriars Bridge. By the 1840s Clowes had expanded the business into one of the world's largest commercial printing concerns using technology developed by Applegarth and Cowper, and employing 600 people.[32]

Steam saw mills replaced traditional methods and engineering firms such as the ironworks of Henry Maudslay (1771–1831), which became Maudslay, Sons and Field in around 1830, moved to a site near Westminster Bridge in 1810. Henry Maudslay was one of the greatest makers of machine tools of the Industrial Revolution, one of his most famous creations being the large screw-cutting lathe.[33] It was also at his works in Lambeth and at the nearby dock, Pedlar's Acre, that they launched in 1832 the first steam ship to be built on the Thames, the *Lord William Bentinck*.[34]

In his *History of the County of Surrey*, Thomas Allen describes the scene in 1831: "The extensive factory of Messrs. Maudslay, supposed to be the most complete in the kingdom. Steam engines, tanks for shipping, and all works connected with various factories."[35]

Indeed Maudslay's works manufactured a diverse range of machinery and machine tools, including mills, locomotives and steam engines, throughout the nineteenth century for customers at home and abroad. The firm worked closely with Marc Isambard Brunel, most famously producing the shield mechanism used for tunneling under the Thames.[36] Maudslay's was situated on a large site between Frazier Street and Westminster Bridge Road, set back from the river and to the east of today's St. Thomas' Hospital. Many great engineering firms that shaped Britain's industrial heritage started life in Lambeth. The Standard Motor Company was founded by Reginald Maudslay, a descendant of Henry, and it was here that The Vauxhall Iron Works on Wandsworth Road made one of the early internal combustion engines called the motor car.[37]

Thomas Field had established a candle workshop at Lambeth Upper Marsh in 1533, but by the 1840s, the firm had expanded to include the manufacture of soap. The making of candles and soap from tallow (rendered beef or mutton fat) was a stinking business. The bone crushing factories in Fore Street contributed to the putrid state of the atmosphere with their crushing and boiling of bones to make fertilizer. In Kennington Lane oil was boiled as part of the process of making floor cloths, at Stangate, closer to the river, the Seysell Asphalte company pumped fumes into the air, and towards Kennington Common the works called Farmer's Vitriol produced sulphuric acid.[38] Smoke and fumes were also produced in vast quantities by the many potteries which began to increase in the eighteenth century and, by the 1840s, dominated the Lambeth waterfront.

Eleanor Coade established her artificial stone works at King's Arms Stairs, by Pedlar's Acre, Lambeth, in 1770, through her connection with Daniel Pincot, a wax modeler for Josiah Wedgewood. Artificial stone had been made in Lambeth by a man called Holt since the early years of the eighteenth century, but it was Pincot who later took over the site and concocted his own mixture of twice-fired glass, lead and clay (lithodipyra) to manufacture artificial stone.[39]

One of the main components of Coade stone was Dorset ball clay, which Eleanor Coade would have known well as she came from Lyme Regis in Dorset. Ball clay is useful because of its high plasticity and is only found in Dorset, Devon and Cornwall[40]; it is a type of Kaolinite sedimentary clay of a fine grain.[41] The carved artificial stone was exported all over the world and in England and London was used by many of the notable architects of the day, like Robert Adam and John Nash. The stoneworks, with its mills, chimneys and kilns, expanded to fill much of the area around Pedlar's Acre and Westminster Bridge, though Coade's ceased making artificial stone around 1843. Back from the river and close by to Coade's stood Maudslay's ironworks on Westminster Bridge Road, and along the riverbank, going downstream, were the Lambeth Waterworks and its intake pipe for drinking water. Next to this stood the Lion Brewery (built 1836 to 1837) and, from 1838, John Fowler's white lead works with two 60-feet tall chimneys and coke ovens.[42]

In 1837 a large Coade stone lion, which today sits on Westminster Bridge, was made to adorn the Lion Brewery. When the Lambeth Waterworks moved to Thames Ditton in 1852, the owner of the Lion Brewery, James Goding, bought the lease of the site and expanded the brewery.[43]

Throughout the world, Lambeth is probably best known for its pottery. Lambeth was the ideal location to produce pottery, with its good water source, transportation links and low lying aspect providing the ideal humid conditions to work with clay.[44] Moreover, there were plenty of large houses ideal for pottery production which were being vacated as Lambeth became a less desirable residential area. The most notable places in Lambeth for pottery manufacture were Glasshouse Stairs, Gun House Stairs and Bridgefoot (at the Vauxhall end of the riverbank), Pedlar's Acre and, until 1763, Norfolk House, on the south side of Lambeth Palace. Norfolk House had once been the residence of Katherine Howard (c. 1521–1542), fifth wife of King Henry VIII and niece of the Duke of Norfolk.

Pottery had been produced in Lambeth since Roman times, as there was a good source of red clay, or London Clay, in the area. London was an insatiable market for all sorts of consumer goods, however, a surprising boost to the pottery trade had been the huge rise in the popularity of hot drinks. The drinking of tea (first drunk on a commercial basis in England in 1654), cof-

The Coade Stone Lion, made for Lambeth's Lion Brewery, now stands at the entrance to West-minster Bridge, in front of the former County Hall (right) and the London Eye. Photograph by David Thomas.

fee (around 1637) and chocolate (around 1657) required a more robust receptacle. In response to this and other market forces, the pothouses of the seventeenth and eighteenth centuries began producing tin-glazed tableware, known as Lambeth Delftware, or tinplate. Tin-glazed pottery required white lime-rich clay, that is, with a high calcite content, which did not occur naturally in the area; the potteries would also have needed a regular supply of sand. The position of Lambeth on the Thames meant that the pothouse owners could easily bring clay in from sources accessible by boat. They imported from sites in Suffolk (Boyton), Norfolk (Winterton and Yarmouth) and Kent (Aylesford).[45]

In 1775 The Earl of Aylesford, of Aylesford, in Kent, granted a lease to claypits on his land: "The Earl has granted a lease of the said claypits for a term of years to a Company of Potters at Lambeth at the yearly rent of £50 with liberty to dig and carry away clay not exceeding 1,000 tuns in a year."[46] Records from the Earl's Estate Book of 1805 show that at least one group of potters from London, presumably Lambeth, was quarrying clay at Court Farm, Aylesford, close to the shores of the River Medway. The clay cost 2s 6d (12½p) per ton, a high cost for the time, no doubt reflecting its quality.[47]

The need to bring in large quantities of raw materials, such as clay, sand and coal, meant that workers outside of London, in Suffolk, Norfolk and in Kent, would have soon heard that there was work to be had in the area. Workers may even have traveled to Lambeth on the barges and hoys bringing in the raw materials.

The production of tin-glazed pottery at Lambeth came under threat towards the end of the eighteenth century from the potteries in Staffordshire, and, in particular, from Josiah Wedgewood, who opened his first London showroom in 1765. Between 1750 and 1846 there was a steady decline in the manufacture of tin-glazed pottery in Lambeth, with only one of an original nine pothouses still in operation. John Wisker, a potter formerly working in Princes Street, Lambeth, took over this last pothouse in Glasshouse Street, near Vauxhall Bridge. After his death in 1835, the factory was taken over by the Singer family, but in 1846 the factory closed to make way for the London and South Western Railway.[48]

Despite fierce competition from Staffordshire, Lambeth had established itself as the centre for pottery in the south and as such the industry was ripe for change and innovation. John Doulton (1793–1873) came to the Lambeth Pottery, Vauxhall Walk, in 1812 from the Fulham pottery, the Fulham Manufacturing Company. Founded in 1688 by the master potter John Dwight, the Fulham pothouse was well known for producing stoneware and Doulton was one of their most accomplished apprentices.[49] By 1815 he was fortunate enough to be able to take a share in the Lambeth company, forming Jones,

Watts and Doulton with Martha Jones and John Watts. The company specialized in ceramic busts, figurines, canning jars and tableware.[50]

In 1820 Jones left and the company changed its name to Doulton and Watts. The business specialized in the production of basic salt-glazed stoneware and swiftly expanded. Part of the company's success was John's realization that stoneware could be used for industrial purposes.[51] In 1826 the business moved to Lambeth High Street, renaming itself Doulton and Company. Like Coade's, Doulton worked with Dorset Clay, and a good supply of sand and stone, which could be shipped by barge to Lambeth, was also available in the West Country.[52] Doulton's new site meant that this and all the company's raw materials and merchandise came in and out of the factory at White Hart Dock in front of Fore Street, right by Great Lemon Court, home to the Osmotherly family in the early 1840s.

Clay was brought from Poole harbor in Dorset to Lambeth by sea on spritsail barges (built at Rotherhithe in London, Whitstable in Kent and the Medway ports of Rochester, Frindsbury and Sittingbourne). These robust barges could carry up to 250 tons of clay at a time, and would also travel up

The shore at Lambeth, and the site of the Doulton dock at the northern end of Fore Street. The first building on the left of the photograph stands today on the site of Great Lemon Court. Photograph by the author.

the Mersey and Trent canals to deliver raw materials to Doulton's competitors in Staffordshire.[53] The barges were the workhorses of the River Thames, being extremely flexible in that they were not only ocean-going but able to navigate through the shallower river waters of the Medway and Thames thanks to their flat bottoms.

It was at about this time that Doulton produced the first ceramic water filter to remove impurities, and in 1835, the device was given royal approval with an order from Queen Victoria for a water filter for her household.[54] Workers at Doulton had no such devices, but even if they had been able to have afforded a water filter it would have most certainly have struggled to purify water drawn directly from the river.

In 1848, Doulton, and their competitor, Stiff's, were advertising glazed stoneware water-closet pans (toilets) with "siphon traps" at seven shillings and sixpence, about 37-and-a-half pence in today's money.[55] Again, such an item would have been far too expensive for the average worker in Lambeth, or anywhere else for that matter. Moreover the average worker would have had nowhere to install such a device, as most lived in temporary rented accommodation.

A list of potters from the *Pigot and Company Directory* of 1832–34 shows how pottery manufacture was well established in the riverside area:

Charles Bloodworth (brown stone), 11 Vauxhall Walk

Doulton and Watts (brown stone and manufacturers of chemical vessels etc), 15 High St.

James Duneau and Co (brown stone), Fore Street

Sarah Green and Son (brown stone), Princes Street

Stephen Green (brown stone), Upper Fore Street

John Higgins (red), Princes Street

David Hill (brown stone), Vauxhall Walk

Samuel Oliver Jones, Princes Street

Dennis Patis (red), Upper Fore Street

John Richard Waters (brown stone and chemical vessels etc), High Street

John Wisker (brown stone and delftware), Princes Street[56]

John Doulton's son, Henry (1820–1897), who would later be knighted by Queen Victoria, joined the company in 1835 and proved to be a driving force in the business. It was he who, at the new Lambeth High Street works, introduced steam technology, and in 1840 installed a massive new kiln for the firing of terracotta sculpture. Doulton expanded further, acquiring other buildings and companies, like Stiff's, Janeway's and Bullock's, and probably some of those listed above in the Pigot's directory, to become one of the biggest employers in the Lambeth area.[57] By 1846, Doulton dominated the

H. Millichamp's terracotta and drainpipe works, circa 1860, on Princes Street near the corner of Salamanca Street and Great Lemon Court. Salt-glazed stoneware pipes are stacked on either side of the factory entrance, ready for shipping and sale. From the Woolley Collection, photograph by William Strudwick. Reproduced by kind permission of Lambeth Archives department.

Lambeth waterfront south of Lambeth Bridge and was one of the area's biggest employers.[58]

Henry's artistic nature gave Doulton an edge over its competitors, though the full effects of this were not to be seen until the 1850s when Doulton joined forces with the Lambeth School of Art. The factory had pioneered the use of stoneware in a range of new markets, and the skill of the workforce was unrivaled. As a result, the factory at Lambeth was the only one that could produce electrical insulators, a line of business which made Doulton's products greatly in demand by the railways and the Post Office telegraphic service.[59] They made fine decorative salt-glaze ware, fine tin-glazed pottery (faience) tile panels and fancy terracotta decorations for public buildings. New decorative effects included faience, impasto, silicon, carrara, marqueterie, chine, and rouge flambe.[60]

It was in Lambeth that the company began producing acid resistant stoneware and glazed piping for London's new sewage system. Yet as Doulton developed a reputation for being at the cutting edge of sanitary technology, in Lambeth the system of cesspits for sewage and the emptying of all

The Doulton Pottery building today in Black Prince Road, Lambeth; the Albert Embankment is in the foreground. Note the distinctive roof and decorative tiled facades. Photograph by the author.

industrial waste into the River Thames continued. Doulton itself was also responsible for filling the Lambeth air with smoke and fumes and for polluting the river water. The working of clay requires the use of water, and any waste, toxic or otherwise, would have been dumped straight into the river. Excess glazes must also have been discarded, comprising of a diverse range of metal oxides, such as lead, tin, cobalt, manganese, iron, copper and antimony.

By the 1840s there were also whiting factories along the Lambeth shoreline which washed and crushed chalk to make whitewash. In 1842 there had been a fireworks maker, Drewell, in Westminster Road, and a fireworks factory, D'Ernst's, in Princes Street, the latter of which blew up spectacularly in March 1842, killing all of the occupants; apparently many barrels of gunpowder had been stored on the premises.[61] There is also evidence of a cement works on the waterfront. An article in *The Salisbury and Winchester Journal* of 1825 mentions White and Company, a cement manufacturer on "the Lambeth side of Millbank."[62] No industry was considered too dirty or too dangerous to be sited at Lambeth.

The *Post Office London Directory* of 1848 lists the jobs of Lambeth residents house by house along Lower Fore Street (numbers 1 to 63) and upper Fore Street (numbers 1 to 40):

> Lower Fore Street: Old Duke's Head [public house], WT Critchfield; Samuel J Addis, junior carver's toolmaker; Robert W Banchard, coal merchant; Matthew Wood, tobacconist; George Smith, whiting manufacturer; Old Red Lion [public house], Mrs. Mary Micklefield; William Ridgward, smith; John Charles and John Field, oil merchants; Charles Cownden, senior boat builder; John Ralph, mast, oar and skull maker; William Crack, barge builder; James and Benjamin Shearin, boat builders; Day and Payne, millers, Malins Wharf; Charles Cownden, junior boat builder; Noulton and Wild, boat builders; Ship [public house], Andrew Wentzell.
>
> Upper Fore Street: Joseph Billes, bone boiler; Abraham, Charles Sedgefield and Henry Crowley, ale brewers; John Howell and Co., patent malt roasters; Jared Terrett Hunt, bone merchant; Ann Points and son, boat builders; Richard Ryder, tobacco pipe maker; Three Merry Boys [public house], John Higgins; Thomas Smith, barge builder; John Barber, bone merchant; Henry and James Cann, bone boilers; James and Richard Nash, barge boat builders; William Hawes, mast, oar and skull makers.[63]

This list of jobs and trades show how a number of service industries grew around the big industries in the area and those with jobs in the factories would most certainly have made additional money at home as and when they could, women and children included. Entertainment was also vital and Lambeth had a vibrant nightlife, attracting the lowest elements of society. Theatres, public houses and prostitution were some of Lambeth's greatest attractions. Astley's Royal Amphitheatre opened in 1774, where monkeys, dogs, pigs and all sorts of acrobats entertained audiences.[64] A handbill of 1846 advertises "Mazeppa! And the Wild Horse," and the second week of "Herr Amidio Neopert, The Great Dutch Bottle Equilibrist."[65]

The Royal Coburg Theatre, the predecessor of today's Old Vic, opened its doors in 1818, following the building of Waterloo Bridge. Music halls, such as the Canterbury Hall, on Westminster Bridge Road, first opened its doors under Mr. Charles Morton, the "father of the music hall." The establishment was named after the pub, the Canterbury Arms, which had stood in Lambeth from the 1600s right up until 1812, when it was burnt down.[66] A handbill for the Canterbury Hall, dating from January 1873, advertises "A splendid staff of stars, including The Marvellous Mystic, Fakir of Oolu, In his Picturesque Garb, Accompanied By The Beautiful Girl! Whom he nightly ENTRANCES in the presence of the audience; and in this state at length — such are his powers — she is seen FLOATING ON AIR ALONE!"[67] Also popular were the so-called penny gaffs and the pubs, which provided cheap entertainment, mainly in the form of melodramatic performances.[68] The public gardens of Lambeth also attracted visitors: Spring Gardens in the 1700s and the famous Vauxhall Gardens, which did not close until 1859.[69]

The roads and trackways leading to Lambeth were not as essential to its development as the river as they were poorly built, often impassable and did not connect Lambeth with its markets as easily or as cheaply as the river. Coaches passed through Lambeth but there were no inns; only the drovers were able to take advantage of the parish's ponds and pubs.[70] Even in 1862, when Mayhew and Binney visited Millbank Penitentiary, the final approach was made by river rather than by road. However, the role of the road in the development of industrialized Britain cannot be overlooked, and is discussed in more detail in Chapter 3. The Turnpike Trusts of the 1700s and the building of Westminster Bridge, in 1750, Blackfriars Bridge, in 1769, Vauxhall Bridge, in 1816, and Waterloo Bridge, in 1817,[71] were all catalysts in opening up the south bank of the River Thames. In addition, The Enclosure Acts of the early 1800s, put into practice by the Lambeth Manor Enclosure Commissioners,[72] formalized and defined land ownership in the area and undoubtedly encouraged and established the development of Lambeth. However, while tolls were still in place on the roads and bridges, it was still cheaper, and probably faster, to transport goods by boat. Bridge tolls were not abolished until 1877, when the Metropolitan Toll Bridges Act of 1877 enabled the Metropolitan Board of Works to buy some of the bridges across the river.[73]

River traffic on the Thames must have been chaotic, with the constant transportation of goods and people, including prisoners. As discussed above, the River Thames linked Lambeth to the sea and to a vast network of tributaries and canals, along which raw materials could be brought from all over the country for the developing industries. The boats too, most of which would have been spritsail barges, would have discharged any waste into the Thames.

An additional factor in Lambeth's development was the building of the railways in the 1830s and '40s. The building of the railways in Britain, the first in the world, was not well planned and there was considerable competition between the different railway companies and the technology that should be developed and employed, such as the gauge size. The building of lines was not well considered, and communities such as Lambeth's took second place to the great rush to create an infrastructure which would further commercial development in the years of the Industrial Revolution. Lambeth's geographical position on the south side of the River Thames, and the fact that it was already industrial rather than a residential, middle-class enclave, made it an easy target for the railway developers and landowners. In Lambeth much of the land had been developed by lessees and they were powerless in the face of landowners selling off land, willingly or not, to the London and South Western Railway Company.

Lord Mayor's Day at Lambeth, November 15, 1845. In the foreground, in front of Lambeth Palace, is the Stationers' Company barge. In the background is a paddle steamer. The river would have been particularly busy on Lord Mayor's Day, but the engraving gives an idea of the chaotic nature of the river and the variety of boats used at the time. Reproduced by kind permission of Lambeth Archives department.

The threat to Britain's sovereignty during the Napoleonic Wars caused great insecurity and a realization that transporting goods and troops by sea was not in Britain's best interest. In the years 1830 to 1831, there was discussion as to the prudence of creating a link between the port of Southampton and London. The company charged with this plan was originally called the Southampton, London and Branch Railway and Dock Company, and the plans included building a branch between Hungerford and the port of Bristol. As with many of the great schemes of the Industrial Revolution, the newly-formed company went into direct competition with another company, in this case the Great Western Railway, which was already employed opening up the great port and industrial center of Bristol. The branch line was therefore abandoned by the Southampton, London and Branch Railway and Dock Company, and in 1834 an Act of Parliament gave the go-ahead for the London and Southampton Railway; construction began almost straight away.[74] However, work progressed slowly as the rival companies continued to argue over branch lines and gauge sizes. An Act of Parliament, the Regulation of Railways Act 1844, helped to formalize the situation.

Initially it was thought to terminate the line at Nine Elms, to the south of Lambeth, at Vauxhall. The line from Nine Elms to Woking Common was the first section to open in 1838, when the company also changed its name to the London and South Western Railway Company. However, Nine Elms was not easily accessible from the centre of London. Here it was harder to cross the river, and road and bridge tolls were an additional difficulty.[75]

There was perhaps another consideration in creating an extension from Nine Elms closer to the center of London. The new railway was a direct link to the south coast and to the port of Southampton. In 1830 the first steamships were introduced on the Solent, speeding up the journey across this stretch of water between the Hampshire coast and the Isle of Wight.[76] Queen Victoria was very fond of the Isle of Wight, having spent some time there as a child. In 1834, The London and Southampton Railway Company's Act enabled the building of a branch line to Portsmouth, the Portsmouth Satellite Railway Company, opening up the Gosport peninsula, the closest point to the Isle of Wight. In 1841, the first locomotive made the journey between Nine Elms and Gosport, and by 1843 Prince Albert made the same journey to meet King Louis Philippe of France at Gosport Station; six days later Queen Victoria accompanied them from London back to Gosport Station.[77]

Queen Victoria and

Queen Victoria, painted in 1840. Watercolor portrait by Aaron Edwin Penley. National Portrait Gallery, London.

Prince Albert acquired Osborne House on the Isle of Wight shortly after this and the house was ready to move into by 1846. To further ease the royal journey, an extension was built from the mainline at Gosport to a new station, right on the coast, the Royal Victoria Station. The royal couple were indeed railway enthusiasts.[78]

Accessibility to the royal family's Isle of Wight holiday home may have been a factor in the building of the branch line from Nine Elms to Waterloo. While Waterloo was not necessarily closer to Buckingham Palace, the journey by road between the two would have perhaps been much more pleasant, as the route from Nine Elms across Vauxhall Bridge passed close to Millbank Penitentiary. A special suite of rooms for visiting dignitaries was even built within the new Waterloo Station.[79]

Waterloo Station was built between Waterloo and Westminster Bridges, offering flexibility for crossing the river. As the latter was the site of one of the ancient crossing points of the River Thames there may have been an element of tradition at work in favoring the building of a new station here. However, as one of the earliest crossings, the north and south banks had also developed more at Westminster than at Vauxhall, and the position of the new Waterloo Station meant that passengers could more easily access the Houses of Parliament, the West End and the City.

The extension scheme from Nine Elms to Waterloo Bridge was devised in 1845. The two-mile line was to be built on a viaduct of 290 arches and six bridges. The viaduct tore through the heart of Lambeth, avoiding certain landmarks such as Vauxhall Gardens and Lambeth Palace, but destroying others, such as the old glassworks, Maudslay's engineering works, the Royal Swimming Baths, All Saints church, and many successful businesses and homes. The Museum of Garden History in Lambeth also relates how "the Canterbury Music Hall had its theatre separated from its entrance by the railway line — patrons walked through a long arch to reach the auditorium, enlivened by an aquarium en route."[80] The London and South Western Railway opened the Waterloo to Nine Elms branch line and Waterloo Station on July 11, 1848.[81] The railway line divided Lambeth in half, its viaduct creating a wall around the industrial riverside, now a ghetto of poverty.

The building of the railway encouraged the opening of hotels, lodging houses and brothels; crime flourished. Lambeth's Museum of Garden History's archive relates how in 1844 Thomas Hood wrote: "'The Bridge of Sighs,' a sentimental account of the suicide by drowning of a young prostitute who jumped from Waterloo Bridge. 'One more unfortunate, Weary of breath, Rashly importunate, Gone to her death!' The epithet stuck; the Bridge of Sighs was visited regularly by London journalists, including Dickens, to witness the miserable procession of women who trailed across the bridge of an evening from the cheap dormitory suburbs of Waterloo and Blackfriars to tout themselves in the theatres and gin palaces of the West End, returning across the river with the dawn."[82]

Lambeth's decline meant that it was the ideal place to build institutions which would have been unacceptable elsewhere in London. In 1815, the Bethlem Hospital was opened for the mentally ill. The building had a facade of Coade stone and was later remodeled by Sydney Smirke, the son of Robert, whose work is discussed later in this chapter. Sydney added a dome to the building, which greatly enhanced its appearance, and today the building houses London's Imperial War Museum. Bethlem Hospital remained a place for the mentally ill until 1864, and there is no doubt that in this age of medical ignorance, patients were not helped as they should have been, as is illustrated by the fact that the hospital became a fashionable destination for Sunday outings.

The Workhouse Test Act of 1723, conceived by Sir Edward Knatchbull, was designed to give relief to the poor. Perhaps unsurprisingly, Lambeth was one of the first places in Britain to have a workhouse, built in 1826 near Lambeth Butts, to the east of the High Street, by the burial ground. Even at this time it was home to 60 people, and by 1777 this had risen to 270. The Lambeth Poor Law parish was formed in 1835 and included the parishes of St. Mary, St. John, Waterloo, Kennington, Brixton and Norwood.[83] The workhouse was feared in Victorian Britain, and Lambeth's institution was bleak and insanitary, but by the authorities it was seen as a solution to dealing with those members of society who could no longer help themselves.

By the 1840s, there was an element of philanthropy in Lambeth, but not on a large scale. Moreover, it extended to the larger community and not just to Lambeth's own working population. St. Thomas' Hospital did not move to Lambeth until 1871, but even at its site in Southwark next to Guy's Hospital, it was Lambeth's closest hospital. The people of Lambeth did not have the luxury of any sort of medical care, and what remedies existed were primitive and subject to ignorance and old wives' tales. Ordinary working people had no access to a doctor, or surgeon, as they were then known. Illness, which was frequent, was treated at home, which is where babies were also delivered. Indeed the surgeon may often have been the person the poor most feared, as the Anatomy Act of 1832 made it legal for a surgeon to claim a body for dissection if there was no money available for burial.[84]

The Lying-In Hospital in Westminster Bridge Road was opened by Dr. John Leake in 1767. Leake's intentions were good, to improve conditions for pauper women in childbirth. The Lying-In Hospital was open to poor women, married or not, from outside the parish as well as those in Lambeth, so not only did it cause a problem for Lambeth Vestry, who were then responsible for those children born in the parish,[85] but it also meant that fewer places were available to local women. While the Lying-in Hospital was most definitely a step in the right direction, it did not ease the hardship of pregnant Lambeth women as much, perhaps, as Leake had hoped.

Also in Westminster Road was the Female Orphan Asylum for around 200 destitute girls, founded in 1758 by Sir John Fielding. The asylum trained the girls in preparation for service in middle-class households. Similarly, at the Magdalen Home on Blackfriars Road, prostitutes were reformed through religious reform with the same purpose, to prepare them for service.[86]

Elementary education was not introduced in Britain until 1870, however, in Lambeth there was some schooling even in the 1840s for the children of the parish. In April 1844, The Ragged School Union was formed in Bloomsbury, to educate deprived children. It was agreed that the schools would only open one or two evenings a week and sometimes only on Sundays. Children at this time were still an important part of the workforce, but the formation of the Union at least recognized a need to educate.

There was a school in Jurston Street which is mentioned by the surgeon John Sewell of Lower Marsh in the Lambeth District Sanitary Reports. Sewell described it as an "infant school" which was attended by 200 pupils in the summer and 150 pupils in the winter; on Sunday evenings it was used as a ragged school for some 300 children. The school was cited by the *Illustrated London News* in 1846 as an example of the good work that was being done for the poor in deprived areas such as Lambeth: "We have selected one of the Society's Schools for illustration, that in Jurston-street, Oakley-street, Lambeth; a locality where the work of reclamation and prevention is much needed. The School is opened on Sunday evenings at six o'clock; and the year's average attendance has been 250 children and 25 teachers. Several distinguished individuals have already visited the Schools in operation; amongst others Lord Ashley, Lord Robert Grosvenor, Lord Sandon, Hon. W.F. Cowper, Charles Dickens, Esq., Lady Troubridge, and Lady Alicia Lambert."[87]

It is not certain if this was the first ragged school in Lambeth or if that honor belongs to the school set up by "Harriet" (Henriette Philipine) Beaufoy under one of the railway arches of the new railway line between Nine Elms and Waterloo, though there is little evidence to support how far Harriet was involved with the project. She was the elder sister of Henry Benjamin Hanbury Beaufoy, and therefore the granddaughter of Mark Beaufoy, the first of the family to come to Lambeth, as discussed above. Harriet must have had a close relationship with Henry and his wife Eliza (née Taylor). Eliza married Henry late in life, having been his companion for many years: she was a "Columbine" at Astley's. Eliza's lowly origins no doubt warmed her to Harriet's work, and when she died in 1847, Henry set up the Beaufoy Ragged Schools in her memory, at a cost of £10,000.[88]

The front cover illustration was painted in 1848 by J.D. Wingfield to show where the new Ragged School would be built. The school was finally built on this site in Doughty Street (now Newport Street) in 1851.[89] A further article published in *The London Illustrated News* described the Lambeth Ragged School in 1851:

> On Wednesday, a handsome building in Lambeth Walk (close upon the South-Western Railway), which has been erected by Mr. Beaufoy of South Lambeth, for the education of the many poor and destitute children in that neighbourhood, was inaugurated at a public meeting of the friends of Ragged Schools in Lambeth; Lord Ashley in the chair. The origin of the school was related to the meeting by Mr. F. Doulton the honorary secretary to the committee, who stated:— In 1845, a few of the destitute and degraded children of Lambeth were accustomed to assemble for instruction, on Sabbath evenings, in a school-room in Palace-yard, near the Palace. In the following year, a few gentlemen in the neighbourhood, at the instance of Lord Ashley, formed themselves into a committee, and afforded the poor children instruction during the week. Soon after, the school was removed to one of the arches of the South-Western Railway Company, kindly granted for that purpose. About this time, the schools excited the sympathy, and attracted the support, of the late Mrs. Beaufoy; and, on her death, her husband intimated his intention of perpetuating her memory and fulfilling her benevolent wishes, by founding the Schools which were opened on Wednesday. The building has cost the sum of £10,000; but the munificent donor has further set apart £4000 for the permanent maintenance of the building. The expenses of tuition will be £250 annually, which is to be raised by subscription. There is accommodation provided in separate apartments for boys and girls, who are to meet for instruction during five week nights, exclusive of Sunday evenings, when religious instruction will be communicated. There is also accommodation for a daily infant school. The Schools are calculated to accommodate about 800 children. There are two large classrooms — one for boys and one for girls; there are also two reception rooms for the training of the children on their first admission, and there are four smaller class-rooms where young persons who show more than usual diligence are taught in the higher branches of education. In the larger class-rooms the committee have erected marble tablets, each bearing the following inscription:—
>
> This Tablet is erected by the Committee of the Lambeth Ragged Schools, as a grateful record of the munificence of HENRY BENJAMIN HANBURY BEAUFOY, Esq., of Caron-place, South Lambeth, by whom these Schools have been built and endowed; and also in grateful remembrance of ELIZA his wife, whose unspeakable private worth has here a fit memorial, and whose benevolence and special kindness to poor children will live in the gratitude of generations who shall enjoy the benefit of these Schools.
>
> "She stretcheth out her hand to the poor; yea, she reacheth forth her hand to the needy."

"Children arise up, and call her blessed."— Prov. xxxi., ver. 20 and 28.

The meeting was opened with prayer by the Rev. Mr. Wix; when Lord Ashley rose and addressed the assembly, eloquently advocating the benefits already derived from the Ragged School system, through which many hundreds had been taken from a state of filth and misery, and raised to one of honorable independence. "There was no reason whatever why Lambeth should not rescue itself from the present disgraceful opprobrium which attached to it. If they exerted themselves in the way he had mentioned, he saw no reason why this district should not vie with any other district in the metropolis, or even with the most favoured parts of the earth." His Lordship concluded by observing that he had no objection to the introduction of any amount of secular knowledge, but it must always be subordinate to moral training.[90]

According to the *Survey of London*, written in 1951, "All but the southern wing was pulled down about 1904 when the railway was widened and the school removed to temporary premises in Auckland Street, Vauxhall and later to Wandsworth Road."[91]

Mark Hanbury Beaufoy J.P., the nephew of Henry Benjamin Hanbury Beaufoy, continued in the Beaufoy's philanthropic footsteps, for when the original Ragged School was sold for re-development, a new school in Black Prince Road was built with the proceeds. The foundation stone of the new Beaufoy Institute was laid by Mark's wife, Mildred Scott Beaufoy, in 1907 and the building was fitted out with Doulton ceramics.[92]

The development of Great Britain as an industrial giant transformed the nation's influence across the world, however, successive governments had neglected the welfare of its workforce and the infrastructure of the towns and cities. Cholera had already struck in 1832, but by the time Waterloo Station was opened in July 1848, London, and in particular the waterside area of Lambeth, was on the brink of one of the worst epidemics the capital had ever seen.

The cholera epidemic of 1848 to 1849 was caused by the drinking of water from the River Thames polluted by human waste. The River Thames was the perfect environment for the cholera bacteria *Vibrio cholerae*, and once Londoners drank the water and became infected, their contaminated sewage reentered the river where the cycle continued. The amount of waste entering the river at Lambeth was excessive, however, it was not only coming from that side of the river. On the north bank of the Thames, on the shore opposite Fore Street, stood the imposing Millbank Penitentiary. The prison had been built on the site of Westminster Abbey Mill, which had been demolished in 1736 for the building of a private house by Sir Robert Grosvenor.[93]

The prison was built in response to the Penitentiary Act of 1779[94] and occupied a piece of marshy land covering around seven acres which did not

"The Penitentiary, Millbank," City of Westminster Archives Centre. The imposing structure of the Penitentiary as it would have been seen from the shore at Lambeth. The barge in the foreground is typical of those used to ferry goods and similar to those which took part in the 100th Medway Barge Match, as discussed in Chapter 3.

abut any important residential areas. The prison had been designed by the philosopher and social reformer Jeremy Bentham (1748–1832) and followed the model of penitentiaries in the United States. Its design was panoptic, that is to give maximum visibility by constant surveillance. Inmates were isolated in separate cells, and any communication between prisoners was forbidden, particularly as they went about their daily tasks of producing items to be sold, such as shoes and mail bags.[95] The purpose of isolation was to reform prisoners, most of whom remained at the penitentiary for around two years, though the longest period of single imprisonment was six years.[96]

Bentham published his ideas in 1791, his ethos being punishment with an appreciation of labor.[97] The design of Millbank Penitentiary was in the form of a wheel, with the governor's house at the centre and six separate pentagonal buildings radiating out, its passages measuring three miles in length.[98] Building began in 1812 and was completed in 1821 (though the inscription on a commerative buttress states the prison was opened in 1816), at a cost of £500,000.[99] The original design was by William Williams, then adapted by Thomas Hardwick, who resigned. John Harvey followed, and was sacked in 1815, and then Robert Smirke finished the project. Smirke was a well-known,

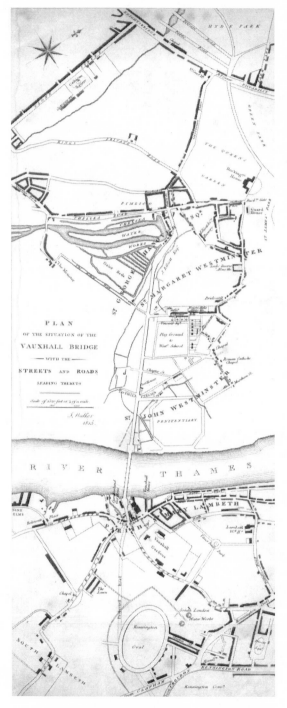

PLAN

OF THE SITUATION OF THE

VAUXHALL BRIDGE

—— WITH THE ——

STREETS AND ROADS

LEADING THERETO

Tory-connected architect who was involved in many famous building projects of the day, including the fiasco of the rebuilding of Strood Church in Kent.[100] It was the Strood builders, Samuel Bakers and Sons (who may also have had a connection with the Baker family at Cooling), who helped Smirke with the foundation problems at Millbank, caused by the marshy ground. Smirke pioneered in Britain the use of making load-bearing foundations from a type of lime concrete and he was also among the first to use load-bearing cast-iron beams in domestic rather than industrial architecture.[101] Samuel Baker junior married Sir Robert Smirke's sister, Sarah, in 1816, and the Bakers and Smirkes continued to collaborate on many London projects, most famous of all being, with Sydney Smirke, Robert's brother, the Dome and Reading Room of the British Library in 1854.[102]

From 1837 to 1844, the

"Plan of the situation of the Vauxhall Bridge with the streets and roads leading thereto." The map drawn by J. Walker in 1815 shows the proximity of the new Millbank Penitentiary to Lambeth. Fore Street and Princes Street are clearly marked on the waterfront, and to the north is Chelsea waterworks. City of Westminster Archives Centre.

Millbank Penitentiary operated as a model to others in London, but by 1848, it was accepted that the prison had ceased to become a model for reform and both Millbank and Pentonville became warehouses for convicts destined for transportation. In his 1862 work *Criminal Prisons of London,* Henry Mayhew described Millbank as "The Convict Depot." Before the American War of Independence, many British convicts had been transported to Maryland and Virginia,[103] but by 1848, Australia was the favored destination and Millbank was the initial repository of those who were then sent by barge to the hulks, such as the *Warrior* at Woolwich. There is evidence, however, that for a time hulks were moored at Millbank itself.

William Baly (1814–1861), physician to Millbank Penitentiary from 1841, wrote to his father at some point between 1837 to 1842. The exact year is unknown, but the letter was written during Baly's period of residence at Brook Street, and after his appointment at the penitentiary. In the letter, Baly writes of the visit to the penitentiary of the Home Secretary, Sir James Graham (1792–1861), regarding the impending government legislation and the possibility that the hulks moored next to the prison would be abandoned.[104]

The hulks, prison ships made famous in Charles Dickens' *Great Expectations,* were decommissioned naval vessels and merchant ships, some of which had been used in the Napoleonic Wars (1805–1815). Home to often thousands of prisoners awaiting a place on a transportation ship to Australia, the hulks were wooden shells, the rigging and equipment of the original ship having been removed. Many of the inmates on board the hulks were imprisoned for years awaiting transportation. Their

William Baly (1814–1861), physician to Millbank Penitentiary. Reproduced by kind permission of the Royal College of Physicians of London.

days began at 5:30 A.M. and ended at 9 P.M., following a day of hard labor onboard and onshore.

Henry Mayhew commented that by 1841, there were 3,552 convicts onboard ships in England, though by 1854 this number had been reduced to 1,298. Conditions aboard the hulks were appalling. Mayhew comments, "So recently as 1841 ... from the report of Mr Peter Bossy, surgeon of the *Warrior* hulk, off Woolwich, which shows that in the year, among 638 convicts on board, there were no less than 400 cases of admission to the hospital, and 38 deaths! ... one of the warders ... remembers seeing the shirts of the prisoners, when hung out upon the rigging, so black with vermin that the linen positively appeared to have been sprinkled with pepper; and that when the cholera broke out on board the convict vessels for the first time, the chaplain refused to bury the dead until there were several corpses aboard...." Mayhew noted that between October 1840 and May 1841, the mortality rate of men on the hulks was greater among those from the middle (7.8 percent) and lower (4.2 percent) decks.[105]

There was no sanitation or running water onboard and by July of 1847, the overcrowding was such and conditions so appalling on the hulks and at Millbank Penitentiary, that in July, questions were raised in Parliament requesting that something should be done.[106] By this time it would appear that any hulks moored at Millbank had been removed, as the parliamentary record, *Hansard,* only refers to the hulks at Woolwich. Nevertheless, the sewage from the penitentiary and the boats transporting convicts from there to Woolwich was still being discharged into the river.

When Millbank was first built, there may have been wells from which prisoners sourced their drinking water.[107] How deep these wells were in the marshy ground and whether they were connected to the river is unknown, however, when Henry Mayhew visited in 1862 he noted that the water was supplied to the prison from the Thames and collected in a large tank:

> We found ourselves in a spacious yard in front of pentagon 6.... Here, in the centre, was an immense oval tank or reservoir.... This was divided into three compartments, and was supplied with water from the Thames, originally for the use of the prisoners. The centre compartment was intended to act as a filter for the water passing from one end of the reservoir to the other; but this was found a failure, and so it certainly appeared, for the colour of the liquid on the filtered side was the light-green opaque tint of diluted *absinthe*.... After the outbreak of the cholera in '54, the several pentagons were provided with water pumped up from the artesian wells in Trafalgar Square.[108]

Excavations carried out at the site in 2001 and 2004 by the AOC Archaeology Group were close to the position Mayhew described. Trench 6 of the excavation "located the south-west corner tower of the prison and a brick drain which ran north-south through the western end of the trench and would have drained water and perhaps sewage ... to the moat to the south."[109] It is not known if the moat had gone by 1848. If it had, then raw sewage would have passed through these drains straight into the Thames, however, certainly even when the moat was in place, it must have drained into the river. Building plans reveal that the water closets for the prison were located on the extremities of the pentagon structures for easy drainage. In his work of 1862, Mayhew describes how prisoners slopped out each morning, "taking care that only one at a time enters the closet."[110] Irrespective of where exactly raw sewage entered the river, water would have been taken back into the penitentiary for consumption.

In *David Copperfield*, written in 1850, but started in 1848, Charles Dickens describes the scene at Millbank:

> We were in the narrow water-side street by Millbank.... A glimpse of the river through a dull gateway ... that one dark glimpse of the river, through the gateway, had instinctively prepared me ... going no farther. The neighbourhood was a dreary one at that time; as oppressive, sad, and solitary by night, as any about London. There were neither wharves nor houses on the melancholy waste of road near the great blank Prison. A sluggish ditch deposited its mud at the prison walls. Coarse grass and rank weeds straggled over all the marshy land in the vicinity. In one part, carcases of houses, inauspiciously begun and never finished, rotted away. In another, the ground was cumbered with rusty iron monsters of steam-boilers, wheels, cranks, pipes, furnaces, paddles, anchors, diving-bells, windmill-sails, and I know not what strange objects, accumulated by some speculator, and grovelling in the dust, underneath which — having sunk into the soil of their own weight in wet weather — they had the appearance of vainly trying to hide themselves. The clash and glare of sundry fiery Works upon the river-side, [of Lambeth] arose by night to disturb everything except the heavy and unbroken smoke that poured out of their chimneys. Slimy gaps and causeways, winding among old wooden piles, with a sickly substance clinging to the latter, like green hair, and the rags of last year's handbills offering rewards for drowned men fluttering above high-water mark, led down through the ooze and slush to the ebb-tide. There was a story that one of the pits dug for the dead in the time of the Great Plague was hereabout; and a blighting influence seemed to have proceeded from it over the whole place. Or else it looked as if it had gradually decomposed into that nightmare condition, out of the overflowings of the polluted stream.[111]

In his *Report on the Mortality of Cholera*, William Farr notes that in Westminster, on the north bank of the River Thames, opposite Lambeth, the cholera epidemic did not begin until June 2, 1849, and Parkes' report does not cover this period. There may have been incidents in the Westminster area prior to June 2, but they have not been recorded, or the record has been lost. Of Westminster, Farr recorded, "110 males and 102 females were deprived of life by cholera, which prevailed in the area with considerable severity...." He went on to say that at Millbank Penitentiary there were 41 deaths out of a total number of inmates of about 1,100, 20 of them occurring from June 21 to July 17. In Westminster St. Margaret parish, in which is situated the Houses of Parliament, "the loss of life from cholera was severely felt." Here the epidemic, according to Farr, started on June 14 and dragged on until October 13, the height being from August 27 to September 23. "In June 7 persons perished from cholera; in July 38; in August 83; in September 89; and in October 6."[112]

When the penitentiary first opened, there was discussion as to whether the prisoners were too well fed. It was agreed in 1822 to reduce their diet, which, in effect, meant cutting down the meat and potato content. This reduction in the ingestion of proteins and vitamins occurred at a time when prisoner numbers were also expanding, but the quantity of food being prepared did not.[113] Moreover, the prison was cold and damp, contributing to a high incidence of pulmonary infections. The prison authorities realised that the cold and poor diet were responsible for the high incidence of illness and tried to improve matters. Dr. A. Copland Hutchinson, then the principal medical officer, and surgeon John Pratt diagnosed both dysentery and scurvy. Despite the authorities' actions to diagnose and prescribe remedies, the real culprit was no doubt the lack of sanitation within the prison, and it is interesting to note that the prison officers who used the same privies as the inmates were also affected with diarrhoea. In the first six months of 1823 there were at least 33 deaths in the prison, their incidence rising as the weather warmed.[114]

Peter McRorie Higgins in his *The Scurvy Scandal at Millbank Penitentiary: A Reassessment* believes that scurvy was a misdiagnosis: "It is impossible to be sure of the diagnosis nearly 200 years after the event — there are a large number of possible food- and water-borne agents, including perhaps most probably amoebic or bacillary dysentery or campybacter, to which the outbreak might be attributed."[115]

Higgins' diagnosis and his description of the bacterial infections caused by the faecal contamination of food and drink are intriguing. It would be unwise to conclude that *Vibrio cholerae* was at work, but it is not impossible that a strain of the pathogen could have already been causing problems in the overcrowded environment at Millbank. In 1823, Millbank Penitentiary was evacuated because of the high incidence of diarrhoea. Many prisoners were released, and of those who remained, the women were moved first to the ophthalmic hospital in Regent's Park, but then to the hulks *Narcissus* and *Heroine*; the men went straight to the hulks *Ethalion* and *Dromedary*. The health of the women fared worst and in 1824 they were released, after which, as far as could be discerned, their illnesses abated. By August, 106 males and 24 females returned to the penitentiary which by then had had improvements made to its sanitation and heating.[116] Reports of the conditions at Millbank between 1824 and 1862, when Mayhew visited, show that these improvements must have been minimal, for the problems at Millbank persisted.

Dr. William Baly was appointed Physician to Millbank Penitentiary in 1841, a position which he held for almost 20 years. Baly was a leading commentator on medical research and development, and was appointed lecturer in forensic medicine at St. Bart's Hospital in the same year. His work at Millbank had begun in 1840, when Dr. Latham, who had taught Baly at University College London, recommended he visit the prison to report on the high incidence of dysentery there. Baly's observations produced many papers, including *Diseases in Prisons*, which in 1847 was to be the basis of his Goulstonian Lectures on Dysentery at the Royal College of Physicians. With William Gull, Baly was part of the Cholera Committee of the Royal Physicians of London set up in 1848, but it was some time before they conceded to Dr. John Snow's theory that water played an important role in the spread of cholera (see Chapter 8). However, it would appear that his lack of certainty over the exact causes of the disease prevented any action being taken to improve sanitation in the penitentiary. The library at the Royal College of Physicians in London holds Baly's letters, and this correspondence reveals the doctor's confusion over how disease arises and is spread. In a letter to his father in about 1841 (during his residence at Brook Street), Baly discusses the possibility that the high incidence of dysentery may be the result of the malaria in the neighborhood. In another letter, dated June 19, 1840, sent to the "Committee of the General Penitentiary, Millbank," he comments on how prisoners' health might be improved by more exercise, fresher air, and most particularly a better diet, including "animal food," i.e. protein.[117]

Sadly, at no point during this period does Baly suggest that the prisoners' drinking water be improved or changed. In his *Report on the Cause and Mode of Diffusion of Epidemic Cholera*, written in 1853, a report prepared for John Ayrton Paris MD DCL FRS, President of the Royal College of Physicians in London, Baly discussed many of William Farr's conclusions, including that of wind direction, which he rules out as the cause of the spread of the disease. He does add, however, that the disease is probably miasmic, due to "morbific *matter*, transportable within limits from place to place by the atmosphere, and capable of increase under favourable conditions in the places to which it is conveyed. For there is no difficulty in supposing that such a matter might attach itself to the surfaces of bodies within these places, so as to remain fixed there and even to increase, as long as the favourable conditions continued, quite independently of subsequent changes in the direction of the wind...."[118]

In his conclusions, Baly still refused to accept Dr. John Snow's theory that cholera was a type of poison acting on the intestines and found in the drinking water taken from rivers and wells.

Yet he did appear to understand that better hygiene, sanitation and drainage would help stop the spread of cholera. Sadly, Baly only reached these conclusions, based on prejudice, arrogance and misunderstanding, in 1853. In 1848, when he was physician at Millbank Penitentiary, the potentially infected fæces of the prisoners were still spewing out into the River Thames, only to be drawn back into the prison again within their own drinking supply. By the summer of 1849, the penitentiary was clearly seen as a source of infection, as this article illustrates from the *Maidstone and South Eastern Gazette:*

> CONVICTS — Much anxiety has been felt during the past week by the inhabitants of Folkestone and Sandgate, at the report that 500 convicts from Millbank Penitentiary were to be located at Shorncliff barracks on account of the increase in cholera at that prison. Upon enquiry, we find that there are no grounds whatsoever for alarm, as only the most healthy of the convicts will be brought here. About 100 arrived by special train on Saturday morning last at Coolinge Bridge near Folkestone, and were marched off to the barracks which had been prepared for their reception, under the superintendence of Capt. GROVE, the governor of the Millbank Penitentiary. The barracks are situated on an eminence, and entirely isolated. A more healthy spot could not be selected.[119]

Closed around 1890, Millbank Penitentiary was demolished for the building of the Tate Gallery, the Royal Army Medical College and Regimental Mess, and the Chelsea College of Art and Design. Three million bricks were salvaged from the site.[120]

Downstream from Millbank Penitentiary, and in full view of Lambeth, being on the opposite side of the river to today's St. Thomas' Hospital, stood the Houses of Parliament. On the evening of October 16, 1834, a fire swept through the Houses of Parliament and the Palace of Westminster. The fire started in a stove in the House of Lords that had been overloaded with the Exchequer's wooden tally sticks. These sticks had been used from medieval times until 1826 to record the collection of taxes, and in 1834 it had been decided to burn the entire collection. In his book *The Annals of London,* John Richardson explained how the London Fire Engine Establishment arrived at 7 P.M. At the height of the fire, 12 fire engines and 64 firemen fought the blaze, which was recorded by a Member of Parliament of the time, Sir John Cam Hobhouse: "The whole building in front of Old Palace Yard was in flames

"The Destruction of the Houses of Lords and Commons by fire on the 16th of October 1834. Drawn on stone by William Heath from a sketch taken by him by the light of the flames, at the end of Abingdon Street." City of Westminster Archives Centre.

and the fire was gaining ground. I assisted in breaking open the entrance to Bennett's cloakroom and then, with several others, rushed upstairs to the Libraries above, next to Bellamy's Eating Rooms. There I directed the men with me to bring down the books from the Libraries, and sent for cabriolets and coaches to carry them over the way to St. Margaret's Church. Shortly afterwards a large body of troops marched down and more fire engines came. The soldiers worked admirably; so did the police."[121]

From Lambeth this scene must have been vivid and quite terrifying. Even today, the position of the Parliament buildings on the edge of this narrow stretch of river makes Lambeth an ideal viewing point, but in the 1800s, spectators standing on the wharves jutting into the river would have been even closer to the conflagration.

By the time the fire had been extinguished all that remained of the Palace of Westminster was Westminster Hall, the crypt of St. Stephen's Chapel (below the Royal Chapel of St. Stephen, where Parliament had sat from 1547 to 1834), the cloisters and the Jewel Tower.[122]

The rebuilding of the Palace of Westminster was decided by the appointment of a Royal Commission and a competition was held to settle the debate on a new design. This was won by the architect Sir Charles Barry (1795–1860; knighted in 1852), who was assisted from 1844 by Augustus Welby North-more Pugin (1812–52). Barry's Perpendicular Gothic design seemed the most appropriate, particularly as a neoclassical design, similar to that favored by Napoleon and the United States for their parliamentary buildings, was deemed unsuitable, having "connotations of revolution and republicanism."[123]

However, the foundation stone for the new Houses of Parliament was not laid until April 27, 1840, the first contract for the "forming, erecting and completing the Cofferdam, River Wall and other Works forming Part of the Foundation of the proposed New Houses of Parliament" being made on September 11, 1837, with the builders Henry and John Lee of Chiswell Street, Finsbury Square, London.[124] The Parliamentary Archives show that drawings for the new buildings were not drawn up until at least 1841; work was not completed until the 1870s.

Thus, in the 1840s, the vista from Lambeth must have been a gloomy one: to the west, the imposing facade of Millbank Penitentiary, and to the east the burnt-out shell of Britain's ancient seat of government. Some even thought that the fire was divine punishment for the parliamentary reforms.[125]

Perhaps the rebuilding of the Palace of Westminster gave the inhabitants

The Houses of Parliament circa 1866 viewed from the first Lambeth Bridge. Reproduced by kind permission of Lambeth Archives department.

Another view of Millbank from Lambeth. The Penitentiary can be seen under a board on which is written "Clayton & Glass Coal Merchants." To the right is the Nag's Head pub, and on the river a paddle steamer can be seen. Watercolor by J. Findlay, Phillips Volumes 1–4/Surrey illustrations. Reproduced by kind permission of Lambeth Archives department.

of Lambeth some cause for hope. King William IV reopened Parliament in February 1835, having given permission for the Houses of Lords and Commons to be temporarily housed in the Painted Chamber and the Court of Requests in the environs of St. Stephen's Chapel and Westminster Palace.[126] The scale of the new construction may have inspired those watching its progress on a daily basis, however, the records for the rebuilding paint a chaotic picture. The length of time it took for the new edifice to be completed indicate that the organization could have been more efficient. *Hansard*, the official report of parliamentary proceedings, shows that by 1847 work was already behind schedule and considerably over budget, almost £1 million having been spent; by 1850, Parliament estimated this had risen to over £2 million.[127]

The rebuilding of the Houses of Parliament most certainly played a role in the development and spread of cholera in the 1848 to 1849 epidemic in Lambeth. The building contracts illustrate the massive scale of the construction. Materials were brought by river to the site from great distances, from places as far apart as Guernsey and Aberdeen, and the numbers of workers on site was colossal: bricklayers, carpenters, masons, plumbers, slaters, smiths, founders and painters. Nowadays the health and safety considerations on construction sites are carefully monitored, but in the 1800s one can be fairly certain that the sanitary conditions of the workers were not paramount and that the river was not just a highway for stone and mortar but also the workers' toilet. In addition, while "superfluous earth and rubbish"[128] was to be taken away, this was only deemed necessary "from time to time."[129] In addition to the number of workers on site, Westminster was still a working place with the Houses of Commons and Lords still sitting; the Courts of Law occupied Westminster Hall.

By January 1849, the construction of the sewers and storm drainage system for new building was giving concern to the authorities, though at this time it was not the discharge of the liquid from the sewers which was so much the problem, but rather their construction and the proximity to the living and working quarters above, both of which might facilitate the escape of smells, or of the dangerous miasma. Henry Austin (1812–1861), the Consulting Engineer for the Metropolitan Commission of Sewers (see Chapter 2), submitted a report, written on August 29, 1848, outlining his worries. Charles Barry's replies are also published in the report and give an insight into the sanitation on the north side of the river from 1848 to 1849.

The sewers of the new building had been constructed to join the existing Abingdon Street sewer to the north, with a total of some 70 to 80 drains emptying into the system, which deposited its contents directly into the River Thames. However, it was the method by which the sewage was held in the system and then emptied into the river which would have further deterio-rated the water quality at this point on the river, and as Barry comments, "During ten hours upon the average in every tide, the outfalls of the public and Palace main sewers are closed by the rise of the tide in the River, and all drainage from the New Palace is consequently stopped for that time period-ically."[130] In other words, sewage would have entered the river at low tide and would not have been flushed away. Most of the sewers along the river oper-ated in the same way, with the sluice gates only opening to deposit their con-tents at low tide.

Austin commented on the shoddy work which had been undertaken in the construction of the sewage system under the new Houses of Parliament. "Several of these upper communications would appear to have been recently made, for the bricks and rubbish knocked out from the openings are still strewn about the sewer.... Mr Barry's attention should be directed to the care-less manner in which this work has been carried on ... brick barrel drains ... wretchedly constructed ... stone-ware pipes; some projecting into the sewer several inches, others stopping several inches short; some broken right away at the mouth by being driven forcibly in.... Some are obstructed at the out-let by bricks and lumps of cement."[131]

The report described how the sewers in question appeared to be con-stantly blocked and poorly ventilated, some sections running above floor lev-els in the vaults of the new construction. In addition, some of these cesspools and sections of these sewers were exposed, one of which passed "within about 12 yards from the basement of the Grand Central Salon connecting the Houses of Lords and Commons."[132] In short, sections of the basement of the new Houses of Parliament were rotting cesspits full of "foul liquid," the accumu-lated muck from the new Houses themselves and the public sewer to the north, and all seeping into the River Thames. Austin described the scene thus: "The noxious gas was bubbling and hissing from the surface as if a great fire were below."[133]

In Barry's defence, he replied to Austin that the drainage of the new Palace of Westminster was "devised and commenced in accordance with the rules and regulations of the late Commission of Sewers for Westminster."[134] Barry stated that in his opinion the sewers had been built properly and he reiterated how the system had been built as low as possible to drain effec-tively into the river. He also added that the system was temporary and in future would be exclusive to the Palace of Westminster. He added:

> Whatever foul deposit may have been found in the Abingdon-street junction of the sewer is wholly due to the foul state of the public sewer in Abingdon Street. The decomposing liquid and solid matter ... is due also to the foul condition of the public sewer in Bridge street, and to the periodical stoppage

of the Palace drainage during the rise of the tide ... at low water the whole of the solid matter and decomposing liquid would pass off if the public sewer were freed from the accumulation of solid matter that has been permitted to collect in it.[135]

Whether this be or be not advisable, it is clear that ample reservoirs for occasional storage under existing circumstances are absolutely necessary in the low situation of the New Palace ... for the immediate discharge of all surface water into the River.[136]

The drainage of the building is as perfect as it can be, all local and other circumstances being duly considered.[137]

While Austin felt that the construction of the sewers beneath the new Houses of Parliament was at fault, neither he nor Barry questioned the fact that raw, rotting sewage was emptying into the River Thames at low tide, and in close proximity to the point of intake of the Lambeth Waterworks Company. This practice continued throughout the summers of 1848 and 1849.

At Lambeth the system of drainage into the Thames was very similar to that which had been devised at the Houses of Parliament. The various sew-

Underneath Hungerford Bridge. To the left, on the shore, can be seen a bump, or earthwork, which may indicate the remains of the intake pipe of the Lambeth Waterworks. The pipe was certainly in this vicinity and the photograph illustrates its proximity to the Houses of Parliament. Photograph by the author.

ers which deposited Lambeth's waste into the Thames had sluice gates at their exits which opened at low tide. Evidence given to the Metropolitan Sanitary Commission in 1848 explained that, depending on the neap and spring tides, the gates to the sewers opened roughly every four to five hours, which meant that their contents were contained in the sewers for about seven hours, all the time emitting an appalling smell. Dr. Wagstaffe, the surgeon from Lambeth who gave evidence at the Commission, not only gave false reassurance to the members that the sewers would be enclosed but also that chemists were being consulted to see if the foul air being given off by the effluent might be burnt off in shafts.[138]

> The Lambeth Waterworks were established between 1775[139] and 1785 between Belvedere Road and the river. The Waterworks were situated downriver from the open sewer which was the Effra tributary, the Houses of Parliament and the heart of Lambeth's industrial area. Before 1834, the waterworks pumped water directly from the river at a point right by Maudslay's ironworks, various potteries, the Lion Brewery and Fowler's lead works. Unsurprisingly, following complaints about its quality, it was then decided to pump water from the *middle* of the river to a reservoir in Brixton, where it was filtered.[140]

At Lambeth in the 1840s, the only source of water was the River Thames, irrespective of what part of the river it came from and whether it was being "filtered" or not at the Brixton reservoir. In his *On The Mode of Communication of Cholera*, Dr. John Snow explained: "Between 1832 and 1849 many changes took place in the water-supply of London. The Southwark Water Company united with the South London Water Company, to form a new Company under the name of the Southwark and Vauxhall Company. The water works at London Bridge were abolished, and the united company derived their supply from the Thames at Battersea Fields, about half-a-mile above Vauxhall Bridge. The Lambeth Water Company continued to obtain their supply opposite to Hungerford Market; but they had established a small reservoir at Brixton."[141]

According to Luke Hebert, writing in 1849:

> The Lambeth water-works are situated upon the banks of the Thames, and the water is forced immediately from the river into the mains, and thence distributed to 16,000 tenants, who consume 1,244,000 gallons daily.
> We have thus given a summary of a more voluminous statement that has appeared in most of the scientific journals, professedly derived from the printed report of a parliamentary commission, appointed a few years ago to inquire into the subject. But we think that every resident of London, after a moment's consideration of the statement made out by the water companies, of their supply, will deem it to be a most overcharged statement of facts. Our own observation upon a great number of houses, leads us to the conclusion,

that instead of 170 gallons to each house daily, there is not that quantity delivered weekly in a majority of cases, or upon an average of the whole. If the water were turned on daily to all the tenants, and the discharge-cocks to all the pipes were prevented from shutting during the period of "laying on," the pipes would be capable of delivering the quantity mentioned. But the facts are, that a great number of the cocks are shut, the cisterns being full; that the majority of them are only open for a few minutes, to receive an addition of a few gallons; and that, so far from being a daily supply to all, the third, fourth, and fifth-rate houses (which constitute the majority,) receive their supplies but twice a week at the utmost, and many of them but once.

The official statements appear to us to be so grossly incorrect that we have not thought it needful to enter into a minute investigation.[142]

As Hebert correctly pointed out, in the 1840s few London residents had the luxury of running water in their homes, let alone clean running water. Standpipes were the commonest means of obtaining water, but in the waterfront areas of Lambeth, even these were absent, as Dr. John Snow explained. "The people in Lower Fore Street, Lambeth, obtained their water by dipping a pail in the Thames, there being no other supply in the street."[143]

In the 1840s, people did not drink the copious amounts of water that we do today. Despite the fact that it was not understood that water could harbor harmful microorganisms, there was certainly suspicion of a cup of water which contained visible dirty matter or smelled strange, though often this would have been disguised by adding flavorings. The popularity of beer and gin among London's working population has been well documented. However, street vendors also sold thirst-quenching beverages such as tea and coffee, ginger beer, lemonade, sweet sherbets, hot elder wine, peppermint water and rice-milk, and in the northern districts of Hampstead and High-gate water carriers also brought water from pumps to those who could afford the service, which included publicans or eating house keepers. In his *London Labour and the London Poor*, of 1849, Henry Mayhew gave a vivid description of vendors selling drinks:

> The water in the stone barrel is spring-water, obtained from the nearest pump, and in hot weather obtained frequently, so as to be "served" in as cool a state as possible. Sometimes lemonade powders are used; they are bought at a chemist's, at 1s. 6d. the pound. "Sherbet" is the same admixture, with cream of tartar instead of tartaric acid. "Raspberry" has, sometimes, the addition of a few crusted raspberries, and a colouring of cochineal, with, generally, a greater degree of sweetening than lemonade. "If cochineal is used for colouring," said one man, "it sometimes turns brown in the sun, and the raspberry don't sell. A little lake's better." "Lemon-juice" is again lemonade, with a slight infusion of saffron to give it a yellow or pale orange colour.

This illustration, entitled "Collecting water from the river, Exeter," shows how water would have been collected at Lambeth. From The history of the cholera in Exeter in 1832 *by Thomas Shapter (London: J. Churchill, 1849). Wellcome Library, London.*

"Nectar," in imitation of Soyer's, has more sugar and less acid than the lemonade; spices, such as cinnamon, is used to flavour it, and the colouring is from lake and saffron.

These "cooling drinks" are sold from the powder or the jar, as I have described, from fountains, and from bottles.

Perhaps the only thing which can be called a cordial or a liqueur sold in the streets (if we except elder wine), is peppermint-water, and of this the sale is very limited. For the first 15 or 20 years of the present century, I was told

by one who spoke from a personal knowledge, "a pepperminter" had two little taps to his keg, which had a division in the interior. From one tap was
extracted "peppermint-water"; from the other, "strong peppermint-water."
The one was at that time 1d. a glass, the other from 2d. to 4d., according to
the size of the glass. With the "strong" beverage was mixed smuggled spirit,
but so strongly impregnated with the odour of the mint, that a passer-by
could not detect the presence of the illicit compound.[144]

It did not really matter how the water was supplied to the residents of
Lambeth, by standpipe or with a bucket, the source was the same, and that
source, the River Thames, had become an open sewer, a repository for industrial waste, for rubbish of every sort, including dead animal bodies. Indeed,
the last live salmon had been fished from the Thames in 1833.[145]

5

Lambeth and the River Thames

Lambeth developed as an industrial hub mainly because of its geographical position. Its low-lying position on the River Thames, away from the City of London, was ideal for polluting factories, as was its proximity to a vast network of land and water routes.

The Thames was essential for the transportation of people and materials, and as the link to natural tributaries, man-made canals and the sea. However, while Lambeth depended on the Thames for transportation, its role as a water source was equally important. Many of the innovative industries which grew up along the shore at Lambeth used the new steam powered machinery, for which a constant source of water was vital. Every type of business and factory needed water, if only to scrub down a counter at the end of the working day, and the growing population of Lambeth depended on the river as their source of drinking water.

In the early days of Lambeth's development, the water supply came from wells, from the Thames and from her tributary, the Effra. Before the development of heavy industry on the Lambeth waterfront the demand for fresh water was much less, moreover, the levels of industrial and human waste which would have drained back into the river were not enough to cause a noticeable depreciation in the water quality. The transformation of Lambeth from a rural backwater to the industrial center of London was already well underway by the end of the eighteenth century. By this time many of the residents of the grand houses with large gardens moved away, complaining that the atmosphere was (already) far too polluted. The subsequent development of the area was rapid and unplanned, with little thought for workers' living conditions or for sanitation, though no doubt the developers thought it fortuitous that waste could be easily disposed of in the river where it would wash away. It was also not understood that the ingestion of water contaminated with human sewage could be the cause of disease.

The mistaken notion that the River Thames would carry waste away contributed to the outbreak of cholera in Lambeth. Many of the migrants who flocked to the district for work had a good understanding of rivers and the sea, having originated from similar areas; they may even have arrived in Lambeth by boat. The design of the barges show this evolution of understanding, as they had been designed to be ocean-worthy, yet flat-bottomed to overcome the river's low tides and sandbanks. However, the migrant population would not have had a deep-rooted understanding of this stretch of the River Thames, and of the unique movement of its waters, and most likely were under the mistaken impression that flowing water which appears clear to the naked eye is safe to drink.

The importance of the crossing points of the River Thames has already been discussed as another reason why Lambeth developed along this stretch of the south bank of the Thames. These crossing points reflect the traditional, ancient places where the river was most shallow and easy to traverse. The Thames of Roman London and earlier was much wider than it is today, and dotted with islands and sandbars, making the crossing from one side of the Thames to the other much easier in certain places, and particularly at Lambeth, which faced Thorney Island, on which the present Westminster Abbey and Houses of Parliament stand. Today, none of the ancient islands remain, the channels between them having been filled by silt, mud and buildings. However, while dredging has taken place in modern times, the floor of the existing river and its banks still hold some clues.

In 2001, the well-known British television archaeology program *Time Team*, broadcast on Channel Four, undertook an examination of the stretch of water around Lambeth and Vauxhall.[1] Taking part in the broadcast was archaeologist Gustav Milne of University of London's Institute of Archaeology. While *Time Team* has been criticized for over-simplifying and detrimentally speeding up the process of an archaeological investigation, it has done much to arouse interest in the study of history and archaeology. Moreover, many of the sites they have featured have been subsequently investigated in the conventional manner, having benefited from the television exposure. Their investigation of the Thames was a snapshot of Milne's extensive work on the river, which continues today in his role as Project Director for the Thames Discovery project. The program made much of the existence of a sand bar between Lambeth's St. Thomas' Hospital and the Houses of Parliament. However, Milne's work has shown that a more likely candidate for the site of a man-made crossing is at Nine Elms, Vauxhall, where a "substantial piled structure" was identified in 1993. Sampling of the wooden remains dates the structure between 1770 and 1260 cal B.C.[2]

Further archaeological investigations, including those under Milne by the Thames Archaeological Survey and the Museum of London's Archaeology Service, suggest that the structure at Nine Elms may have had a spiritual significance.[3] Close to this point two of the Thames' tributaries, the Tyburn and the Effra, empty fresh water into the saline tidal river. The movement of water at this point may also have been significant to the ancient observer, and copper alloy spearheads unearthed here associated with the wooden structure may have been deposited deliberately and may indicate ritual behavior.[4]

By the 1840s, the view from the shore at Vauxhall would most certainly have not aroused spiritual feelings. William Farr (1807–1883) was the first Compiler of Abstracts for the General Register Office,[5] which was established in 1838. Farr understood the value of statistics and their use in determining the cause of disease and epidemics such as cholera. In 1852 he brought his statistics and hypotheses together in a single volume entitled *Report on the Mortality of Cholera in England 1848–49*. In his report, Farr noted, "The contents of the greater part of the drains, sinks, and water-closets of this vast city and of the 2,360,000 people on its sides, are discharged through the sewers into its waters; which, scarcely sullied by the primitive inhabitants, have now lost all their clearness and purity. The dark, turbid, dirty waters from half-stagnant sewers are agitated by the tides, but are not purified until they reach the sea."[6]

Lambeth is situated between two bends on the Thames, delineated by Vauxhall Bridge to the south and Waterloo Bridge to the north. Before the building of the Victoria and Albert Embankments and modern dredging, this marshy, low-lying stretch of the Thames flooded regularly, and by the fifteenth century (or earlier), measures had already been taken to keep the river at bay with the building of Narrow Wall. Today Belvedere Road follows roughly the same line, well back from the river and behind the Royal Festival Hall.[7]

Marshy, low-lying Lambeth was an extension of the shoreline, most of the area being under the high water mark. In the 1840s, the area was prone to regular flooding, filling the lower levels of the houses, the streets and courtyards with sewage from the open sewers. The sewers were constructed in such a way on the flat low-lying land that there was not enough drop in them to flush their contents immediately out into the river. The various sewers which deposited Lambeth's waste into the Thames had sluice gates at their exits which opened at low tide. Evidence given to the Metropolitan Sanitary Commission in 1848 explained that depending on the neap and spring tides, the gates to the sewers opened roughly every four to five hours.[8] Today at low tide it is still possible to see how narrow and shallow the river is at this point.

At low tide at Lambeth in the 1840s, the river may have been narrower still. In addition, variations in the levels of mud and silt deposits on the Lambeth shore, together with moored barges, other obstacles and detritus, would have created pools of warmer, brackish, stagnant water. Such pools, as discussed below, would have been ideal for the reproduction of microorganisms such as cholera, and also for the collection of drinking water.

Today the River Thames behaves much the same as it would have done in the 1840s. From Teddington Lock, which was first built in 1810[9] about eight miles to the southwest of Lambeth as the crow flies, the river meanders in the same way and under a similar number of bridges. Fresh water moving downstream from Teddington only begins to mix with tidal salt water in the area around Battersea, just upriver from Lambeth. At Lambeth, on an ebb tide, a body of water will move some way downstream, but because of the considerable distance to the sea and the number of bends in the river, the same body of water will flow back again on the next flood tide. While water speeds vary along the river, it can take anything from three weeks to three months for a body of water to pass from Teddington Lock to the sea. In the summer, with reduced rainfall, the process slows considerably and it is estimated that in the warmer months the "net daily seaward movement [from Teddington to the sea] ... may be only 0.6 to 1.2 miles."[10]

It was the physician Dr. John Snow (1813–1858) who finally convinced the medical community that cholera was a waterborne disease. In his 1849 *On the Mode of Communication of Cholera* he commented on the state of the Thames in the cholera epidemic of 1854, the outbreak which followed that of 1848 to 1849:

> The Thames in London is a very large body of water, and if the whole of it flowed into the sea every day, the liquid which flows down the sewers in twelve hours would form but a very small part of it; but it must be remembered that the quantity of water which passes out to sea, with the ebb of every tide, is only equal to that which flows over Teddington Lock, and from a few small tributary streams. In hot dry weather this quantity is moreover greatly diminished by the evaporation taking place from the immense surface of water exposed between Richmond and Gravesend, so that the river becomes a kind of prolonged lake, the same water passing twice a day to and fro through London, and receiving the excrement of its two millions and more of inhabitants, which keeps accumulating till there is a fall of rain.[11]

Waste continually deposited into the river at Lambeth would not have been flushed away quickly and would have passed up and down the shoreline for a considerable amount of time, perhaps for the entirety of the summer. In the *Reports and Correspondence Respecting the Drainage of the new Palace at Westminster* by the Metropolitan Commission of Sewers, January, 1849, as discussed in the previous chapter, Charles Barry writes of the tides with respect to the new sewage system: "That during ten hours upon the average in every tide, the outfalls of the public and Palace main sewers are closed by the rise of the tide in the River, and all drainage from the New palace is consequently stopped for that time periodically."[12]

From this account it is clear that at Lambeth the tide would have been out twice a day and it is during this time that the sewage would have poured from the outfall pipe at the Houses of Parliament, remaining on the shore, and awaiting the incoming tide. This sewer was still linked to the existing Abingdon Street sewer, to the north of the river, with a total of some 70 to 80 drains emptying into the system. Just a few hundred yards upstream two other tributaries of the Thames, the Effra and the Tyburn, both open sewers by the 1840s, emptied their waste. A little further downstream from Westminster, as illustrated below, was the intake pipe of the Lambeth Waterworks. The waterworks did not supply the riverfront areas of Lambeth, as there were no standpipes there, but rather it pumped the tainted water of the Thames to residents farther afield, as William Farr explains in his *Report on the Mortality of Cholera*: "Lambeth Water Company and Southwark Water Company — The waters of the Thames between Waterloo Bridge and the Hungerford Suspension Bridge, supply parts of the districts of Lambeth, St. Saviour, St. George Southwark, Newington, and Camberwell; the other parts of these districts being supplied from Battersea by the Southwark Company. The mortality from cholera was at the rate of 136 in 10,000. In the district of Lambeth the mortality was 120, St. Saviour 153, St. George Southwark 164, Newington 144, Camberwell 97, in 10,000."[13]

In his *Mode on the Communication of Cholera*, Dr. John Snow drew up a table to show the correlation between the water supply from the River Thames and the number of deaths from cholera in the middle of 1849. He noted, "In every district to which the supply of the Southwark and Vauxhall, or the Lambeth Water Company extends, the cholera was more fatal than in any other district whatever." The table showed that at Lambeth out of an estimated population of 134,768, 1,618 people had already died from cholera. Other districts supplied by the Lambeth Company were St. George, Southwark, where there were 836 deaths out of an estimated population of 50,900, and Camberwell, where there were 504 deaths out of an estimated population of 51,714.[14]

In the cholera epidemic of 1848 to 1849, most of those infected with the disease suffered at home, where they also died, as in the majority of cases death comes quickly after the first cholera symptoms are manifested. In the 1840s, there was no general system of health care, and some of the London hospitals, such as Guy's in Southwark, would not admit patients who were suspected of suffering from cholera as they could not be certain that it was not contagious.[15] Some of the hospitals, such as St. Bartholomew's (St. Bart's) to the north of the river, in Spitalfields, continued to admit patients. It must be considered that this was not necessarily because the surgeons felt they could cure the cholera, but because they needed to be able to experiment with potential cures and also to have the opportunity to dissect the bodies of cholera victims to gain a greater understanding of the pathology of the disease. The records for this period for St. Bart's Hospital still exist, and an analysis of a sample of the deaths from cholera at St. Bart's from the autumn of 1848 to the summer of 1849 show that nearly all of the deaths from this sample occurred among those living close to the Fleet River. The Fleet, and indeed all the tributaries of the Thames, had become dumping grounds for every sort of waste, including human sewage, yet for the poorer members of society, they were still a source of water and many of them fed into existing wells and water supply systems.[16] *The Times* newspaper reported at the height of the cholera epidemic in August 1849: "The numerous attacks of cholera, and the many fatal cases, in the parish of St. Bride's, all occurred within a few yards of the Fleet-ditch."[17]

According to John G. Avery in his *The Cholera Years*, "In March to May 1848, 29,000 cubic yards of raw sewage made its way into the Thames where many of the private water companies drew their source of drinking water. By February 1849, this had alarmingly grown to 80,000 cubic yards."[18]

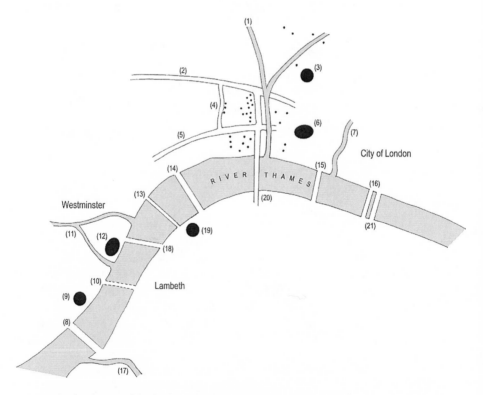

A sample selection of deaths from cholera at St. Bartholomew's Hospital, London, from October, 1848, to July, 1849. Dots indicate the residences of victims.[19] Illustration by the author, redrawn by Alexander Thomas. Number key is on page 127.

KEY TO MAP NUMBERS

1. *The Fleet River*
2. *Holborn*
3. *St. Bartholomew's Hospital*
4. *Fetter Lane*
5. *Fleet Street*
6. *St. Paul's Cathedral*
7. *The Walbrook River*
8. *Vauxhall Bridge*
9. *Millbank Penitentiary*
10. *Proposed site of Lambeth Bridge (built 1862)*
11. *The Tyburn River*
12. *Westminster Palace and the Houses of Parliament and the site of Thorney Island*
13. *Hungerford Bridge*
14. *Waterloo Bridge*
15. *Southwark Bridge*
16. *New London Bridge*
17. *The Effra River*
18. *Westminster Bridge*
19. *Lambeth Waterworks*
20. *Blackfriars Bridge, leading to Bridge Street and Fleet Market (now New Bridge Street and Farringdon Street)*
21. *Old London Bridge and the approximate site of the Roman crossing*

William Farr, in his *Report on the Mortality of Cholera*, realized that the Thames and its tributaries, in effect the capital's water supply, may have something to do with the cause and spread of cholera. However, he was still convinced by the miasmic theory and that the height at which a population lived was significant. His theory that miasma, or bad air, was the cause of cholera was supported by the fact that the Thames was a "large evaporating surface."[20]

Farr noted that in the summer, when temperatures were higher, greater evaporation would occur and this process released "tainted vapours" into the air, of which the London fog was evidence. He recorded temperatures throughout the epidemic of 1848 to 1849 to show how the prevalence of cholera decreased and increased:

The cholera reached London in the new epidemic from about October 1848; it prevailed through the winter and destroyed 94 lives in the second week of January; when the temperature of the Thames was 37°[F]; it declined rapidly through April and May; the night temperature of the Thames then rose to 62°[F] in the week ending June 2nd; with some fluctuations it went up to 68°[F] in July, and remained above 60°[F] until the middle of September (week ending September 15th). The deaths from cholera registered [in the whole of London] during each of the 16 weeks were 9, 22, 42, 49, 124, 152, 339, 678, 783, 926, 823, 1,230, 1,272, 1,663, 2,026, 1,682. The mean night temperature of the Thames fell to 56°[F]; the deaths from cholera to 839 in the week September 16–22; the temperature gradually fell to 38°[F] on the last week of November, when there was only *one* death from cholera registered.[21]

Thus Farr makes a direct correlation between the temperature of the water of the Thames and the vehemence of the epidemic. He noted also that deaths increased in the districts closer to the river, most notably on the south side at Wandsworth, Lambeth, St. Saviour, St. Olave, Bermondsey and Rotherhithe. Farr goes on to discuss the work of a Mr. Glaisher of the Royal Observatory at Greenwich who made scientific calculations to estimate the amount of vapor evaporated from the Thames. Glaisher estimated that 1,857.6 gallons of water evaporated from an acre of the River Thames per day, though he could not be certain how much of the decomposed organic matter within it would be inhaled by the population.

Farr drew a table to show the relationship between place of residence and deaths from cholera, as follows. It is clear from his statistics that in Lambeth deaths from cholera were significantly higher because of the higher density of people living in low-cost accommodation, their proximity to the river, and from where they were drawing their water.

London Group of Districts	Deaths from Cholera to 10,000 Persons Living	Density of Population (Persons to an Acre)	Elevation in Feet Above High Water Mark (Trinity) [i.e., the Trinity Standard, Thames High Water Mark]	Annual Value of Houses ([Financial] Year Ending April 5, 1843) in £s
Supplied with water From the Thames Above Battersea	15	72	105	82
Supplied with water from the New River, the Lea, and the Ravensbourne	48	137	42	44
Supplied with water taken from the Thames, between Battersea and Waterloo Bridges	123	73	5	31

Farr went on to note that the "mortality of the 19 highest districts was at the rate of 33 in 10,000, and of the lowest 19 districts 100 in 10,000.

Notwithstanding the disturbance produced by the operation of other causes, the mortality from cholera in London bore a certain constant relation to the elevation of the soil, as is evident when the districts are arranged by groups in the order of altitude."[22]

His discussion of those living at a higher elevation above the river Thames is extensive and stretches to many pages in his *Report on the Mortality of Cholera*. Farr drew diagrams, devised formulae, and compiled tables, clearly convinced that elevation was a factor in cholera mortality rates. Next he looked at the density of population and wealth, and was perplexed that "in all the 6 districts supplied by the water of the Thames, from Kew and Hammersmith, the mortality from cholera is low; but the mortality is lowest in the three densest districts which happen to be only half as wealthy as the rest."[23]

What Farr did not consider in this section of his argument was how the quality of water varied in the river. Kew and Hammersmith are further upstream from Lambeth and Battersea, and while these areas had sewage discharging into their stretch of the Thames, as there was nowhere else for the sewage to go, the water here was still cleaner and not as conducive to *Vibrio cholerae*, particularly as the saline water of the flood tide only reached as far as Battersea.

Farr realized that a higher density of population did play some part in increasing mortality, and wealth also played a part in decreasing it, though his statistics painted a confused picture and he found it hard to draw a definite conclusion. However, he was able to conclude that the wealthier population who lived in the elevated districts above the Thames definitely fared better than their poorer counterparts in the low-lying Lambeth, and were less likely to die of cholera.

In his conclusion, Farr conceded that water probably did play a part in the spread of cholera, but not because the impurities within it were ingested, but because they were inhaled:

> The epidemic began and was most fatal in the ports on the coast; and in ascending the rivers step by step, we saw it grow less and less fatal. It became probable that a certain relation existed between elevation and the power of cholera to destroy life. The more exact information which we possess respecting the London districts establishes this connection beyond doubt.
>
> As we ascend, the pressure of the atmosphere diminishes, the temperature decreases, the fall of water increases, the vegetation varies, and successive families of plants and animals appear in different zones of elevation. The waters roll along the surface of the rocks, or filter through them and the porous strata of the earth to burst out below — the sources of rivers, or of tributaries which carry disintegrated rocks, with the remains and excretions of vegetables, animals or men, in every stage of decomposition. The deposits in stagnant places, and at the estuaries, show the kind and quantity of mixed

matter which the laden rivers carry down and deposit on the low margins of the sea at the tidal confluences of the fresh and salt waters ... it is evident that the refuse matter of the first town will pass through the second; of the first and second through the third ... to the lowest town. The drainage of the towns is difficult on the low ground and the impurities lie on the surface, or filter into the earth. The wells and all the water is infected.

The river, the canals, the docks, and the soil of a port may be viewed as a large basin ... undergoing infusion and distillation at varying temperatures; and as the aqueous vapour which is given off ascends, it will be impregnated with a quantity of the products of the chemical action going on below, variable in amount, but necessarily greatest in the lowest and foulest parts. The emanations, mixing with the superincumbent atmosphere, ascend like smoke.

From an eminence on summer evenings, when the sun has set, exhalations are often seen rising at the bottoms of valleys, over rivers, wet meadows, or low streets; the thickness of the fog diminishing and disappearing in upper air. The evaporation is most abundant in the day; but so long as the temperature of the air is high, it sustains the vapour in an invisible body.

The amount of organic matter, then, in the atmosphere, we breathe, and in the waters, will differ at different elevations. It is established by observation that cholera is most fatal in the low towns, and in the low parts of London; where ... the greatest quantity of organic matter is in a state of chemical action ... cholera ... is the result of some *change* in the *chemical action* of this matter; leaving it open for further inquiry to determine whether, in England, the change is spontaneous, or the result of the introduction of a zymotic matter from beyond the seas; whether the poison enters the human frame in air or water, through the skin, the mucous membranes, or the air cells of the lungs.

The cause of cholera is some chemical modification of organic matter; and here is the great practical fact — that *although elevation of habitation, with purity of air and purity of water, does not shut out the cause of cholera, it reduces its effects to insignificance.*[24]

While the majority of the scientific hierarchy at this time were in agreement that disease was spread by foul air, most acknowledged, like Farr, that this was probably not the full story. The study of bacteriology was in its infancy at this time, held back by limited research, prejudice and arrogance in the medical community. By 1848 Dr. John Snow had already deduced that drinking water contaminated with human sewage was probably the cause of cholera, but what no one yet knew was how in warm summers, the low-lying brackish river at Lambeth was the ideal breeding ground for *Vibrio cholerae*.

6

The Lambeth District Sanitary Reports

By 1847 the Whig government of Lord John Russell was well aware that cholera was likely to appear again in Britain. Diarrhea, dysentery and *English* cholera were common in the summer, but a full-blown epidemic was a frightening prospect with the memory of the 1832 outbreak still vivid in the population's memory. Following his extensive work on the matter, Edwin Chadwick was convinced living conditions and disease were interlinked and took on the role of Royal Commissioner on London Sanitation as an opportunity to improve living conditions for the urban poor, especially in London.

The Royal Commission began its work in September 1847, and while there is no direct reference in the *First Report* of the Commission to the Lambeth District Sanitary Reports, they were likely conducted with a view to submission to the Royal Commission, or as a fact-gathering exercise prior to, and perhaps even following, the evidence which was given (see Chapter 2). Although a complete set no longer exists, the headings of the reports and the dates inspections were undertaken confirm this hypothesis. A Central Sanitary Committee was set up in the Parish of Lambeth in or before January 1848. This committee set up subcommittees for the various districts of Lambeth which undertook a number of inspections. Some of these inspections were more detailed than others, some may never have taken place at all, as a great deal of plagiarism appears to have taken place. However, those which contain the most detail follow a similar scheme to Chadwick's 1842 *Report on the Sanitary Condition of the Labouring Population of Great Britain* (see Chapter 2).

The reports were written in two or three phases, in January and February 1848, where observations and recommendations taken during local visits were noted, and then in July of the same year, when the Sub Committees submitted a follow-up document. Lambeth was divided up into districts and subdivisions of the districts for the purposes of the reports and which were bordered to the north and west by Westminster and the River Thames, and to the east and south by Southwark, Newington, Camberwell, Dulwich, Norwood and Croydon, Streatham, Clapham, and Battersea. The areas visited also included Kennington, Stockwell and Brixton.

The reports were compiled by the members of the District Sanitary Sub Committees for Lambeth's Central Sanitary Committee with the aim of iden-

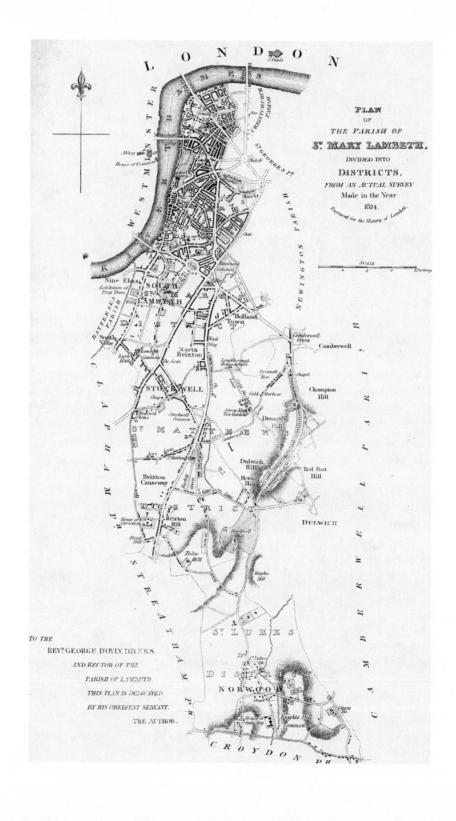

tifying correlations between sanitary conditions and health. Most of the reports concluded that there was a link between poor sanitation and ill health, and they cited the following common causes. Lambeth was filthy, stinking and low-lying, in effect sinking slowly into the mud of the marshland. The housing for the poor people of Lambeth had been built too quickly and in a shoddy fashion without proper foundations, their level in the ground made worse by the building up of roads above ground level and the piles of detritus and muck heaped up on the roads and footpaths each day. The houses in Lambeth were prone to damp not just because of their low-lying situation but also because they had been packed tightly together and lacked ventilation; some houses had been built right up to factories emitting noxious fumes and bugs. The piles of muck in the streets had, in many cases, been there for years and while some effort was made following the first phase of reporting by the Sub Committees to clear these away, it became evident that the men employed to clear the rubbish were demanding additional money from the local residents for the privilege, a service the poor of Lambeth simply could not afford. The accumulation of muck was made worse by the poor drainage of the area and the fact that houses had been built without connecting the cesspools and privies (toilets) to the main drains and sewers. In every case, the main sewers were open, though a couple were covered over following preliminary reporting, and far too shallow for their purpose, being the boundary ditches between the parishes, and no doubt also between the fields of the once-rural Lambeth. The deeper sewers in the south of Lambeth had once carried the clear waters of the River Effra, and to the east of Waterloo Station, residents made similar use of the River Neckinger, which emptied into the Thames much farther downriver, to the east of the Tower of London.

Living conditions in Lambeth were worst in the areas along the bank of the river in Upper and Lower Fore Street and Princes Street. This was the most densely populated area, where factory workers and the purveyors of every kind of trade lived in tenements some eight to a room with no running water, and overflowing privies and cesspools; there were none of the new flushing water closets here. One of the Sub Committees to the south of the district, in St. Mark's, commented that less running water was possibly a good thing as there was nowhere for it to go. Indeed, the areas beyond the riverbank appeared to have an adequate supply of water, though none of the reports mentioned that its supply was sporadic or that the quality was appalling. An article in *The Times* newspaper of July 24, 1848, commenting on the visits of

Opposite: *Plan of the Parish of St. Mary Lambeth divided into Districts. From an actual survey made in the year 1824. This image was reproduced by kind permission of Lambeth Archives department.*

Lower Fore Street, circa 1860. The gulley down the centre of the road was for the disposal of excess household waste, including sewage. From the Woolley Collection, photograph by William Strudwick. This image was reproduced by kind permission of Lambeth Archives department.

the Lambeth Sub Committees, revealed: "About 800 poor families live in this immediate spot ... the water is laid on by pipes only, no cisterns being provided, so that when it comes in the people are compelled to fill what vessels they have, which has to last them until it comes on again."[1]

It is difficult to form a fair impression of the conclusions of the Sub Committees when some documents are missing, however, the views of its members were certainly mixed, and it would appear from the above statement in *The Times* that some of their information may be misleading. On the one hand there are some members who appear to have copied the reports of others into their own words (perhaps so that they did not have to revisit the areas concerned), and who blamed the poor, the Irish in particular, for their own lack of cleanliness. However, there is also concern for the poor and their desperate, but impossible, situation, which lends an air of frustration to some of the reports. Many of the members of the Sub Committee clearly felt deeply for the plight of the poor in Lambeth and became angry when little was done between January and July to remedy the situation; the Reverend James Gillman is one example. The overriding fear was that with the warmer weather cholera would return and the Sub Committees' efforts to halt its progress would be in vain. In short, Lambeth was on the brink of epidemic.

Lower Fore Street circa 1860. To the front of the photograph on the right-hand side is the access to the foreshore and Brennand's Dock, which at the time of this photograph would have already been occupied by Mr. Wentzell. From the Woolley Collection, photograph by William Strudwick. This image was reproduced by kind permission of Lambeth Archives department.

A document included with the District Sanitary Reports dating from April 8, 1852, revealed the situation at Fore Street, supporting Dr. John Snow's observations in his *On the Mode of Communication of Cholera* that residents in this area had no piped water and had to take their water from the river by bucket. The document in question is titled *The Report of the Surveyors of Highways of the Parish of Lambeth on the Obstruction of Brennand's Dock, Frying Pan Alley and Lion and Lamb Passage*.[2] The first part of the document discussed the dock situated at Lower Fore Street and a barge which had been moored there by a Mr. Wentzell, causing an obstruction. The barge was roofed and used as a boathouse, so had become a permanent fixture. Mr. Wentzell had commenced a lease on the premises on July 3, 1849, at the height of the cholera epidemic. However, the date of leasing was crucial as it proved that the practice of drawing water from the river for consumption occurred prior to this. The lease contained a covenant to wharf and embank the premises, and a clause regarding the river "to be used gratis at all reasonable times by all such inhabitants of Lambeth as shall find it convenient to resort thereto for the purpose of procuring water, for the use of themselves, their families and Cattle but not for sale."[3]

The document went on to describe how this spot was the original landing place for the Horseferry "there anciently used ... from a Bank on the opposite side of the river Thames heretofore belonging to the Convent of Westminster and containing on the west side thereof towards the River 41 Feet on the east side thereof towards Fore Street 47 feet 9 inches."[4] A detailed description of the contents of the remaining reports followed, district by district, starting with St. Mary Lambeth. The parish map illustrated above gives an overview of the area.

St. Mary's Lambeth

First Report of the Sub-Committee for the District of the Parish Church of St. Mary Lambeth to the Central Sanitary Committee.

The report noted that on January 3, 1848, and for the purposes of reporting, the district was divided into 13 divisions. It is not clear if reports were undertaken for each of these areas, but if they were then only a handful survive. Visits to the assigned districts in Lambeth St. Mary were carried out that week and their observations were presented to the District Sanitary Committee on January 11 and 12, 1848, as follows.

The Sub Committee noted that there were open sewers on the north side of Chester Street, Lower Kennington Lane, Mead Row and the east side of Regent Street. These and the open sewers on each side of Bank Street "are very bad and offensive."[5] Many of the houses in the area had cesspools and the state of these and the privies was not good and required some attention. With regard to the privies, there were simply not enough of them, especially in Asylum Place, where five houses shared a single privy. In Little East Place there were only three privies for the use of 30 families. The privies were also bad at Bonnet's Buildings, Brook Street and East Street, and where they were situated close to the houses "emitted a considerable effluvium some remain long unemptied."[6]

In Richmond Street, a heavily populated area, the drainage was bad and the stench in some of the houses was intolerable and seriously affected the health of the residents. The supply of water was generally abundant, but the roads and footpaths were not in a good state. There was an accumulation of "dust [refuse] and rubbish" that the Sub Committee blamed on the residents and scavengers and which was especially bad from Fore Street down to the river. The Sub Committee discussed the matter with the local residents, "the poor, who complained that the scavengers would not remove the rubbish without a fee being paid."[7]

The Sub Committee remarked on the offensive trades in the area, including the boiling of oil at the cloth factory in Kennington Lane and the smell

The rear of dwellings in Upper Fore Street, circa 1860. Note the holes in the walls leading from the privies. This image was reproduced by kind permission of Lambeth Archives department.

from bone crushing factories in Fore Street, all of which they felt was detrimental to heath. The smell from the bone crushing factories was mentioned many times in the reports and in contemporary writings. In conclusion, the Sub Committee commented that the state of health was good and there was not so much sickness "as might have been expected."[8]

The Sub Committee reported again in February, 1848, when they stated that their district was divided into three portions. Either the first report contained an error or, more likely, the February report covered three areas within the original thirteen cited in January. Considering the streets covered in the February report, the latter is the more likely conclusion.

In Cardigan Street, the drainage was deficient. At the back of this street and Devonshire Street there was an open ditch "of worst description into which houses in both streets drain — the soil of the privies being exposed to view and presenting a most disgusting appearance."[9] In Devonshire Street there were no drains and refuse was thrown into the street. Barrett Street had no connection to the sewer; in Queens Place (New Street) and Orsett Street, where there were houses belonging to a Mr. Coombs of South Lambeth, there were holes dug into the gardens for refuse. In Orsett Street there was a gutter in the middle of the road for the use of all the houses. In Catherine Street and Cottage Place there was also no drainage, and the former residents threw their slops into a gutter in the road. The houses to the right of Park Street had no drains and the ditch belonging to Vauxhall Gardens and Vauxhall Walk was "full of nauseous filth."[10]

The roads in Cardigan Street, Queens Place (New Street), Frances Street, New Street and Wickham Street were all higher than the ground floor of the houses, indeed in Catherine Street, the road was a good three feet higher. At the bottom of Cardigan Street there was a large piggery; the Sub Committee noted that pigs were also kept at Queens Place (New Street) and at 17 Devonshire Street. The houses in Cardigan Street were small, with two to four rooms each, averaging about 12-feet square; the houses were dirty and crowded, and the situation was much the same in Queens Place (New Street).

Sickness was not too bad in the area and the supply of water in all cases was good according to the Sub Committee. They noted complaints from the residents regarding contractors not removing the *dust* and in many cases money had been demanded of them to take the rubbish away. The report concluded that the people were glad the Sub Committee had made their visit and they were glad that someone was trying to help them, though the visitors worried about the drainage and that typhus fever and cholera would return in the summer.

Second Report of the Sub Committee for the District of the Parish Church of St. Mary Lambeth to the Central Sanitary Committee (undated).

The report noted that since January 12, 1848, the Sub Committee had met twice and had further information to report, as follows.

At Pleasant Place, on the north side of Elliott's Row, the open sewers were most foul and offensive and there were complaints by local residents in hot weather and before rain. The situation appeared to have become worse in the past two years than at anytime in the 20 years before. At 21 Elliott's Row the Sub Committee noted, "The privy is in the back kitchen and empties itself into the sewer thus making a direct communication with the house. No. 22 has an open sewer on three sides, sickness (typhus fever) of children in this house was attributed to the pestilential effluvia arising from the corrupt and stagnant matter in the sewer — which in this part is very foul: the complaints were rather of the effluvia than the drainage."[11]

The Report continued:

> The open sewer before mentioned continues at the back of the houses on the south side of Bird St. [possibly Burd Street], where it is in the most foul state possible; full of putrescent matter, vegetable and animal contributions from privies, from a skinners and curriers etc. etc. It was so offensive that the visitors were glad to hasten from it.
>
> The whole of Canterbury Place consisting of nearly 40 houses at rental of about £35 per annum with few exceptions have not any communication with the sewers notwithstanding a large one was built in the middle of the road a few years ago. There are cesspools at the back which can be emptied only into the Gardens, or the contents carried through the houses.

In Little Canterbury Place there were no drains and the cesspools were overflowing, many houses were lower than the road; at number 29 "the water used is discoloured and tainted and the family unhealthy from the defective drainage."[12]

In Church Street, especially between Pratt Street and the distillery, the houses were badly drained. At Norfolk Row, Norfolk Place and Horrinds Cottages there were no drains, and the privies were full and offensive in Norfolk Row where steam rose from the grating of a private drain belonging to the distillery. The smell of this was very bad and impregnated with gas tar. The smell of the candle factory nearby was also very offensive. In Norfolk Place the privies adjoined the houses in a yard "not 2 feet wide — the walls are stained nearly to the ceiling — the paper falls off and everything is shortly covered with a filthy incrustation."[13] The situation was worse at Horrinds Cottages, where "the soil from the privies, especially at no. 5 oozes out, and is prevented running into the houses only by straw being laid down in the yards."[14]

The health in the district was generally good, except for in Norfolk Row, where the amount of sickness was blamed on the steam from the sewer and the candle factory. There was also sickness at Graves Cottages, which was blamed on the dreadful state of the cesspools and the accumulation of rubbish.

At Lambeth Walk, on the north side and from the east end to Saville Place, the drainage was also very bad. Here the cesspools at the back were very offensive in the summer and, on the opposite side of the road, the back of the houses drained into a sewer in St. Albans Street. There was an accumulation of filth at the back of the houses in Lambeth Walk, especially at the west end. There was a bad smell of fish offal at numbers 34 and 162 emanating from gratings in the road. The south side of South Street was also badly drained and the houses were very damp, "the water not being carried off at all but sinking into the ground."[15] Windmill Court was in a disgusting condition, there appeared to be only two privies to 30 families. In Harpurs Walk, there was one privy for the whole court, serving six houses, and at Pennells Place the privies were bad and "dangerously ruinous." The houses on the south side of Chester Street had no drainage, and in Edward Street, where there were around ten houses, the situation was the same. In one house the occupants kept pigs and boiled bones: "There is no drain; a part of the waste liquor only is conveyed by pails to an adjoining grating."[16]

In Providence Place and Charles Place the drains were very bad, as was the effluvia; the houses in Charles Place were connected to a sewer but "the stench is abominable."[17] In Providence Place and Earl Street there was a "great accumulation of soil and offensive matter in almost every yard," and in Dawson's Rents, Joseph's Place, the soil from the privies in the Butts "was oozing thro" the walls of inhabited rooms (in this place there was but one privy for 10 families).[18] In King Street and Earl Street, where there were 47 houses, more than half did not have enough drains, and at number 47 there was no outlet. The privy to this house was under the staircase and "so situated as to impregnate the water supplied for domestic use."[19]

In James Mews the drains were blocked and the water was overflowing; in Newport Street the drainage had been cut off from the remaining houses by the works undertaken by the building of the railway. At Duke's Head Court the drain was bad, on the east side of Fore Street there was no sewer, and at number 12 King's Head Yard the drain appeared to run under the house, giving off a terrible smell. Edward Street was constantly engulfed by the smell and smoke from a furnace boiling bones. In William Street there was a large piggery, and at Doughty Street, at the back of a butcher's, there was a square pit full of offal which served as a drain for the slaughterhouse. The Sub Committee also noted in the margin of the report that cows were also kept near here. The area was also impregnated with the smell of the factory in Fore Street belonging to Mr. Mitchell, a tallow melter and bone

Work Yard, Doughty Street, a view of the southwest side taken from the cow yard. In the fore-ground are three houses, dust heaps and sheds occupied by John Wright, the fronts of which faced Adams Row. Watercolor by D. Wingfield, July 7, 1848. This image was reproduced by kind permission of Lambeth Archives department.

crusher. A resident next door to the factory complained to the Sub Commit-tee of bone flies and of the bone bugs which crept through the walls.

With regard to the state of the roads, at Hercules Buildings, the situa-tion was not good. Edward Street was badly cleansed, and King Street, Lam-beth Walk and Joseph Place were "filthy" with "many nuisances."[20] At Norfolk Row, *dust* was thrown in front of the houses, and in Doughty Street the roads were also filthy with dung and rubbish at the back of the houses adjoining the Butts; the road was in bad repair and almost impassable. The supply of water was generally good, with two exceptions, though the Sub Committee did explain the nature of these exceptions. The report concluded with the statement that the poor people of the district were constantly complaining about the state of the area.

St. John's Waterloo

First and Second Reports of the Sub-Committee for the District of St. John's Waterloo to the Central Sanitary Committee.

This document included both reports and was dated January, 1848. The district covered the east side of Waterloo Road and the west side of Cornwall Road to the north of Lambeth.

In Le Grand Place, Waterloo Road, the houses were small, with four rooms, each occupied by 10 or 12 people and all very poor. Only two of the houses had small backyards with privies, which were in a terrible state; here were six other privies for the common use of the other houses and they were all most offensive. In Cornwall Place and Cornwall Road the houses were also small. The privies were in the front courts as there were no backyards, but the drainage was good. At the corner of Mason Street on Cornwall Road there was a cow yard, with another yard opposite which was used to deposit the dung, and it was noted that this area was often full. In Williams Place, by Cornwall Road, the houses were occupied by costermongers (fruit, fish and vegetable street vendors). The houses were divided by a narrow passage in which there was little light, and there were yards behind with privies. These were in a disgusting state as there was no drainage and they were overflowing. At Providence Place the drains were being cleared, and this had also occurred in Cammons Place, which was clean.

The Sub Committee begged the Central Committee to sort out Church Terrace, Church Street, Pear Tree Street and Cornwall Road, however, a further visit in July 1848 revealed that the area was still unfit for human habitation, and while in Le Grand Place some changes had taken place, it was still filthy.

An additional report for Waterloo Road, Mark Road and from Vine Street to the waterside was undertaken and dated January 12, 1848. This Sub Committee, perhaps the same group as above, reported that the area was quite respectable and well drained. The report commented on the ditch behind the houses on Belvedere Road, which continued behind Vine Street to Sutton Street, but did not remark on its condition. However, of the road from Vine Street to York Road, its condition was "shameful," like the "waves of the sea" and very muddy.[21]

St. Thomas' District

First Report of the Sub-Committee for the District of St. Thomas' Lambeth to the Central Sanitary Committee

This report was written on January 14, 1848 by Mr. J.W. Weeks, who presumably was a member of the Sub Committee who visited this part of Lambeth in the north of the district.

Mr. Weeks commented first on Jurston Street which was in a wretched condition. There was rubbish in the streets and an open drain, which was once the boundary ditch between St. Thomas' and St. George's parishes. This ditch was open almost the entire length from Christchurch Workhouse to the Westminster Road and was full of dead cats and dogs. There had been many deaths in the weeks leading up to the writing of the report.

Weeks commented that in Jurston Street the Sub Committee "found a number of pigs, the stench was so great that we could scarcely remain near the spot to make further enquiries."[22]

Hooper Street, the road running parallel to Jurston Street, was in an even worse condition, though there was a good water supply. The cesspools were overflowing, the drains were imperfect and the houses small, with one family to a room. There was a distinct lack of cleanliness among the people themselves and in their houses, especially among the Irish who lived in these streets. The worst street of all was Harriet Street, where the dirt of many years had been left to rot in the streets: "The dirt of all kinds have been left to accumulate for years in several portions of the street. It was thrown up into great heaps so as to convey the idea of so many dung-hills in the centre of the street — no drains — and cesspools in a bad state and all of this within a few yards of the Lower Marsh."[23]

In Gloucester Street, the Sub Committee encountered a man who kept ten pigs in his cellar. They advised him to get rid of his stock as soon as possible, which they reported he had agreed to as he believed the animals were harming his health. In Charles Street the drains were bad and the cesspools almost full; in Short Street there was a cow yard with no drain, which in heavy rain became badly flooded. To the front of the houses in Robert's Place there was a narrow passage which served as a dumping ground for stinking rubbish; the Sub Committee observed this became very bad when it rained.

A further report was written in February 1848 by the surgeon John Sewell, of 59 Lower Marsh.[24] Sewell noted that there were three Sub Committees in this district, and that this was a joint report, which explains why there is some repetition. However, there is also the possibility that some information was shared between members of the Sub Committee to save members having to make personal visits.

In New Street, Mitre Street and Queen Street to the north of the District, and in the same area as discussed earlier by Christchurch Workhouse, the Sub Committee noted pools of water in and to the sides of the roads, as drainage was inadequate. The sewer running under number 32 Queen Street at the back of Christchurch Workhouse was in a terrible state, but the landlord had done nothing about it. The report also mentioned the cow yard in Short Street, but then went on to discuss the Victoria Theatre. Today the Victoria Theatre is known as the Old Vic theatre, and while it has undergone many refurbishments and changes, it still stands in the same spot as it did in the 1840s. In the District Sanitary Report, Sewell described how the east and west sides of the Victoria Theatre were used as a public toilet by theatregoers.

At Cottage Place, Webber Street, there were seven houses and a donkey stable. The area which was occupied by costermongers was a problem as it was filthy; there was a dust heap, the drainage was bad and there was not enough water. The Apollo Buildings, Hooper Street, Jurston Street, Frances Street, Harriott Street, Providence Row, Whiting Street and Charles Street were all filthy with rubbish in the roads and no drainage. Harriott Street was especially bad as the rubbish had been allowed to accumulate for several years. The cesspools were also in a bad state and again "all within a few yards of the Lower Marsh." This area was occupied by the poorest of society with one family to each room. The situation was particularly bad in Frances Street, which was occupied mainly by Irish families. At number 28, seven rooms were occupied by seven families, totaling 13 adults and 24 children, and this was typical of the area. The cesspools were full, the drainage bad and many people kept pigs: "A man in Gloucester Street has 10 pigs in his cellar and on opening his front door the stench was dreadful."[25]

The area also had many open ditches which contained dead animals, decomposing matter and discharge from the privies. Sewell also noted that in Jurston Street there was an "infant school" with 200 pupils in the summer and 150 pupils in the winter, which on Sunday evenings was used as a ragged school for some 300 children from poor families (see Chapter 4). However, the school was bounded to the north by a street "in a wretched condition a large portion being covered with stagnant water and quantities of mud composed of ashes and decomposed vegetables and all kinds of refuse."[26] By the playground there were pigsties and to the south an open ditch. While the supply of water to the district was good, Sewell concluded as follows: "From the open ditches, bad drainage, filthy state of the Streets, and want of cleanliness in the Houses of the poor generally, the Subcommittee fear that should it please God to visit London with that awful scourge, the Cholera, the state of St. Thomas's District would augment the spread of that disease to an alarming extent to more healthy localities."[27]

St. Thomas' must have been divided into at least two divisions, as another report was conducted for the area by Mr. James Guthrie, Mr. William Musselwhite and Mr. William Wilson. The areas they visited were Pollar Buildings, Providence Row, Whiting Street, Mary's Buildings, Isabella Street, and Thomas's Street. The houses in the area were low in the ground, sometimes with one family per house and a lodger, but there were also some houses divided into two apartments, one on the ground floor and one on the first floor. In the houses where the poor were living, the rooms were smaller and more confined. The streets were dirty and the footpaths separating buildings were in a filthy state; in rainy weather there were pools of water and a lot of mud. The buildings were enclosed by passages which were difficult to pass through as they were full of rubbish heaps of mud and ashes, from 18 to 24 inches deep. There were pigs everywhere, often running about freely, enjoying the muddy environment. The drains were in a bad state and one was blocked where it joined the sewer. The privies too were in a dreadful condition and ran into each other before reaching the sewer. The Sub Committee commented:

> Into one of these plague spots we entered and no sooner was the outer door opened than the stench immediately met our nostrils warning us to retreat from a place so nauseous so unfit for human existence, or human sight.
>
> But the greatest nuisance in this neighbourhood is to be mentioned. It is a long drain almost uncovered in its whole extent leading from Westminster Road on the one side nearly to ... Christchurch Workhouse in the most filthy abominable state imaginable, containing within it the discharge from water Closets in a stagnant state, dead animals of various kinds, vegetable matter in a state of putrification and decomposition emitting a stench and effluvia strong enough to contaminate the whole neighbourhood with the most noxious miasmata calculated to give rise to, and a focus for the attraction of the most fatal epidemics.[28]

The Second Report was written on July 25, 1848, by Mr. J.W. Weeks, Mr. John Sewell, Mr. W. Musselwhite and Mr. Jennings.

By July the drainage was still the same — deficient — with the open ditches terrible at this time of year. The situation in Hooper Street, Jurston Street and Short Street had also not improved, with the residents still throwing their rubbish into the street and complaining, despite the fact this was a problem of their own making, in the opinion of the Sub Committee. However, the Sub Committee had discovered that throughout the district a system did exist to take rubbish away, but residents had to pay for the privilege. The poor were simply unable to do this, and the report suggested they would rather have the rubbish on the street.

A new drain had been constructed on Boundary Row, which John Sewell commented on further in a letter to the Sub Committee and which is discussed below. However, while the main ditch had been covered, the tributaries running into it had not, which caused a dreadful problem for the residents of Queen Street who lived near a part of the open section. The smell was no better than before, and the Sub Committee concluded that all the sewers should be covered.

In a letter dated June 15, 1848, Mr. John Sewell, a member of the Sub

Committee and a surgeon, of 59 Lower Marsh, discussed the same ditch, known as the Black Ditch. The ditch ran along Boundary Row towards Black-friars Road and Sewell wondered if it had been covered over in response to the work of the Lambeth Sanitary Committee. Everyone he had spoken to was very glad this had been done and he urged that all the sewers in Lambeth should have the same treatment.

St. Mark's District

The following report was titled *District No 1, Lower Kennington Lane to Kennington Cross* and appeared to be a part of others belonging to this area. The report was conducted by Mr. John Ashley, Mr. Edward Jenkins and Mr. Thomas Law.

In Newington Road there was a common sewer. The drainage was not bad, but many houses deposited their waste into a large ditch at the back of Kennington Common. At Lower Kennington Lane there was another large common sewer and most of the houses in this district had cesspools in the yards and gardens. The houses at Bennett's Buildings, Kennington Lane, were small tenements "wretchedly inhabited," lying low and with bad drainage, their privies and cesspools overflowing; there was fever prevalent in the area. In the area of Regency Square the drainage was poor and there were the "most miserable houses," filthy with no drainage, the cesspools in a bad state and the privies "scarcely deep enough to contain the soil."[29] Pleasance Row in Lower Kennington Lane, on the right-hand side, had no connection to the common sewer, the street having been raised many times. As a result the basements of the houses were below street level and the cesspools and privies were constantly overflowing. Most of the houses in this district had cesspools with some or no connection to the main sewer. The report concluded: "It would appear that all parties would gladly avail themselves of the advantage of the Common sewers but that the expense of doing so deters them, and the unwillingness of tenants to lay out money upon the landlord's property."[30]

The next report for Division 2 of the District of St. Mark's was similar to the previous one in that there was no formal heading. However, the areas clearly form part of the same district in the south of Lambeth. The report covered Clapham Road to Dorset Street, South Lambeth, and was undertaken by Mr. Thomas Grey, Mr. Stephen H. Ayers and Mr. John Snell.

The drainage in this area was bad and there were deaths from fever in this crowded area: "The use of cesspools being in most cases resorted to in order to avoid the expense of carrying to the main drainage, or sewers, altho' these latter are in many parts available for the purpose while others for want of this or of suitable cesspools are in a very bad state: especially those in Little William Street, and Ebenezer Place where there is an uncovered surface drain."[31] An open sewer ran through South Lambeth. The houses here were badly constructed and ventilated, though there were no complaints about the water supply. The roads were bad, too muddy to walk along or even to go to church. The Sub Committee recommended that the open sewer running at the back of Kennington Oval (which probably formed part of the River Effra, a Thames tributary) should be covered. The area was in need of drains to connect the area to the main sewers, and the cesspools needed inspecting, cleaning and the introduction of traps.

A report for District number 3 was dated January 29, 1848. This covered the area of Clapham Road, east to the church, to Holland Street by St. Ann's Road, to Russell Gardens, and Brixton Road back to the church, and was conducted by Mr. M. Mulhus, Mr. Robert Nisham, Mr. John Williamson and Mr. Thomas Davies.

The Sub Committee noted that the drainage was defective in this area, and that in most places there were no common or deep sewers and only small road drains or cesspools which needed constant emptying. In Russell Gardens there were no drains, the houses had no sinks and everything had to be emptied into privy cesspools or a public "link" at the front of the houses. There was a "dust bin for all refuse,"[32] but the cesspools overflowed onto the public way. There was, however, a good water supply.

The report for District number 4 for St. Mark's covered Brixton Road to Loughborough Road and was undertaken by Mr. Currey, Mr. Boult and Mr. Mullins.

Here the drainage and sewers were good and everything appeared most respectable. However, from Loughborough Lane to the first part of Coldharbour Lane there were no sewers. At Bloxham Buildings the situation was very bad, with 11to 14 people per house, bad drains, privies and cesspools at the front.

The report for District number 5 of St. Mark's covered the north side of Camberwell Road from Kennington Common to Camberwell Green in Lambeth, and north to the ditch which bounded the Parish of Lambeth. The Sub Committee comprised of the Rev. George Grieg, Mr. John Barrup, Mr. Cornelius Wheeler, Mr. Jenkin Joel and Mr. Joseph Collings; their visit was conducted on Wednesday, January 19, 1848.

The drains in the area were imperfect and the new sewer under Camberwell New Road appeared not to be in use, even though it would have been of great use in the district. Open ditches which had once served as boundaries were now sewers, collecting waste from the cesspools and the kitchens The Sub Committee recommended that these ditches should be covered.

Some cesspools were generally in good order but needed cleaning out once every five years, others were found to be overflowing. The cottages had wash houses and privies which were common to all. Most houses in the district were small, with two to six rooms of eight to ten feet square housing families of eight, and at rents of 3/9 (about 15p) to 7/- (35p) per week, usually eight people to a family. There was an ample water supply and while the roads were in a reasonable condition, there was the occasional accumulation of mud in places; the only *nuisance* in the area was the catgut factory owned by Mr. Farmer.

District Number 7 included Lansdown Road to the north of Wandsworth Road, and from Priory Road to Vauxhall Gate; the Sub Committee comprised of Mr. James Humphreys, a chandler, Mr. Solomon Knight, Mr. Harbin, Mr. Linford and Mr. W.H. Mason. The report was most likely written in January or February as it mentioned the frost and the recent fatal outbreak of influenza.

The Sub Committee noted that there were no sewers in the area, just ditches which presumably were the old parish boundaries between Lambeth and Battersea. The ditches were in a terrible condition and one crossed the road at Nine Elms. At Clarke's Place, Vauxhall, at the southern tip of Lambeth, there were piggeries, the refuse from which ran off into the drains and remained on the surface, to "grow green there." The cesspools were bad and there was no way of getting rid of the surplus refuse. Water was plentiful, but the Sub Committee wondered if it might not be better not to use so much water as there was nowhere for it to go.

The Sub Committee blamed the "irresponsible public office"[33] for conditions in the area. The houses comprised of small rooms, with usually one family to a room and sometimes four families in a single house. Fever was prevalent and the people were close to starvation:

> To talk to *the poor* who have usually more than enough to do with the struggle to obtain an adequate supply of the most ordinary food indispensible to the maintenance of human life, their families and themselves, to talk to such about *the adoption of measures for the promotion of cleanliness and the importance of the ventilation of their houses and Courts etc* is likely we fear, how kindly so ever expressed, to be productive beyond a loss of time on both sides; whilst as respects *the Owners of the Houses* they are probably much better acquainted with their state of Reparation than we can pretend, or at any rate might deem it advisable to tell them.[34]

A solution to part of the problem in the area, according to the Sub Committee, was to connect the area to the sewers in the Clapham South, Lambeth and Wandsworth Roads. That development had gone on in the area without regard to sanitation was the fault of the late Commissions of Sewers, the report concluded:

Now fortunately abolished ... who during so long a succession of years abstracted large sums of money from the pockets of the people. Neither ought we to be much surprised ... when we learn from ... the Metropolitan Commissioners of Sewers.... They had had cases of Sewers which did not discharge, running in *contrary* directions, from want of proper levels. Without an Ordnance Survey they had been *going on* in the dark; and the loss which had been occasioned by that *want of attention* was enormous. In one district, that of Holborn and Finsbury [in north London], an outlay of £260,000 would be necessary to remedy the *defects* of the existing System of Drainage. Indeed it was possible that a *great portion* of the money which had been expected in London for drainage would be found to have been *thrown away*.

As to the state of the Works in the *South District* [i.e. Lambeth], Mr. Austin stated, "that the late Commission proposed to lay out £100,000 in works, *the whole* of which would probably *stand in the way* of future improvements. Were a plan of converging drainage carried out in the same area, there would be a saving in the whole district of between £300,000 and £400,000." And this, on the *sole* authority ... of *the New Commission*, do those *Extinct* Bodies stand clearly convicted ... of the most gross and culpable Ignorance of the duties of the Office to which they were appointed ... in the discharge of their Functions, of an equally reckless and scandalous waste of the Public Property.[35]

The Second Report, completed in July, 1848, was succinct, and commented that the ditches at the back of Kennington Common and at Nine Elms were still a problem, as was the drainage in the area.

Trinity District

First Reports of the Sub-Committee for the Districts of Trinity Church Trinity District to the Central Sanitary Committee.

Sub Committee Division Number 1 of the above district reported in January 1848, and comprised of the Rev. Frederick R. Perry and Mr. Delamore. The Sub Committee visited Penlington Place, Allen Street, Homer Street, Carlisle Street, Little Park Place, Park Place and Cottage Place.

The report noted that to the east of Penlington Place there was a sewer but it was not connected to the houses there. Most of the houses had cesspools which were in a terrible state. In Allen Street, the effluent from the cesspools was carried off by barrel drains running along the backs of the houses, though the last two houses were unable to use this facility; in Homer Street the situation was similar. Little Park Place had no benefit from the ditch which had recently been converted to a sewer. Some residents kept pigs, which many locals complained about. The houses were small but the area was not as densely populated as other areas in Lambeth. To the north side of Park Place there was a barrel drain which the Sub Committee noted had caused some illness; the report quoted a local surgeon as having said, "The effluvia arising from the drains had caused the illness of all the members of the family."[36] To the south side of the road the houses had cesspools and these houses, like so many in Lambeth, were lower than the road and consequently very damp; at the top of the street there was a muck heap.

In Carlisle Street there was no drainage and the houses were not attached to the sewer. In Cottage Place there was the same "irregular drainage" as in Little Park Place. Again, here the cesspools were terrible and the locals kept pigs. The Sub Committee believed that the landlords were at fault for not connecting the houses to sewers and the district authorities were at fault for not removing the refuse. The report concluded by saying that the supply of water was good in the entire district.

The report for Division number 2 in Trinity District was presented in the form of a letter from the Rev. James Gillman of 3 China Terrace, Lambeth, and included information provided by other members of the Sub Committee, Mr. Thomas Coater and Mr. I. Allanson. The report included the following observations:

> In visiting The Upper Marsh, the neighbours complain of the house no 33 keeping a great many pigs, sometimes as many as twenty four are kept in a yard about 3 yards sq and in summertime very offensive, and in Brooks Court at the back of no 33 the drainage is very bad and a great accumulation of dirt and other nuisance also in Vestry Place in the same Court the drain is stopped by the Railway being made but the supply of water is good.
>
> In St. George's Place Upper Marsh there are suspended wooden drains and very leaky consequently the stench is very great especially in the summer the inhabitants of no 4 could not live in it; and the Committee noticed a soap manufactory in Carlisle Lane altho' the neighbours made no complaint and the drains were good, but in Carlisle Square no drains, and a Slaughter House in the rear, and the cesspool very bad, the inhabitants had all been ill last summer, and complained very much of the stench from the Privies.
>
> In the other parts of the Division, we found the sewers and the drains tolerably good.[37]

The Sub Committee for Division 3 of the Trinity District reported on January 10, 1848, and comprised Mr. William Thomas Nixon, churchwarden, and Mr. Robert Hicks, Guardian of the Poor.

On the west side of Upper Marsh, the houses had privies but there were no sewers and effluent drained into ditches on Mr. Buckley's premises. At Pembroke Place the houses were newly built, the privies clean and the water supply good, but effluent still emptied into cesspools which drained into the same ditches as those on Upper Marsh. The situation was the same in Mason Street

Garden Court, Heathfield Place, Frederic Place and Masons Place, the houses in which were all owned by Mr. Buckley. At Stangate Mews there were stables, warehouses and workshops, but on the vacant ground nearby there were heaps of ashes and manure; again this area was the property of Mr. Buckley. A major problem in the area was the drain running through Mr. Buckley's premises and which the Sub Committee noted the late Commission of Sewers "always prevented being covered over."[38] The east side of Felix Street was very dilapidated and poor. There was no sewer and the drain at the back of

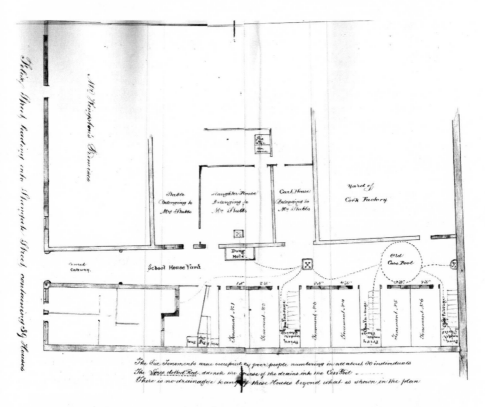

A plan of six tenements in School House Yard on the corner of Westminster Bridge Road and Felix Street from the 1848 Lambeth District Sanitary Reports. From top left, and in a clockwise direction, the annotations read: "Mr Kingston's premises; stable belonging to Mrs Stubbs; slaughterhouse belonging to Mrs Stubbs; cart house belonging to Mrs Stubbs; Yard of Cork Factory; Old Cess Pool, open passageway and privy under stairs; Tenements 6 and 5, open passageway and privy under stairs; Tenements 4 and 3, open passageway and privy under stairs; Tenements 2 and 1, privy, pig sty, privy." Above the slaughterhouse is a pig sty and hen house. An annotation accompanying the plan reads: "The six tenements were occupied by poor people numbering in all about 80 individuals. The dotted lines denote the course of the drains into the Cess Pool. There is no drainage to any of these houses beyond what is shown in the plan." This image was reproduced by kind permission of Lambeth Archives department.

the houses emptied into the Stangate sewer. The roads in this area were very bad, though the people in the area were decent, with the exception of those in Felix Street itself. The report concluded that School House Yard in Felix Street was "the most objectionable place under our inspection."[39]

The Sub Committee for Division 4 for Trinity District comprised Mr. John Jalland, Mr. (possibly John) Archbutt and Mr. George Webb, and reported on January 10, 1848, regarding the west side of Felix Street, the north side of Bridge Road, Amphitheatre Row and Stangate.

The Sub Committee reported that the west side of Felix Street was in a terrible state, which was the landlord's fault. The worst houses were numbers 2, 5, 10, 11 and 12, the latter three of which were unfit for human habitation, though there were still people living there. According to the report, the problem was that the residents "are of dirty habits which such habitations afford no means of correcting."[40] The rooms in the houses measured 10 feet by 7 feet, and there were no windows at the back. However, there was a good water supply and the drains and cesspools on the whole were in good order, though they were used by a lot of people. There was good ventilation at the back of the houses, which were at the side of Astley's Theatre. Only one person was ill.

In Amphitheatre Row the residents were slightly better, but the street was still very dirty because of the way the houses were situated with the stabling for the theatre to the rear, which meant there was no ventilation. At the front of the houses the only way for light to enter was through a grating which was very close to the sewer. With regard to Astley's Theatre, there were no specific problems, however, this contrasted to the situation closer to the river. The report considered the premises which had been occupied by the boat builder Mr. Lyon and which were now occupied by Mr. Hearn. Mr. Hearn was a dust contractor who was in the business of collecting horse manure to be taken away by barges. There was evidently a problem with an accumulation of manure, however, the Sub Committee was assured that the piles of dung contained no human waste. The Seysell Asphalt Company works were open and clean, but there was a dreadful smell. On the riverbank, at the entrance to the "ancient dock"[41] adjoining the Red Lion Brewery, there was a large pile of manure which had accumulated at the livery stables.

The Sub Committee did not inspect Westminster Bridge Road as everything appeared in good order in that area. Their main concern, and in conclusion to their report, was that the dust contractors were not taking refuse away from small tenants.

A separate report referred to "District No 6," probably part of Trinity Division. It was written by Mr. Richard Ablee, Mr. Washington Lee, Mr. Alfred Engelbuck and Mr. John Northy.

The houses in Bond Street, Vauxhall, were in a bad state and many pigs were kept in the area, which was filthy with dung piled up against the walls. In Miles Street, Vauxhall, there was an open sewer in a filthy state. In Southampton Street West, close to the Southampton Railway, there was also an open sewer which was in a dreadful state as all the refuse from the local water closets and the station accumulated there. In Spring Place, Wandsworth Road, there was no sewer. The houses had cesspools and the residents threw their slops into the road. On the west side of Wandsworth Road the houses were small and built on swampy land. The damp rose up the walls of the houses above the levels of the upper floors, making them unfit for habitation. At the boundary of Lambeth and Clapham the open sewer was in a bad state, and in South Lambeth on the road to Vauxhall, there were open sewers on both sides of the road.

An additional report for the Trinity District is a synopsis of some of the earlier observations. It was written on February 4, 1848, by the Rev. James Gillman, who was a member of the Sub Committee for Division 3.

Gillman noted that in Trinity District, drainage was mainly by cesspools and that most of these were not in a bad condition. There were no sewers in many of the streets and the one in Stangate needed to be repaired, all of which was causing illness in the area. The cellar of 41 Carlisle Lane overflowed with effluent and the suspended wooden drains in George's Place, Upper Marsh, were leaking. In Mason Street some of the houses had no backyards and so the cesspools were situated under the back rooms of the houses. Some houses had been built quite recently and to a reasonable standard, with the exception of those in Felix Street, where numbers 2, 5, 10, 11 and 12 were unfit for human habitation. The water supply was good but "not of the best quality,"[42] and the roads and paths were muddy and in a bad state of repair. The Seysell Asphalt Company and Mr. Hearn's manure piles were both mentioned again, as were the soap makers, bone boilers, the offal from butchers' shops and a dung heap in Chisam Yard.

Finally, there was a letter included in the Trinity District Reports addressed to the Rev. Mr. Gillman and Mr. Farmer, which included some details not mentioned in earlier reports. The letter commented on the Stangate sewer and the bad state of the cesspools, but it also remarked on the state of Crosier Street, where the landlord, Mr. Crook, had promised repairs; some, but not all, of which seem to have been carried out.

The roads were also in a bad state of repair with an accumulation of muck, moreover, some houses had cesspools, and some were drained. In Garden Row the houses were drained but the privies were in a bad state and the rooms of the houses were small, damp and dirty. In Mary Street there was no drain and, as the road was higher than that of Crosier Street, it acted as a gulley for the waste. In Paris Street the road was fair, though there were no drains and the houses had cesspools. The Cesspools from Stangate Street overflowed into Palace New Road and into Mr. Hicks' premises, although the report does not clarify if this is the same Mr. Hicks who was the Guardian of the Poor and on the Sub Committee for Trinity District Division 3.

The Second Report for the Trinity Division, written on July 26, 1848, by the Rev. Gillman was brief. It stated that since the last report there had been no changes, and because of the warmer weather, the smells in the area were even worse. The dust nuisance had improved, but several cases of scarlatina and typhus had been reported.

All Saints District

First Report of the Sub-Committee for the District of All Saints Church to the Central Sanitary Committee.

The Sub Committee of the All Saints Division reported in January, 1848, and included Mr. W. Merritt, Warden of All Saints, Mr. Manners and the Rev. A. Peat.

The Sub Committee reported that in Artichoke Court and Granby Place the drains were bad. The two large open ditches in the area were in a dreadful state. One ran between Granby Street and James Street and along Barnes Terrace, and the other between James Street and Lower Marsh. There were many pigsties and slaughterhouses in the area; the houses were not too badly crowded but they were dirty and badly ventilated. The courts and alleys were full of rubbish and filth and residents complained that the dust heaps should be removed.

In the Second Report for All Saints District, written in July, 1848, by the Rev. A. Peat, Mr. Thomas Merritt, Mr. Elliott, Mr. Nickels and Mr. W.H. Manners, the situation did not appear to have changed very much. The ditch between Granby Street and James Street was still bad, but as the land nearby belonged to the railway, it was hoped that it may be eradicated once works proceeded. The ditch between James Street and Lower Marsh, however, was still in an appalling state.

Stockwell Chapel District

First Report of the Sub-Committee for the District of Stockwell Chapel to the Central Sanitary Committee.

The First Report for this district was written on January 25, 1848. The

Sub Committee was appointed by Kennington Vestry, rather than Lambeth, and covered the area of Old Stockwell within the boundaries of Clapham Road and Rise, Stockwell Place, Love Lane, the south side of Robert Street (Brixton Road) to Angel House and "thence by diagonal line" to the point where Bedford Road met Acre Lane. The Sub Committee included Mr. Dodd, a surgeon, and the Rev. H. Clissold; their visit was undertaken on Tuesday, January 18, 1848. Their observations were similar to those in the north of the district, in other words, bad drainage, damp and a profusion of pigsties. The report also included the following information which illustrates the chaotic state of the authorities at the time:

> Mr Harbon an old and intelligent shopkeeper in this street said that instead of facilities being offered to the poor to encourage and induce them to make branch drains, they were impeded and prevented by the fees or payment required for every branch drain which broke into the street drain, and that until such fees were remitted and aids granted, the poor man would never make a branch drain at all and would submit to the overflowing cesspools, unable as he was to do more than provide labour and the materials of brick and mortar, without encountering other expenses. Mr Harbon observed that these fees and the trouble occasioned by notices required etc operated as a bar to the making of branch drains, where most required for sanitary improvements [sic].[43]

By the time of the Second Report of July 26, 1848, the Sub Committee noted that many of the problems regarding waste in the streets had been resolved by better communication with the manure dealers. However, the problems with the infrastructure of the drainage system remained, particularly as the landlords of the properties in the area did not see the drains as their responsibility: "As to the impossibility of ... getting any effectual level for drainage ... until ... [the area] ... is provided with a good main sewer as to occasion a fall for the household drains: a necessity for which is daily becoming more pressing by the erection of so many Towns.... Until this improvement in main sewerage shall have been effected, they have reason to expect that but little good can be done in house or street drainage in that locality."[44]

Included with the report was a letter written on July 25, 1848, from a local surgeon, Dr. Owen. The letter discussed the case in the first week of July of a woman in East Street, Stockwell, "a case of *English Cholera*."[45] The patient had been suffering from diarrhea for two to three days and Dr. Owen describes how she had a "cold surface," a "leaden countenance,"[46] and an irregular pulse. She had been vomiting and excreting in spasms and had cramps in the legs: in effect many of the symptoms of Asiatic cholera. However, the woman was better by the following day and the surgeon commented that these symptoms were not uncommon at this time of year. Dr. Owen could not find any obvious causes for these outbreaks but believed the poor drainage of the area may have had something to do with this, as well as the prevalence of other diseases, such as scarlatina: "Puddles of stagnant dirty water or decomposing vegetable matter and putrelage discharging especially during warmer weather most offensive exhalations.... Cholera Pestilence in all probability now approaching us."[47]

The Rev. James Gillman and Mr. Robert Hicks of the Trinity Sub Committees were clearly concerned that something should be done to improve the sanitation and living conditions of the area. They compiled a synopsis of the First Reports, though it is clear from the Second reports undertaken in July that their efforts were to a large degree wasted:

> Proposed Extracts from Reports for Surveyors of Highways and Trustees of the Lambeth Improvement Act. Prepared by Mr. Gillman and Mr. Hicks, February, 1848.
>
> Brook Street — cesspool to privy separated from kitchen by a single brick wall, through which the fluid contents ooze into the kitchen creating an intolerable nuisance.
>
> Brook Street in general — the same complaint as above applies to many houses in this street.
>
> Floor Cloth manufactory in Kennington Lane — the boiling of oil complained of as detrimental to health.
>
> Fore Street bone crushing factories — The smell complained of as a great nuisance. The Bone Bugs creep through the wall into the next house. [The report was annotated in pencil with "Boneflies."]
>
> Edward Street — At no. [number not included] Pigs are kept and [?] boiled the chimney complain of [?].
>
> East Street — The cesspools require emptying.
>
> Joseph's Place, Dawson's rents — The contents of privys [sic] from houses in the Butts oozing through the walls of inhabited rooms.
>
> Norfolk Place, Norfolk Row, Horrinds Cottages — Privies run over.
>
> William Street — a large Piggery.
>
> Doughty Street — a pit at the back of a Butcher's in Lambeth walk receives all the offal of the slaughter-house.
>
> Norfolk Row — Unhealthy from the steam arising through grating of a private drain.
>
> Lambeth walk, South side west End — Heaps of filth at the backs of the Houses, annoy neighbours.
>
> Lambeth Walk — An offensive smell arises from a grating in the Road opposite no 34 and on the opposite side of the Road at no 162 [the latter part pertaining to no 162 has been crossed out in pencil].
>
> Cardigan Street — Piggery at the bottom of the street.
>
> Queen's place — ditto.
>
> 17 Devonshire Street — ditto.
>
> No 41 Carlisle Lane — Cellar of the house overflowed with the contents of a privy or drain.

Mary Street, Crosier Street, Little Park Place, Pembroke Place — Cesspools complained of.

George's Place, Upper Marsh — there are suspended wooden drains very leaky and emitting much stench.

Carlisle Square — cesspools bad.

Stangate — Seysell Asphalt smell is complained of.

Hearns Wharf, late Searle — Complaint that manure and other offensive matter is deposited previous to embarking the same.

Carlisle Lane — a soap makers, a bone boilers is very offensive.

Carlisle Square — A Slaughter-house in the rear is complained of.

School House Yard — ditto.

Felix Street — ditto.

Park Place — Muck heap found at the top of the street — Pigs kept.

Little Park Place — Pigs kept.

Brooks Court — ditto.

Cottage Place St. John's district Waterloo — dust heap at the end.

Bond place — Dust and rubbish suffered to accumulate under the houses.

Gravel Place, Waterloo Road — Priveys [sic] dirty and offensive.

Mason Street — ditto.

Cornwall road — A large offensive dung heap.

Williams Place, Cornwall Road — priveys [sic] overflow.

All Saints District near the Lower Marsh — Slaughter-houses and pig-styes complained of but the precise sites of the nuisance not pointed out.

Robert's Place — Accumulation of filth.

Victoria House — nuisance for want of urinals.

Apollo Buildings, Hooper Street, Jurston Street, Francis Street, Harriett Street, Providence Row, Whiting Street — The cesspools generally are full and offensive.

Near Kennington Common — Farmer's Vitriol Works and a Cat-gut manufactory at Fields Cottages complained of.

Clarts [?] Place, Bond Street, Vauxhall — Piggeries.

Garden Row, Stangate — The Drains from the privey creates a nuisance in no. 1, 2 and 5 of Garden Row.

A general complaint on the subject of dust.[48]

On July 24, 1849, *The Times* newspaper published a report on the Lambeth Sub Committees' investigations "to ascertain whether the extraordinary number of deaths that is daily taking place from cholera is attributable to the want of proper sanitary arrangements. The result of the inquiry, so far as it has at present been made, shows that unless some speedy means be adopted for removing the pestilential smells occasioned by the various obnoxious works carried on, the spread of the disease would be most fearful."[49]

The following day, a notice was put up in Lambeth by Mr. W.T. Logan, the Clerk of Lambeth Workhouse, forbidding by law the throwing of refuse into the streets. How the people of Lambeth were expected not to throw their rubbish into the streets when there was no collection and nowhere else for it to go is perplexing. Equally perplexing is the attitude of the Lambeth Board of Guardians in the case of Mr. J.T. Mitchell, a longstanding medical officer of the parish. Exhausted by his efforts to tend the sick and dying in the epidemic and in desperate need of more pay for medicines, Mitchell resigned, in the hope that his gesture would spur the guardians into action. To the contrary, they accepted his resignation.[50]

7

The Cholera Outbreak

What statistics there are for deaths from cholera in 1848 for Lambeth are inaccurate and in many ways misleading. At the time there was much discussion as to whether sufferers from diarrhea were indeed suffering from cholera at all; there is also the possibility that the causes of some deaths were even altered or suppressed to avert widespread panic, though there is no solid evidence for this. The figures for 1849 are much more precise. Out of a population of around 115,888 in Lambeth, 1,618 died of cholera, a figure which increases to 1,894 when deaths from diarrhea are included. Some of the largest contributors to these figures were the 187 deaths from cholera (126) and diarrhea (26) at the Union Workhouse on Prince's Road. The areas which butted on to Lambeth were also badly affected. In St. George Southwark there was a total number of 961 deaths, and in Newington there was a total number of 1,042 deaths from cholera and diarrhoea.[1]

The figures relating to the registration of death from cholera were put together by William Farr (1807–1883). Farr was a doctor by training, having studied in Paris and London.[2] He became the first Compiler of Abstracts for the General Register Office,[3] which was established in 1838. Paid an initial salary of £350 per annum,[4] Farr worked under the first Registrar General, Thomas Henry Lister, and then under the second, George Graham; his career spanned around forty years until 1880. Farr understood the value of statistics and their use in determining the cause of epidemics such as cholera. A letter from Farr accompanying the first annual report by the Registrar General expressed his view: "Diseases are more easily prevented than cured, and the first step in their prevention is the discovery of their existing causes. The Registry will show the agency of these causes by numerical facts."[5]

In his time as Compiler of Abstracts, Farr, advised by Edwin Chadwick, helped to ensure that the Registration Act which enforced the registration of births and deaths in 1837 was amended to include the cause of death. Farr was also instrumental in standardizing the structure of the ten-yearly census so that population data could be compared more easily.[6] In addition, it was Farr who published the *Weekly Return* of the General Register Office, a statistical analysis of deaths, which also appeared in *The Times* newspaper, as discussed below. Farr was an ardent supporter of public health reform and used his work to put forward his own views, which included the need for state intervention. His influence on successive Whig administrations certainly influenced Parliament's slow but growing recognition of the need for social reform.[7]

In 1852, Farr compiled his *Report on the Mortality of Cholera in England 1848–40*, which gave a detailed account of the deaths from cholera and his hypotheses for the causes of the disease. These he worked out statistically by comparing "explanatory variables": death rates from cholera and all causes, elevation, density of housing (per house and per acre), wealth (by average house value in a district, and by average house value per head of the population in a district), poor rate, annual mortality, and water supply.[8]

For Lambeth, these variables were as follows. Deaths from cholera per 10,000 inhabitants, 120; deaths from all causes from 1838–44, 233; elevation, three feet above Trinity high water mark; persons living to an acre, 34; average annual value of a house, £28; average number of persons living per house, 7; amount in pence paid for relief of poor to every £1 of house rent annually, 17 pence (1/- 5d), or 7p today. However, Farr's figures were misleading as they took into account those areas of Lambeth which were better off and more sparsely populated. Nevertheless, his statistics show that in 1849 alone, Lambeth suffered the worst number of fatalities from cholera of all the districts of London.

William Farr (1807–1883), the first Compiler of Abstracts for the General Register Office. Photograph published in Vital Statistics: a memorial volume of selections from the reports and writings of William Farr *(London: The Sanitary Institute, 1885). Wellcome Library, London.*

Dr. John Snow, in his 1849 *On the Mode of Communication of Cholera*, included a table from Dr. Guy of King's College Hospital "showing the occupations of 4,312 males of fifteen years and upwards"[9] who died of cholera in the 1848 to 1849 epidemic. In London the highest mortalities were sailors (299, 1 in 24), weavers (102, 1 in 36), hawkers (67, 1 in 22) and coal porters and heavers (53, 1 in 32).[10]

In London from October 1848 to December 1849 the total number of deaths was as follows.[11]

Deaths from Cholera in London as *registered* each week.

Farr notes that this is different to the number of deaths which actually occurred.

1848			1849	
October	122		January	262
November	215		February	182
December	131		March	73
Total	468		April	9
			May	13
			June	246
			July	1,952
			August	4,251
			September	6,644
			October	464
			November	27
			December	3
			Total	14,126

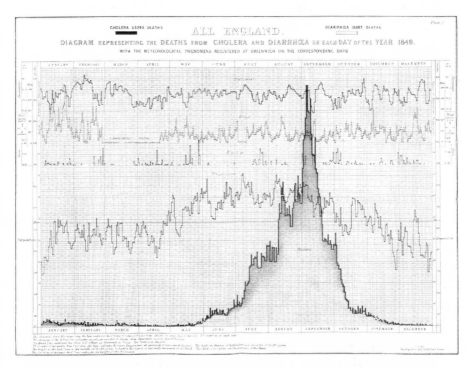

"All England. Diagram representing the deaths from cholera and diarrhoea on each day of the year 1849. With the meteorological phenomena registered at Greenwich on the Corresponding Days."[12] *Farr plotted deaths from cholera against (from top to bottom), the barometer, wind, rain and temperature. Farr was certain that the most important influence in the spread of cholera was the wind. Wellcome Library, London.*

In his *Report on the Mortality of Cholera in England 1848–49* Farr drew several diagrams to show deaths from cholera and to show how cholera had spread throughout England.

The Lambeth District Sanitary Reports show that in 1848 the authorities were aware cholera could return, not just because the conditions appeared to be favorable but because it was well known that epidemics had broken out overseas and were gradually coming closer and closer to Britain's shores. In his role as Metropolitan Commissioner of Sewers (see Chapter 2), and fearful of an epidemic, Edwin Chadwick demanded that Assistant Surveyor Lovick instigate the flushing out of the River Thames every two to three months to eradicate the bad smells emanating from the sewers, which for the many of those who supported the theory that disease was transmitted by bad smells was essential to avoid a cholera epidemic. From March to May 1848, 29,000 cubic yards of effluent were flushed into the river, and between September 1848 and February 1849 another 80,000 cubic yards were flushed. Not only was this an unpopular move, as the Thames became more polluted, but it is evident from the Lambeth District Sanitary Reports that this cannot have been particularly effective, as in Lambeth, for example, the smells from the sewers continued to be particularly offensive. Worse, the flushing of organic matter into the Thames would have encouraged the growth and spread of the *Vibrio cholerae* bacteria. The mortality rate from cholera rose in London: 246 in June, 1,952 in July, 4,251 in August, to a peak of 6,644 in September,[13] though it is important to note that this period was also very warm.

Vibrio Cholerae is endemic to the mouth of the River Ganges in India.[14] The first incidences of cholera in humans no doubt occurred before documentation began, but there are accounts of a disease resembling cholera in ancient Sanskrit, Chinese and Greek texts, and it was certainly reported by the Portuguese who visited India in the sixteenth century.[15] The first pandemic erupted in India in 1817, but it is no coincidence that cholera did not spread to Europe until the 1820s, when travel had become faster, more frequent and more common. As discussed in Chapter 2, *Vibrio cholerae* can survive for long periods in an estuarine environment, perhaps years, and while it can travel distances in water, there is no evidence as yet that it can traverse whole oceans by itself or by its association with phytoplankton and zooplankton. The rapid spread of cholera by land was by human contact and through the pollution of estuarine environments by contaminated human waste; by sea, cholera was transported by boat and by ship.

The diagram shows the routes by which cholera traveled from India to Europe and the Americas, which follow the course of human travel. It had been thought that cholera was transmitted by the winds as its progress so closely matched their course, however, ships necessarily follow the same routes, and it was in this way that cholera was transmitted from one port to another. *Vibrio cholerae* was carried by the ships' passengers and in the waste emptied from ships' bilges. Bacteria would have been discharged from ships into an environment conducive to its survival, as many ports are situated in the mouths of brackish estuaries.

Until recently it had been thought that the 1848 cholera outbreak originated in Kabul, Afghanistan, in 1845, where it arose during a hot summer. By the following year cholera had reached the Middle East, killing 12,000 people in Teheran out of a population of 60,000; it then moved on to Russia and to Europe.[16] However, recent research has shown, as discussed in Chapter 2, that it is possible that the cholera epidemics in London throughout the nineteenth century may not have been isolated outbreaks, only brought to the capital from the sites of other outbreaks. As it is now understood that *Vibrio cholerae* can withstand cooler winter temperatures and mutate itself into a *dormant* state, it is possible that the bacteria had already become endemic in some British estuarine environments, and perhaps the River Thames, since

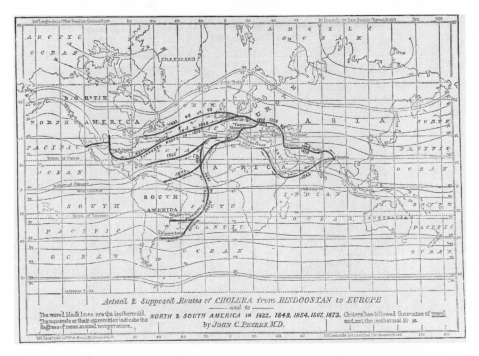

The Actual and Supposed Routes of Cholera from Hindoostan to Europe and to North America in 1832, 1848, 1854, 1867 and 1873, John Peters, 1885, from A Treatise on Asiatic Cholera *by Edmund Charles Wendt (New York: W. Wood, 1885), 68–71. Wellcome Library, London.*

the earliest cases were recorded in 1821, or since 1831, when the first epidemic broke out in the port of Gateshead in the north of England.[17]

The sporadic way in which the disease manifested itself in London from the summer of 1848 suggests that this may be the case. Therefore it is possible that different strains of cholera were causing cholera and cholera-like symptoms in London, and by the hot summer of 1849, conditions were perfect in the River Thames for the deadliest strain, *Vibrio cholerae* O1, to do its worst. The origins of the cholera epidemic were therefore possibly twofold. On the one hand *Vibrio cholerae* was brought to London by ship, but an endemic strain may have already been present in British estuaries.

The first official case of cholera in Britain occurred in October 1848, however, it is likely that the disease had struck well before this, as noted by the surgeon Dr. Edmund A. Parkes (1819–1876): "It has been stated in some of the medical journals, that several cases, very much resembling the Asiatic cholera, occurred in London during the summer and early autumn of 1848."[18] Observations of a case of *English Cholera* in July 1848 by Dr. John Sewell, a surgeon in Lambeth (as included in the Lambeth District Sanitary Reports), confirmed Parkes' view.[19] However, the lack of documentation relating to the early cases of the cholera outbreak may also have been because surgeons were trying to play down the reemergence of the disease in order to avoid mass panic. Parkes alludes to this possibility: "Mr Haden believed it to be an advanced case of the approaching epidemic of that disease, and not to be simply a case of the common English or bilious cholera."[20] In other words, Mr. Haden was voicing the fears which others were refusing to admit.

Dr. Edmund Parkes had some considerable experience of cholera, having worked in India, at Madras and Moulmein, as Assistant Surgeon to the 84th (York and Lancaster) Regiment. When he retired from the army in 1845, he set up practice in London, but continued to write papers, in particular on cholera. Later, in 1855, he was dispatched by the government to the Crimea to set up a hospital in Renkioi in the Dardanelles to "relieve the pressure upon the hospitals at Scutari."[21] In 1849, when Parkes was acting as Assistant Physician to University College Hospital London, he wrote *An Inquiry into the Bearing of the Earliest Cases of Cholera, which Occurred in London During the Present Epidemic, on the Strict Theory of Contagion.* His report begins with the following information: "The following Inquiry originated in a request made by Dr. Parkes, by the General Board of Health, that he should examine into the evidence which might be derived for or against the doctrine of Contagion, by an analysis of the early cases of cholera in London."[22]

In his report, Parkes believed it was likely cholera had already arrived in London by July 1848, however, he was careful to note that the first case of which he was made aware was the only case in the neighborhood. His under-

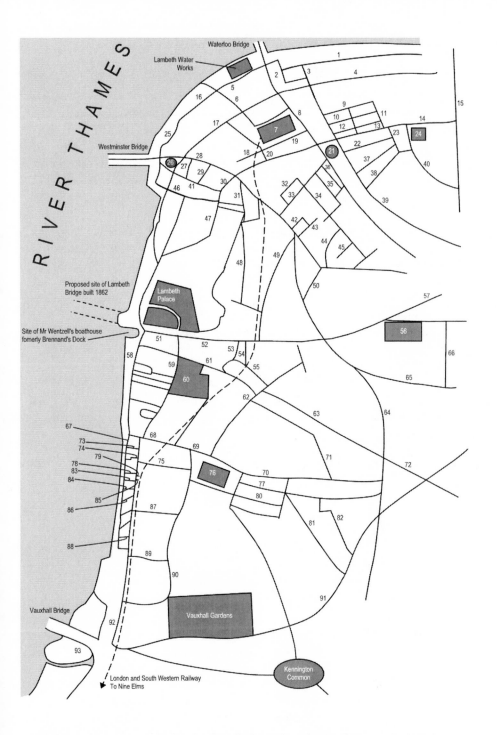

A diagram of the streets and landmarks of Lambeth in 1848 and 1849. Illustration by the author, redrawn by Alexander Thomas. Number key is on pages 166–168.

standing of the contagious nature of the disease meant that had this case been cholera, it would have claimed other victims. However, recent research has identified many strains of *Vibrio cholerae*. *Vibrio cholerae* O1 possesses the antigen O1, which produces the cholera toxin known as CT+,[23] and it is this strain which is the most dangerous and causes fatalities. Work by Waldor and Mekalanos (see Chapter 2) suggested that the structural genes for the cholera toxin are "encoded by a filamentous bacteriophage," a virus which has infected the cholera bacterium, and it is the infection process in the human gut which causes the activation of the pathogenic virus.[24]

However, there is also a non-O1 strain which may still induce diarrhea in humans. Up until the end of the twentieth century it was thought that the "only reservoir of toxigenic *V. cholerae* O1 ... was the human intestine."[25] However, the scientists Citarella and Colwell[26] discovered that the O1 and non-O1 strains are in fact a single species, and may live in a shared aquatic environment; moreover, they can remain in a dormant state for years. In other words, the isolated cases Parkes noted may well have all been victims of cholera. A report in *The Times* of August 1855, by which time the understanding of cholera in Britain and London was considerably better, indicated that this may well have been the case: "It would appear that there is no longer any doubt that diarrhoea and cholera, when they prevail together endemically, are different degrees of the same disease, produced by the same causes, and aggravated by the same influences."[27]

1. Commercial Road
2. Bond Street
3. Cornwall Road
4. Upper Stamford Street
5. Belvedere Road
6. Vine Street
7. Waterloo Station
8. Waterloo Road
9. Brad Street (going east-west) and with Brad Pace (going north-south)
10. Woolton Street
11. Cross Street
12. Canterbury Street
13. New Cut
14. Charlotte Street
15. Blackfriars Road
16. Narrow Wall
17. York Road

18. James Street
19. Granby Street or Henry Street
20. Lambeth Marsh (going east-west)
21. Victoria Theatre (today's Old Vic)
22. New Street
23. Short Street
24. Christchurch Workhouse
25. Pedlar's Acre
26. Astley's Theatre
27. Felix Street
28. Westminster Bridge Road
29. Mason Street
30. Upper Marsh
31. Carlisle Lane
32. Charles Street
33. Oakley Road
34. Gloucester Street
35. Isabella Street
36. Thomas Street
37. Mitre Street
38. Queen Street
39. Webber Street
40. Black Ditch
41. Stangate Street
42. Burd Street
43. Frances Street
44. Hooper Street
45. Jurston Street
46. Crosier Street
47. Love Lane
48. Carlisle Place
49. Hercules Buildings
50. Mead Row
51. Church Street
52. Canterbury Place
53. Pratt Street
54. Windmill Street
55. Mill Street
56. Bethlem Hospital
57. Lambeth Road

58. Lower Fore Street
59. Lambeth High Street
60. Lambeth Burial Ground
61. Paradise Row/Street
62. Lambeth Walk
63. East Street
64. Walcot Place
65. Pleasant Row
66. Elliott's Row
67. Upper Fore Street
68. Broad Street
69. Lambeth Butts
70. Princes Road
71. Regent Street
72. Chester Street
73. Naked Boy Alley
74. Frying Pan Alley
75. Salamanca Street
76. Lambeth Workhouse
77. Park Street
78. Stone Wharf
79. Great Lemon Court
80. Orsett Street
81. Devonshire Street
82. Cardigan Street
83. Free Court
84. Fox Alley
85. Lemon Court
86. Bull Alley
87. Anderson's Walk
88. New Street
89. Glasshouse Street
90. Vauxhall Walk
91. Kennington Lane
92. Vauxhall Row
93. South London Water Works, later known as the Southwark and Vauxhall Water Company

Another case which aroused Parkes' suspicions occurred in Wandsworth, to the southwest of Lambeth. It does not appear that this person died, though

Parkes noted that later on in the year there were further cases in Wandsworth, which may support the theory that the cases he noted were a demonstration of different strains of cholera. Another case was in Southwark, closer still to Lambeth, in the New Kent Road, a spur off the old Watling Street. The man, John Dean, died within a few hours, and according to Parkes an inquest was held as there was suspicion Dean had been poisoned. However, the doctor who attended him, Mr. Fairbrother, was sure that Dean had died from Asiatic cholera, the common name for the disease.

Further on in his inquiry, Parkes discussed the Registrar General's Report, which listed cases in August and September of "common autumnal cholera"[28] and added that as they "did not exceed the average ... there is no trace of the epidemic of cholera in England."[29] By September 30, four further cases had been reported, by October 7, 13 more, and Parkes listed where these outbreaks had occurred: Old Street, West London, Bethnal Green, Spitalfields, Whitechapel, St. George's in the east of London, Stepney, Rotherhithe, Greenwich and Orsett Street in Lambeth, a few streets back from the waterfront and close to Lambeth Workhouse.

The case of John Harnold on September 22, 1848, was considered by Dr. John Snow (1813–1858) to be the first confirmed case of the epidemic, particularly as the person carrying the disease arrived from an area where cholera was already at epidemic levels.[30] Harnold had traveled by steamer from Hamburg in Germany, and made his way to Horsleydown in Southwark, close to Lambeth. Parkes questioned whether Harnold had in fact become infected in Southwark as this was an area where "cholera was commencing to prevail."[31] However, Parkes concluded that it was most likely Harnold had contracted cholera in Hamburg as the second engineer had also fallen ill onboard the steamer. Parkes related that the victim's clothes and bedding were thrown overboard, somewhere on the approach to the north Kent coast, close to Gravesend, where the boat was quarantined for about six hours. It is possible that the tainted clothing and bedding may even have added to the spread of the epidemic in the London and north Kent area, as the waters at this point in the estuary may have been conducive to the *Vibrio cholerae* bacteria.

Cholera was transmitted in London by the drinking of contaminated water. The spread of cholera via this contaminated fluid was varied. Victims may have drunk river water and used it in the preparation of food. Transmission also occurred with poor hygiene, by touching surfaces tainted by contaminated fluids and then touching one's mouth. In this respect the overflowing privies of Lambeth were an excellent source of infection in a community where people would have rarely washed their hands. Street food would also have been a source of infection as food may have been handled with dirty hands. Costermongers, the purveyors of fruit on the streets, were known to store their wares under the family bed.[32]

In his *On the Mode of Communication of Cholera,* John Snow noted similar behavior: "It is not unlikely that some cases of cholera which spring up without any apparent connection with previous cases, may be communicated through articles of diet. It is the practice of poor people, who gain a living by selling fruit and other articles in the streets to keep their stock in very crowded rooms in which they live, and, when visiting out-patients of a medical charity a few years ago, I often saw baskets of fruit pushed under the beds of sick patients, in close proximity with the chamber utensils."[33] Goods stored in this way would most certainly have become contaminated had the occupier of that same bed been suffering from cholera. Rats, mice, flies and other flying insects may also have transmitted the bacteria on their feet. *Vibrio cholerae* can also be ingested by eating shellfish, like oysters and crabs. The eating of raw oysters caught in contaminated water was a common way to become infected with cholera; *Vibrio cholerae* O1 can also live for many weeks inside crabs, which need to be cooked for some time to destroy the pathogen.[34]

As discussed in Chapter 2, recent work on the ecology of *Vibrio cholerae* O1[35] has shown that the pathogen produces the enzyme chitinase, the purpose of which is to dissolve chitin, a component of the exoskeletons of copepods, the plankton group with which *Vibrio cholerae* associates in its natural environment. Chitin is an insoluble polymer and contains carbon and nitrogen, which are essential nutrients for marine microorganisms such as *Vibrio cholerae.* Scientists observing the progress of cholera outbreaks in recent years have noticed that they occur with an increase in phytoplankton and zooplankton blooms in estuarine and costal environments and further research has shown that *Vibrio cholerae* can "sense, attach to, and degrade natural chitin surfaces" in an aquatic environment.[36]

The attachment of *Vibrio cholerae* to chitin is one of the factors which makes the pathogen so dangerous to humans and, as the work by Nalin et al. at the University of Maryland School of Medicine reveals, "Pandemic strains of *V. cholerae* of O-group 1 serotype might adsorb onto and multiply on contaminated chitinous fauna, including crabs, shrimp, or zooplankton. Adsorption appears to occur more readily at pH 6.2 than at 7.3 and may therefore be more likely to occur in estuaries than in ocean water. It is possible that chitin of previously cooked but recontaminated crabs or other crustacea, like the powdered crabshell used in these studies, could be a substrate for vibrio multiplication and might permit survival of stomach acid by V. cholerae on chitin particles ingested during a meal."[37] Additional work by Wachsmuth, Blake and Olsvik showed "*V. cholerae* O1 adheres to chitin, and survival of chitin-absorbed *V. cholerae* in a dilute hydrochloric acid solution of approximately the same pH as human gastric acid is prolonged.... Chitin is also a component of crustacean shells and may protect adsorbed *V. cholerae* O1 from destruction by heat as well as by gastric acid."[38]

With regard to the first official case of 1848, that of John Harnold, Parkes noted that "Harnold ... entered a place where cholera was commencing to prevail," confirming his suspicion of the likelihood of other unrecorded cases. The next cholera victim was the first in Lambeth, though Parkes did not explain how the disease arose there. However, he does suspect that it may have been by human contact. He endeavored to trace the movements of the victims he recorded to try and understand the means of cholera contagion.

John Murphy, aged 22, lived at number 26 Lower Fore Street in the waterfront area of Lambeth. Though Parkes did not say so, from his name, it is likely he was an Irish immigrant. Parkes did note, however, that he was "a labourer in the adjoining gas-works, but out of employ and badly fed."[39] On September 30, 1848, Murphy visited his cousin at Kensal Green in northwest London. By the late evening of the same day he was seriously ill and, by 8:30 the following morning, he was dead. There is a possibility that Murphy may have contracted cholera somewhere along his journey, but Parkes did not consider this. Following Murphy's death, there were a series of cases in Chelsea, further upriver from Lambeth, and then Jane Langham, aged 27, in Harp Court off Fleet Street. Many of the cholera victims in this area were admitted to St. Bartholomew's Hospital in Smithfield, just to the north of St. Paul's Cathedral. This case is not mentioned in the surviving records as Jane Langham did not die from her infection. However, many of the other victims in this area contracted cholera because they obtained their water from the Fleet River (see Chapter 4), an open sewer and tributary to the Thames. In his *On the Mode of the Communication of Cholera*, Dr. John Snow commented, "The inhabitants of Harp Court, Fleet Street, were in the habit, at that time, of procuring water from St. Bride's pump, which was afterwards closed on the representation of Mr. Hutchinson, surgeon, of Farringdon Street, in consequence of its having, been found that the well had a communication with the Fleet Ditch sewer, up which the tide flows from the Thames."[40]

The next victim was another associated with the river, a man onboard the convict hulk *Justitia*, off Woolwich, and his symptoms were violent and rapid. It is impossible to tell from this whether the epidemic was becoming more virulent or that this victim was simply more susceptible to the pathogen. With regard to this case, Dr. Snow commented, "I was informed ... that the hulk *Justitia* was supplied with spring water from the Woolwich Arsenal; but it is not improbable that water was occasionally taken from the Thames alongside, as was constantly the practice in some of the other hulks, and amongst the shipping generally."

By the end of September, Edwin Chadwick, in his new role as Commissioner to the Board of Health, had contacted the Poor Law Board to ensure that regulations were put in place for the Poor Law Guardians to deal with a cholera epidemic.[41] Chadwick sent Dr. Sutherland and Dr. Grainger to Hamburg to try and glean further information about the epidemic, and Sir William Pym, Superintendent of Quarantine at the Privy Council Office, declared a quarantine.[42] At around the same time, cholera cases were reported in Sunderland and on a Prussian ship which had docked in the northern port of Hull. On September 28, the Nuisances Removal and Diseases Prevention Act, which had been passed in Parliament on August 7, came into force and effectively stripped Pym's department of any authority, giving control to Chadwick's Board of Health, though the department was not ready to take any immediate action.[43]

The *First Notification of Cholera* in the United Kingdom was published by Chadwick's Board on October 5, 1848, followed by the *Second* on October 31, when detailed regulations were also completed, and *Regulations* on November 3. Articles published in the medical press at the time show that the board was in chaos, producing contradictory advice and still in conflict with Pym's Quarantine Department.[44]

The ninth case of cholera recorded by Parkes was again in Lambeth, on October 4, 1848, just a few days after the first occurrence. The next victim was James George, aged 40, a butcher's carter of 29 Lower Fore Street. Parkes noted that George and Murphy were not acquainted, though they may have met casually in the street on the evening of Murphy's return from Kensal Green. He concluded that George's infection "must have been through the particles of poison floating over the neighbourhood."[45] Indeed, Murphy and George may well have not had any contact at all, and both were infected by an already contaminated water supply in Lambeth. George fell ill on the morning of October 4, but, according to Parkes, as he was used to having stomach upsets, he and his wife ignored the symptoms and, after taking a dose of brandy and rhubarb, he made his way to Newgate Market in the City of London. His symptoms worsened in the churchyard of St. Paul's cathedral, where he began to vomit and suffered *purging* (diarrhoea).[46] George was taken to St. Bartholomew's Hospital, where he died at 9 o'clock that evening. The Registers of Deaths at St. Bart's show George's wife did not claim his body, and may have given her consent for the corpse to be dissected in exchange for a free burial by the hospital. The records show that the body underwent a postmortem, but the purpose of the procedure would probably have been research and experimentation as surgeons were impatient to understand how cholera killed its victims. Following the postmortem, the body was dealt with by the undertaker James Barnard of the Old Bailey, a regular visitor to the hospital, as the records cite his name many times.[47]

St. Bart's had a burial ground in Seward Street, less than half a mile to the north of the hospital, in today's Islington, which had been consecrated especially for the poor who died at the hospital: "In the Parish of St. Luke being the hospital's freehold hath been appropriated and consecrated for buying ground for the poor patients who dye [sic] in this hospital ... no Bodies but such of the Poor Patients who dye in the hospital should be suffered to be buried there."[48]

The 1832 Anatomy Act permitted anatomical research on bodies from the workhouses and prisons or by donation in exchange for free burial. For many paupers, such an offer may not have been welcome as there was considerable prejudice against anatomical research and dissection, mainly on religious grounds as the resurrection of the body was key to the beliefs of Victorian Christians. John Abernethy (1764–1831) was surgeon at St. Bart's from 1815 to 1827 and he, like most surgeons in London at the time, knew the importance of anatomical research to further the understanding of the human body and disease. Abernethy felt that unclaimed bodies were an ideal resource and gave evidence before the Select Committee on Anatomy in 1828, "which was appointed to investigate the methods of obtaining bodies for dissection, and the law affecting people who obtained them."[49] There was tremendous opposition — and fear — to the practice of the grave robbers or so-called "body snatchers" of the past and legislation was needed to regulate the supply of dead bodies and for consent to be given where necessary and appropriate by the family of the deceased. The 1832 Act achieved its purpose and the illicit trade in bodies disappeared.

The records for the postmortem of James George no longer exist. However, it is clear from records at St. Thomas' Hospital during the 1854 cholera epidemic that postmortems were dissection by any other name, or at least anatomical research, as any opportunity to explore the workings of the human body were relished by the surgeons of the day. For the surgeons, anatomical investigations were vital to try and understand how cholera attacked the human digestive system. Their work in this period shows that they understood severe dehydration took place and that this also caused a thickening of the blood. However, without an understanding of bacteriology, they could not grasp the cycle and process of the infection (see Chapter 2).

On October 4, 1848, Parkes reported that James George's daughter also fell ill with cholera. This may be Eliza, who is recorded in the 1851 Census.[50] She too was admitted to St. Bartholomew's Hospital under Dr. Burrows, but her attack was not severe and she recovered; her admittance to the hospital is therefore not recorded on the death register with that of her father.

At the same time as cholera was taking hold in Lambeth, it was also spreading in Chelsea, Southwark, Spitalfields (by St. Bart's Hospital),

Bermondsey (near Long Lane, where there was an open ditch, no doubt used as a sewer), and the hulk *Justitia* in Woolwich. There were also many cases among sailors who had been living onboard ship in the Pool of London and a case on a hospital ship moored off Greenwich; all less than a week since John Harnold had arrived in Southwark from Hamburg.[51]

The next case, in Lower Fore Street, Lambeth, was the cousin of John Murphy, a John Healy, aged 25. Healy had also worked at the gasworks and, like Murphy, had lost his job. Healy fell ill on the morning of October 5 and while it seemed he might recover, by the sixth day he had a black tongue and had fallen into a coma; he too subsequently died. Parkes noted that he was a temperate man, as many thought excess alcohol consumption contributed to susceptibility to cholera, and that he also did not eat well, "being sometimes thirty-six hours without food." Indeed, research has shown that regular drinking and poor nourishment do increase susceptibility to infection as both disrupt the production of gastric acid. *Vibrio cholerae* is most dangerous to those with a weakened immune system, and as it is sensitive to acidic environments, those with low levels of stomach acid are even more prone to infection.

Parkes calculated that between September 28 and October 10, 1848, there were 28 reported cases of cholera, but news had clearly spread of an impending epidemic, as on October 13, *The Times* newspaper carried the following advertisements:

> Bowel Complaints Cures and Cholera prevented ... Shillcock's Anti-Cholera Specific ... is earnestly recommended.
>
> The cholera having reached our shores ... it becomes the duty of all persons to be prepared. The Hindoo Anti-Cholera Compound ... proved eminently successful during the very worst period of cholera, at Archangel in Russia ... 1831.[52]

In addition, from October 11, the paper began publishing the weekly mortality rates from cholera compiled by William Farr at the General Register Office and listing the areas where the victims had died. The first report contains the details of the 11-month-old daughter of a chair maker who lived in Orsett Street, Lambeth. The article commented that "in the centre of the road there is an open drain, which at times is very offensive, the drainage to the house is very bad, and the scarlatina has been prevalent."[53]

While we know now that the cause of the child's cholera came from a tainted water supply, it is interesting to note that scarlatina (scarlet fever) had been prevalent in Lambeth at the time. Scarlet fever is caused by a streptococcal bacteria and is often accompanied by vomiting and abdominal pain. There is the possibility that these cases may not have been scarlet fever at all, but rather mild cases of cholera. Moreover, the sickness which was constantly prevalent in the Lambeth tenements meant that residents, and in particular

children and the elderly, would have had a very low resistance to any virulent disease such as cholera.

By October 25, *The Times* was publishing a regular, separate column on
The Cholera in which it noted 45 had died that week from the disease in London. One of these was another victim in Lambeth, a waiter, aged 41, who
lived in Devonshire Street,[54] close to Kennington Lane, just south of Fore
Street and a little back from the waterfront.

By November 1, 1848, the number of deaths from cholera had fallen to
34, and by 4 November to 6, and there were no reported fatalities in Lambeth. Parkes did not record any notable incidences for this period, but he did
give a hint as to why the rate of deaths may have fallen off: "In London ...
[the cholera] having been partially developed in the remarkable weather which
ushered in the month of October."[55] While Parkes does not explain precisely
what he means by "remarkable," it is likely that the weather was unseason-
ably mild in October 1848, and this would certainly have facilitated the growth
of *Vibrio cholerae* in the waters of the River Thames.

On November 3, Chadwick's *Regulations* were published, one of the
instructions of which were for the local Guardians to send their officers to
make reports on the worst areas in order that they might be cleansed. In the
event of an epidemic, Chadwick's Board recommended "dispensaries, houses
of refuge ... and house-to-house visitation."[56] By November 8, the number
of deaths from cholera rose again, to 65, and *The Times* gave a clue as to why
this may have been: "The long continuance of wet weather." Heavy rain would
have caused many sewage ditches to overflow and seep into the drinking water
supply, such as wells. However, it is possible that while temperatures may have
been cooling, the rain may have provided the *Vibrio cholerae* with an opportunity to breed in shallower, warmer pools of water on the edge of the river,
an environment rich in sediment and another essential ingredient for the survival of the pathogen. Many of the cases in this week in November occurred
in Lambeth and already outbreaks were occurring in exactly those streets
which the Lambeth District Sanitary Sub Committees had predicted:

> Printer, 45 years, "Asiatic cholera (10 hours)." Boy, 4 years, "English cholera
> (24 hours)." Waterloo, 2d Part.— At 18, Jurston-street, son of a waterman, 2
> years, "diarrhoea and sickness merging into cholera (5 days)." 18, Jurston-
> street, son of a waterman, 14 years, "cholera (68 hours)." At 9, Cheltenham-
> place, a beerseller, 57 years ... cholera Asiatica (18 hours)." At Jurston-street,
> labourer, 41 years, "cholera (16 hours)." At 17, Agnes-street, wife of a porter,
> 30 years, "Asiatic cholera (12 hours)." Lambeth Church 2d Part.— M., 23
> years, "cholera (10 hours)." This man was a licensed hawker. He was intoxi-
> cated on the Saturday, and locked up until Monday, when he was discharged,
> and took a hearty supper of pork, greens and potatoes at night. He was
> seized with cholera at 2 o'clock A.M. on Tuesday and died on the same day.—

Kennington, 1st part.— At 26 Ely-place, hammerman to a blacksmith, 22 years, "malignant cholera (nine and a-half hours)." At 3, William-street, Dorset-street, daughter of a bricklayer, 14 years, "cholera (12½ hours)." At the Lodge, South Lambeth, daughter of a solicitor, two years and eight months, "cholera (16½ hours)."[57]

By the week ending November 15, the deaths from cholera in London were 65. In Lambeth, fatalities occurred first in Eaton Street, New Cut, which was "densely inhabited, ill cleansed and drained."[58] One of the deaths was of a woman street seller who "lived selling trifles in the streets and at public-houses."[59] Deaths also occurred in John Street off Belvedere Road, Chel-tenham Place, Jurston Street, Oakley Street, and Devonshire Street. By November 22, there had been an additional 54 deaths from cholera, with fatal-ities in Lambeth at Mitre Place, Broadwall, (where the wife and two daugh-ters of a coachmaker died), Jurston Street, Charles Place, and Union Street.[60]

By the last week of November, deaths from cholera in London had fallen once more, to 30.[61] On November 30, the first death occurred in Lambeth Workhouse, of a man "seized in a court leading out of Glasshouse-street, Vauxhall, and was only admitted to the house a few hours before death."[62]

At the beginning of 1849, the cholera persisted. William Farr noted there were two deaths from cholera in the riverfront area of Lambeth in January, which may include the death on January 16 in Burdett Street, near Waterloo Road; there were also two deaths to the east of Vauxhall towards Kennington Lane. Then, on February 3, there was a death from cholera in Whitehorse Street, and by March 17, there had been 1,191 cases of cholera and 609 deaths.

By June 1849, as temperatures began to rise, deaths from cholera also rose and the authorities were aware that they were in the midst of a new and deadly epidemic. The first death in June in Lambeth was on June 15 in Agnes Street near Waterloo Road, that of a 54-year-old wife of a carpenter. On June 23 there was a case close by in Short Street, one of the areas singled out in The Lambeth District Sanitary Reports. On June 26, Kezia and Mathilda Hilliard were admitted to St. Bart's Hospital. They resided in New Court, New Street, which is just off Short Street and close to the Victoria Theatre, today's Old Vic. It is not known why Kezia and her daughter were in the area around St. Bart's Hospital. Perhaps they were visiting friends, perhaps they were doing some business for Kezia's husband, George, who was a wheel-wright. Kezia Kerrenhappuch, whose maiden name is unknown, married George Hilliard before 1836, possibly in the Medway Towns. Their son Jesse was born in 1836 and then a daughter, Harriet Amelia, in 1838, who was chris-tened in the Medway Towns at Chatham's parish church, St. Mary's, on Dock Road on October 3, 1838; Mathilda arrived in about 1841.[63]

On their admittance to St. Bart's Hospital, Kezia suffered from cholera for 16 hours before dying, but Mathilda struggled with the disease for a whole day. Their bodies were taken by the undertaker James Barnard of the Old Bailey, though Mathilda's first underwent a postmortem. The body of an eight-year-old child who had died of the disease most of London's surgeons wanted to understand must have been a source of fascination. Mother and daughter were buried at the hospital's graveyard in Seward Street.

On June 27 there was another death in Lower Fore Street. The waterfront area was badly affected, and William Farr noted especially the following streets: High Street, Duke's Head Court, Felix Street, Vauxhall Walk, Lambeth Walk, Upper Marsh, Canterbury Place, Broad Street, Hercules Buildings, Glasshouse Street, North Street (Vauxhall Walk), Salamanca Street, Royal Street and Fore Street.[64] From June 29 to July 2 inclusive, three people died of cholera at number 2 Ferry Street. On July 3 there was a death in James Street, and on July 9 and 10, at Duke's Head Court, a silver-chaser and his son died.[65]

Throughout the first two weeks of July the temperature rose into the 80s, and in this period there were around 233 deaths from cholera in Lambeth.[66] The summer of 1849 was one of the loveliest in terms of climate, as was recorded retrospectively in October that year in *The Times*: "Never has the sun shone upon the inhabitants of London with such enduring splendour as ... 1849. Never has the air been more balmy and elastic, nor the nights more cloudy and brilliant. The absence of rain or watery vapour for the last eight months has been the great characteristic of the time.... It was in the midst of this illusive splendour that the destroying angel was sent forth by the Almighty on his deadly mission.... The warm sunny air became impregnated, we know not how, with qualities destructive to human life."[67]

By July 18, 1849, the total number of deaths in London from cholera had risen to 1,369; in that week the deaths (339) were double those of the previous week. In the past six weeks, deaths from cholera were 22, 42, 49, 124, 152 and 339, and 387 of these deaths were on the south side of the river; the highest toll was in Lambeth.[68]

By the middle of the month, cholera was well established at Millbank Penitentiary and on the prison hulks *Hebe, Wye, Justitia, Unité* (a convict hospital) and the *Warrior* off Woolwich. The *Warrior* was not as badly affected as the others and the authorities realized this had something to do with its position on the river, being farther from the Plumstead marshes. An article in *The Times* of July 18 noted that "a sewer empties itself near the *Justitia,* and another larger one is near the *Warrior*. Both are offensive."[69] It was decided to move the hulks *Hebe, Wye* and *Unité* further upriver towards the dockyard. It is not known whether this decision was undertaken, but certainly any movement of the hulks upriver, closer to Lambeth, would have made the situation worse.

In the same issue of the newspaper, the situation at Millbank Penitentiary was discussed. Here too cholera was raging and while the link between cholera at Millbank and in the hulks was not considered, it must have been a factor. The penitentiary was a holding place for convicts who were subsequently transferred to the hulks prior to transportation onboard sailing ships to Australia. The article discussed the inquest of the prisoners Thomas Morcon and James Kinman, who had died of cholera in Millbank. Dr. William Baly, the physician at Millbank, gave evidence and spoke of his attempt to cure the patients by wrapping them in wet sheets and blankets, as had been recommended by *The Times* newspaper. Baly added that there were already eight cases of cholera at the prison and each of them had been supplied daily with a half-pint of Barclay and Perkins' beer. He also revealed that the prison authorities were considering transferring around 600 prisoners to the Sussex coast to escape the epidemic.[70]

On July 16, in the Kennington Lane area, there were 14 deaths, six of which were in the workhouse. On July 21, an outbreak began at number 3 Grove Place, Lambeth. The landlady was the first to die. The illness began in church and she was "removed during Divine service."[71] (The next victim to die in Grove Place was not until August.) A few days later, on July 24, *The Times* published an article highlighting the situation in Lambeth. It reported that "several gentlemen connected with the parish and borough of Lambeth have been making a sanitary inspection of the borough, with a view to ascertain whether the extraordinary number of deaths that is daily taking place from cholera is attributable to the want of proper sanitary arrangements. The result of the inquiry, so far as it has at present been made, shows that unless some speedy means be adopted for removing the pestilential smells occasioned by the various obnoxious works carried on, the spread of the disease will be most fearful."[72]

The Sub Committees of the Lambeth District Sanitary Committee made their investigations of the borough a year earlier, in January, February and July, 1848. It is not clear if the gentlemen conducting the investigations in July 1849 are the same, however, their conclusions were identical, and it is useful to note that even with cholera raging in the district nothing had been done to improve the insanitary living conditions in Lambeth.

The article in *The Times* explains it was the noxious fumes of the Lambeth factories in the waterfront stretch between Lambeth Palace and Vauxhall Bridge which were to blame:

> "A street called Upper and Lower Fore-street ... cut off by the gas works belonging to the Vauxhall Company. In this street are bone-boilers, soap-

makers, tallow-melters ... and other equally unwholesome trades. A large number of poor families live in this street, in little low houses, the rooms of which are scarcely high enough for a person to stand upright in; scarcely any of these houses have privies, the dust heap appearing to be the common receptacle for all filth. The tide from the Thames flows up to the doors, and when it recedes it leaves all the filth from its banks opposite the houses, the stench from which when it dries is fearful. Behind it ... Princes-street ... literally studded with courts and alleys, all densely inhabited by poor persons ... bone-houses ... soapboilers ... grease-works.... When the bone-boilers are at work, which is almost every day, it is next to impossible for a stranger to pass through the street without being compelled to vomit.... About 800 poor families live on this immediate spot.[73]

The description repeated much of what was reported in the Sanitary Reports from the Sub Committee of the St. Mary's and Trinity Districts (see Chapter 6).

The article went on to comment that Dr. William Baly at Millbank Penitentiary was certain that these noxious fumes were spreading the cholera. A description of the area behind the waterfront painted a picture as grim as that in the waterfront area itself with families living in single rooms, single privies for several houses and water arriving sporadically via pipes, so that any water had to be held in vessels for use. The water in these pipes was pumped from the Thames by the Lambeth Waterworks by Westminster Bridge. The article explained that few of these houses had drains and that the cellar of one house in particular had become a dump for all types of waste, including human excrement. Indeed, the streets and alleyways were strewn with rubbish of every sort, the worst areas being Gloucester Street, Wellington Place, Salamanca Place, Brothers Row, King's Head Court, Ferry Street, Duke's Head Court, Faircloth Court, Glasshouse Street and York Wharf (see Chapter 6). The description also included the open sewers which ran alongside the road and into which emptied the effluent from the factories. The article concluded with the following statement: "As soon as the gentlemen have completed their survey, which will be in a day or two, they intend to present a report to the parochial authorities and demand the removal of those nuisances."[74]

On July 25 there was an inquest into the death of a shoemaker, aged 20, who had died of cholera at number 5 Bate's Buildings, Broadwall, again in the vicinity of Short Street, Lambeth. Farr noted that Bate's Buildings was one of the "narrow courts in Broadwall, crossing the boundary sewer." It is this sewer which gained such a reputation in the reports of the District Sanitary Committees and was known as the Black Ditch. Farr noted that half the number of deaths due to cholera had occurred near this boundary ditch, and at Bate's Buildings these included the younger sister and mother of the shoemaker, and perhaps even his father, who was ill with cholera at the time of Farr's writing and whose fate went unrecorded.[75]

The following day, Ann Osmotherly died at 11 Princes Street, right behind Fore Street, one of the worst areas of Lambeth, where there was no running water. Ann's death certificate stated that she suffered for 24 hours and that James, her husband, was present at the death. Ann was 51 years old and left behind six children: Emma, aged 19, Sarah, aged 17, James William, aged 14, Mary, aged 12, Hannah, aged 10, and George, aged 8. The youngest daughter, Lucy Charlotte, had died a few months earlier, just before the Christmas of 1848. Lucy had died of smallpox after being ill for two weeks; she had not been vaccinated, no doubt because her parents simply could not afford to do so.

On July 26 there was a storm in London,[76] causing flooding and the contents of the cesspools, drains and sewers to overflow and mix with the water supply. By the end of July, the total number of deaths from cholera in London had risen to 1,741. In that week alone, 106 died in Lambeth, once again the worst of the areas south of the river. The temperature was still high, though like any English summer, variable. The following day, a report in *The Times* discussed the inquest of Ann Tiptaff, aged 68, of Queen Street, by Webber Street in Lambeth, who had died of cholera. She lived by an open sewer and her son was convinced that the foul stench emanating from the ditch was the cause of her illness and that it should be enclosed. An inquiry discovered that the sewer was flushed daily by the River Thames "by order of the Commissioners of the Sewers." The coroner questioned the logic of this, stating, "Of what use can that be; because of course, when the tide recedes it would bring the soil back?"[77] A Mr. Adcock, who had attended Mrs. Tiptaff with the surgeon Dr. Brooks, replied that he thought the sewage was discharged at Rotherhithe. It is not made clear whether Adcock said this in ignorance or to deceive, but he was quickly reminded that the sewage was discharged at Waterloo Bridge. The discussion considered other deaths from cholera which had occurred near another open sewer at Broadwall, and concluded that it was the flushing of the drains that was causing the problem as it was "disturbing and discharging all the sulphuretted hydrogen in the deposit."[78] It was agreed that the Lambeth Inspector and Board of Guardians should be notified so that the drains could be covered.

On July 26, the 34-year-old wife of a shoemaker died at number 80 James Street. Farr noted of the area, "This spot lies quite in a hollow; it was built on very marshy ground, the drainage is defective, and there are ditches partially filled up, which often serve as receptacles for decayed vegetables, stinking fish etc. With few exceptions the deaths have occurred to persons extremely poor, residing generally in one room, and in dirty narrow streets."[79]

Farr also reported that in the June and July period, at 10 Mitre Place, Broadwall, again mentioned in the District Sanitary Reports, the three children of a laborer all died within a three-day span. "At No. 15 Eaton-street, a mother and a son. At No. 60 Cornwall-road, on July 30th, the widow of a cooper and 2 children; and on July 29th at No. 11 Brad-street, the daughters of a compositor died."[80]

Farr noted that the streets affected worst in the June–July period were Roupell Street, Mitre Place (Broadwall), Whitehorse Street, Eaton Street, Cornwall Road, New Street, Little Windmill Street, Salutation Place, Le Grand Place and Wootton Street. In July and August, deaths exceeded births by 53.[81] On July 30, Members of Parliament discussed the possibility of not sitting through August "when the ... cholera, the bone houses in Lambeth, and St. Margaret's churchyard, would infallibly carry off a few dozen honourable members."[82] It is interesting to consider that Parliament was more concerned to leave the area to protect themselves rather than remedy the situation directly across the river or in the nearby churchyard.

By August, the death toll had risen further, with 783 deaths recorded in the last week of July, the greatest number of mortalities occurring south of the river, in Lambeth, with 111 deaths. The temperature had dropped a little, however, to an average of just under 60°F.[83] The following day, *The Times* published a notice which had been issued by W.T. Logan, the Clerk of Lambeth Workhouse, in response to their article on the Lambeth Sanitary Sub-Committee's investigation: "Caution. The guardians of the poor in the parish of Lambeth hereby give notice that if any person or persons shall upon any of the roads, streets, lanes, mews, courts, alleys, passages, public ways or open spaces within the said parish, throw, or lay, or cause, permit or suffer to be thrown or laid, or to remain, any ashes, dust, offal, dung, manure ... vegetables, or any other filth or refuse whatsoever, such person or persons so offending will be proceeded against, and dealt with according to the law."[84] How the population of Lambeth were expected to comply with this new regulation went unrecorded.

On August 4, a letter appeared in *The Times* from Mr. J. T. Mitchell of Kennington Common regarding the conduct of the Lambeth Board of Guardians, their medical officers and the help given by them to the poor of the district. Mr. Mitchell, a medical officer of the parish for some 18 years, and two assistants were appointed by the Lambeth Board of Guardians, which he pointed out included a medical man, as directed by Chadwick's Board of Health. He stated that in the last week of July they had attended the homes of 1,028 inhabitants of the area, which included 59 cases of Asiatic cholera and 141 cases of diarrhea and "ordinary" cholera. The distinction between the three types of illness being that Asiatic cholera was the most serious and had

symptoms which were likely to be fatal. Whether there was any real difference between the three is impossible to tell. Mitchell related how he and his
assistants worked night and day and were so exhausted one of the assistants
had resigned. He complained that his salary was too low and barely covered
the cost of the medicines he was expected to provide. Worse, when he appealed
to the Board of Guardians on July 26 to recruit another assistant and to ask
for help from other medical professionals in the tending of the poor, he was
met with indifference. By the Tuesday morning, which was the same day as
the next meeting of the board, Mitchell decided to tender his conditional resignation, no doubt in the hope that this might spur the board into action;
his resignation was immediately accepted. Mitchell's conclusion was that the
Board of Guardians of Lambeth should not have responsibility for the poor
and that this should be entrusted to the government. Mitchell added that
despite the fact he was no longer employed by the board, he would continue
to work with the poor until a successor was found.[85]

Mitchell's letter to the board asked for an additional ten shillings (50p)
per patient for every cholera sufferer he should visit. He noted that in other
areas of the district the board were already paying this amount to some medical officers. He concluded that to cover the number of cholera sufferers he
needed a team of six, rather than three, and noted that some of the medical
officers in Lambeth refused to attend cases at night, and even in the day,
increasing the burden on others.

In the same issue of *The Times* newspaper, there was a report of another
case of cholera in Lambeth, that of Henry Hopping, a tailor aged 49, and his
wife Jane, aged 40. Their deaths had caused a stir in the neighborhood of the
Lower Marsh in Lambeth as they had died most suddenly of cholera and were
found dead together, leading to concerns by the male deceased's brother,
Thomas, that they had been poisoned. They lived in the top back room of a
house above a shop in the Lower Marsh. The room had been locked from the
inside, so there was clearly no foul play, and inside Mrs. Hopping was found
on the bed, Mr. Hopping seated beside her; "both faces bore a very distressed
appearance."[86] The door had had to be forced open, not just because it was
locked but because a "portion of sofa-bed was placed against it." There was
vomit and excrement around the room and Mr. Sewell, the surgeon who
investigated, found a quantity of prepared chalk water and gum, which had
been used as medicine, but which he knew would do no good whatsoever in
curing the symptoms of cholera.

Mr. Sewell is the same John Sewell who was a member of the St. Thomas'
District Sanitary Sub Committee in Lambeth and who lived at 59 Lower
Marsh. He performed postmortem examinations on the Hoppings and noted
"the heart and vessels containing thick black blood, the viscera in the chest

being collapsed to half the usual size, slight general inflammation of the stomach and intestines, the gall bladder filled with dark green bile, and an entire absence of any urine, which had apparently been suppressed for some time. There was serious effusion in the intestines, corresponding with rice-water evacuations." He had no doubt their deaths arose from cholera.[87]

Neighbors gave their opinion on the sort of people the Hoppings were to try and shed some light on their deaths. The lady who lived in the top front room, Sophia Jefferies, said the couple drank a lot, ate a little and would fight, indeed Jefferies had "seen the woman with her face bruised and her eyes blackened by her husband's violence."[88] In addition, they talked so loudly everyone could hear their conversation. Jefferies became concerned when she had seen Mr. Hopping on the Monday morning but then, knowing they were both locked in their room, heard no sound whatsoever, which was definitely out of character for the couple; she called Mr. Malden, who ran a shop in Lower Marsh. At the inquest the coroner thought it odd that the neighbors had not heard the Hoppings vomiting when they had said they could hear every word of a conversation, but concluded that their deaths must have been particularly sudden, a conclusion to which Mr. Sewell concurred. One mystery remained in the Hoppings' case, and that was why the section of sofa bed had been placed against their door. The fact was that the bedstead had been broken for some time and the room was so tiny that the only way the cupboard could be opened was to move parts of the bedstead over against the door.

William Farr also noted an increase in the number of cases in the area around Lower Marsh, Short Street and the boundary ditch at this time. Farr noted that the area was "subject to effluvia from bad drainage,"[89] but he concluded that the heightened number of cases in the area was most likely because of the crowded environment and "indifferent food."[90] The Board of Health was frustrated by the inaction by the local Boards of Guardians. "Repeatedly and earnestly," said the Board of Health, "[we] urged on the Boards of Guardians ... the importance ... of making immediate arrangements ... but our representations were made in vain. The Local Authorities could not be induced to carry into effect the preventative measures we proposed, and we ourselves had no means of putting them into practice. Our entire staff consisted of two medical inspectors, one of whom was laboriously and exclusively occupied in grappling with the epidemic in Scotland."[91] In order to take control of the situation, Lord Ashley of the Board managed to secure an amendment to the Nuisance Removal Act which enabled them to "summon witnesses, to direct measures of precaution to overcrowded graveyards, and to prosecute for willful neglect or violation of its provisions."[92]

Reports vary as to when house-to-house visitation started in earnest, but on August 6, *The Times* reported an improvement in cholera deaths, which it credited to the house-to-house visits organized by the Board of Health in areas such as Lambeth. Considering Mr. Mitchell's account above, and the fact that at this time the board was still trying to put the system into operation, it is possible that the report may be exaggerated. In addition, the same report stated that conditions in the prisons were easing and that at Millbank Penitentiary there had been only one case in the prior week and that it had been mild. The report did not confirm if the majority of the prisoners had been transferred to the Sussex coast, as had been earlier discussed. Despite such optimism, the number of deaths that week in Lambeth was 203 and the low-lying areas to the south of the river were still the worst affected. Indeed, two days later, the optimism had faded and *The Times* reported, "It is unsatisfactory to observe that the constant increase of mortality which commenced in the second week of July was maintained in the week ending Saturday last."[93]

The newspaper reported the number of deaths in London for the past six weeks: 49, 124, 152, 339, 678, 783 and 926. The number of deaths from diarrhea had dropped, however. This may have been because earlier cases had been caused by the nontoxic strain of *Vibrio cholerae*. That week there were 143 deaths in Lambeth and the average temperature was 59.5°F, though on some days the temperature rose well into the seventies.

On August 10, at number 4 Globe Court in Regent Street, Lambeth, towards the south of the district and close to Lambeth Workhouse, the son of a bonnet-shape maker died. Farr said of this area, "A narrow, badly-ventilated court, running between Regent-street and King-street. Two-roomed houses and very confined."[94] On the same day, an article was published in *The Times* regarding an inquest into a death from cholera at Brixton jail. The coroner quizzed Mr. W. Harris, surgeon to the jail, about the prisoners' diet and their environment. Mr. Billinghurst, a member of the jury, asked Mr. Harris, "If the reservoir of the Lambeth waterworks which is in front of the prison, was not very injurious to the inmates. The coroner said he thought not, for the water would clear the air. Mr. Billinghurst observed that when the deposit from it was let off it passed down the sewers, and was exposed to the air at the station-house, where it went into the river Effra, and then the stench became almost abominable."[95] A letter the following day to *The Times* from "an inhabitant of South Lambeth" demanded "to arrest that direful nuisance, the open ditch sewer called the Effra."[96]

On August 11 the daughter of a shoemaker died at 36 Windmill Row, an area "filthy in the extreme."[97] On August 12, cholera claimed its next victim at 3 Grove Place, a girl aged 14. On the 13th of the same month in Little Windmill Street a laborer living at number 12 finally succumbed to the disease after suffering for over 50 hours. Farr noted, just as the District Sanitary Report Sub Committee had done of the area, that it was "filthy and dirty ... chiefly inhabited by Irish families and vendors of decayed fruit, fried fish, or vegetables."[98] Farr's description adds weight to the theory that the street vendors of Lambeth may have contributed to the spread of cholera by their practice of storing goods in an insanitary environment.

Protests continued to appear in *The Times* newspaper deploring the state of the streets in Lambeth and how such protestations to the Board of Health were still being ignored. Of particular concern was the waterfront area of Fore Street and Ferry Street where "deposits, which had been left by the tide, of a most offensive nature — such as dead dogs and cats, human excrement ... emitting a most offensive odour."[99] The state of this area had been reported on similarly in the Lambeth District Sanitary Reports. The writer reiterated concern for the boneyard in Princes Street, owned by Jared Hunt, where "bones which are taken by the butchers from the meat whilst it is in a raw state ... are taken to Mr. Hunt's yard to the extent of several tons daily, and as they lay sometimes for weeks ... become putrid and emit a most poisonous effluvia."[100] The article concluded with the comment, "There is no greater proof required than the registrar's returns [of deaths], which show that the cholera was 500 per cent worse in this borough than in any other part of the metropolis."[101]

William Farr was certain that the deaths in the area of north Lambeth around the boundary ditch were due to effluvia, or bad smells emanating from it and carried by the wind. Proof came when a cowkeeper in Little Duke Street, whose wife had died of cholera at the beginning of the month, also lost several of his cows; these too had succumbed to the effluvia, in Farr's opinion.

On August 14 an artist at 20 Brad Street died. Farr noted that the area was "frequently one mass of mud and water."[102] The middle of August saw a slight drop in the rate of deaths, even in Lambeth, and in the week ending August 14, deaths had fallen to 28; *The Times* attributed this to better care and better medication. By August 22 the newspaper reported that the epidemic has been so severe in London that of a population of 2,206,600, nearly one in every thousand inhabitants had died every week. After the false optimism of the week before, mortality again increased in Lambeth, and it is clear that the complacency of the Board of Health and the efforts of the medical profession were inadequate in the face of such a virulent epidemic.

The epidemic continued to rage around the Black Ditch. On August 15 the epidemic claimed another victim, a 31-year-old laborer, living at 3 Victoria Place. On August 15, there was another death in New Street, at number 5, of a single woman who caught cholera but then, according to Farr, died of typhus. On the 16th, in the same house, the son of a smith fell ill with scarlatina, but after four days, he was suffering from cholera and died. On August 18 a coachmaker died in Glasshouse Street. On August 19, the 69-year-old wife of a journeyman carpenter died in Vauxhall Row, and on the same day the son of a laborer died in Frances Street. Farr said of this area, "Densely crowded with Irish, of dirty, intemperate habits; a long open sewer runs parallel to it. Pigs, ducks etc, kept in the vicinity ... numerous have been the attacks ... 9 of which were fatal."[103]

On the same day, the 49-year-old widow of a bricklayer died in Isabella Place after having suffered from cholera for three days. Farr said of Isabella Place, "The most filthy in the district; the entrance is not more than 4 feet wide; there are or 6 or 8 dilapidated houses in it of 2 rooms each, all front, no air through them, and in each room containing a family; a recess on the left is the receptacle of all manner of filth, dust, decayed vegetables, fish guts etc. The stench is very bad at all times."[104]

Also on August 19, a woman aged 25 died at 21 Pleasant Place, where "in front of this row of houses is an open sewer."[105] Four days later there was another death in Cornwall Road of a widow aged 60 who had cared for a younger victim a few days earlier, and fell ill shortly after washing the clothes of the deceased. On the same day there was the death of a potter's son at 3 Granby's Buildings in Vauxhall Walk. Farr commented of the area, "An unhealthy neighbourhood, ill cleansed and drained and surrounded by bone-crushers, potteries, soap makers, and other offensive establishments."[106]

The Board of Health secured finance that same day, August 23, to appoint a Principal Medical Inspector and four assistants who were responsible for the worst affected districts of London. Their reports enabled the Board to issue "Special Orders to the vestries or Unions bidding them appoint and pay the said visitors, and put the whole medical force of the Union at their inspector's disposal."[107] It is likely that Lambeth took advantage of the scheme, but perhaps not throughout the entire borough, as by September 11, the public were still demanding visitations.

On August 25 the daughter of a wharf laborer died at 24 Neville Street in Vauxhall, and Farr noted that the cholera had been particularly bad in this street, which was "newly-built and tolerably clean."[108] On August 26, a man died at 6 Church Terrace, which overlooked the graveyard, about which Farr commented, "The churchyard ... now so often opened for funerals that effluvia must enter the surrounding houses."[109]

Cholera continued to rage through the area around the Victoria Theatre. On the 27th of the month, at 14 Whitehorse Street, the fourth death occurred at number 14, that of a lighterman.[110] On August 28 there was another death in Globe Court off Regent Street, the son of a law stationer and the fifth from the same family, including the mother and her children, the father having deserted them. Farr noted that another death had also occurred next door.[111] On August 29 the next victim died at 3 Grove Place, a woman aged 24, and a girl aged 8 was severely attacked but survived. At 14 Apollo Buildings, the son of a tailor died. Farr says of this area, "This small spot abounds with noxious effluvia. The privies are most offensive, and the water scarcely fit to drink; heaps of refuse matter thrown about by the costermongers. Pigs, horses, rabbits, and all sorts of animals are kept here. The fish, vegetables etc in which the people deal are at night frequently placed under the bed. There are 2 cats'-meat dealers in Apollo-buildings, the stench from which is much complained of."[112]

At Grove Place, the outbreak continued the following day with the husband of the landlady developing symptoms, but recovering. Farr noted that Grove Place was very near James Street and was "a most filthy spot.... There is a very bad smell in the house [number 3 Grove Place], which cannot be traced."[113] Perhaps like many of the houses in the area there was a sewer or ditch running beneath the property, or effluent was simply seeping into the marshy ground.

In the first two days of September, there were 51 deaths from cholera and 7 of diarrhea in Lambeth, and *The Times* reported that it was the worst affected area in London. On September 1, the sixth death in Le Grand Place occurred, that of the daughter of a journeyman carpenter, on the 2nd the daughter of a butcher died at 16 James Street; on September 3 a surgeon aged 45 years, who was ill for only eight hours, died at Carlisle Place, Carlisle Street.[114] On September 4 a widow died at 2 Graves Cottages in Saunders Street, "the state of the premises ... highly prejudicial to health,"[115] and on the 6th and 7th, there were two deaths at Barrett Street, a lithographic printer and his son. Of Barrett Street, Farr commented, "At the back of these premises there are a number of pigs kept by a neighbour; the stench is so bad that they frequently cannot have the back door or window open."[116] Also on September 7, a coal porter in Little Windmill Street died, and on the 8th a laborer, aged 17, at John Street, off Cornwall Road. Farr said of the Waterloo Road area and of James Street in particular, "The attacks and deaths in this street have been more severe than in any other part of this district; it was built on a swamp — the ditches formerly complained of are now filled up."[117]

By the beginning of September it is clear from a letter to *The Times* from "A Working man" of Lambeth that nothing had yet been done about the state of the streets and the lack of sanitation. The letter expressed the frustration and incomprehension that nothing had been done: "There is an inspector of nuisances appointed by the parish; but to expect anything from a parochial officer, who is, to a certain extent, the servant of the influential proprietors of the manufactories in question is in vain. The Board of Health may be doing great things in other quarters (although we do not hear where), but more fruitful fields for its staff to be "up and doing" can scarcely be found."[118] The letter implied that the parochial officers of Lambeth, which must have included some members of the Sanitary Sub Committees, were under the influence of the factory owners, or were factory owners themselves. The theory prevalent at the time that cholera was transmitted by foul smells was perhaps part of the reason why nothing happened in Lambeth. If it were thought that the emissions from the factories played a role in the spread of the disease, it is likely that the factory owners would have done everything in their power to prevent the closure of their businesses. The idea that the factory owners were trying to prevent change was repeated by another letter, published in response to the first on the following day, September 4, 1849: "Mr Grainger, the inspector of the Board of Health, has, I believe, with others, inspected these places [the bone-boiling factories], but nothing has been done to remedy the evil. The proprietor of one of these premises resides on the spot, and may, perhaps, have represented to the officers that he and his family enjoy good health, and that consequently it cannot be injurious; but the public think differently and complaints are very numerous."[119]

In the same issue of *The Times* newspaper, a copy of a memorial was published, signed by the Archbishop of Canterbury, five of Lambeth's surgeons and "other inhabitants." The notice put the blame for the cholera epidemic ("larger than any other parish round London")[120] firmly at the door of the Lambeth factory owners, namely Jared Tarett Hunt (bone merchant and manure merchant, Upper Fore Street), Henry and James Cann (bone boilers, 40 Upper Fore Street), John H. Barber (melter and bone merchant, 87 Upper Fore Street),[121] H. J. Bellis, George Lamb, and "others." The effluvia emanating from their works was so bad it caused passersby to vomit. The notice asked "that immediate measures may be adopted by your hon. Board [the Board of Health] to put down this intolerable nuisance, which has produced an unusual mortality in this densely populated district."[122]

William Farr believed that the epidemic was at its peak on about September 8, when 13 people in the Waterloo Road area died in that one day, and eleven the next. On September 8 the son of a chemist died at 9 Thomas Place in Gibson Street. Farr related the comments of the boy's father: "There are 3 gulley-holes [probably cesspools] within 20 yards of each other in this street, the smells from which are so offensive as to alarm the residents. Thomas-place is a narrow, confined spot."[123] On September 9 and 10 a further 60 died of cholera in Lambeth and another five of diarrhea. On September 10, there was another death in James Street, at number 12, a bricklayer, and the seventeenth case in the street. Farr commented on the pigsty and slaughterhouse at the back of the house "which are much complained of."[124]

Another letter to *The Times*, on September 8, appealed for the railway arches to be employed as wash houses to try and help alleviate the filth in the district.[125]

However, the situation was so grave that on September 10, a group of the local people decided to hold a public meeting at the Ship Tavern in Fore Street, Lambeth, in view of "the pressing necessity for improving the dwellings of the poor, as the only means of arresting this dreadful pestilence."[126]

The meeting was chaired by a Mr. Newman, and a Mr. Cochrane was the first to speak. He expressed the alarm of the people of Lambeth gripped by the terrible epidemic. He explained how a policeman was now stationed at the gate of the burial ground to control the people entering, so great were the number of funerals currently taking place. That day there had been 42 burials, not an unusual figure, as the daily average was around 40 to 45; even before the peak of the epidemic there had been 20 to 30.

Cochrane declared that the cholera epidemic was "the direct interposition of a wise and all-seeing Providence," in other words, the number of deaths were by the hand of God, however, as the cholera has only affected

A view of the Ship Tavern, Lower Fore Street, Lambeth. This photograph was taken after the building of Lambeth Bridge in 1862 and the tavern may have had a different appearance in 1849. Mr. Wentzell's boatyard was well established and the roofed barge of which the Surveyors of Highways complained (see Chapter 6) appears to have been removed. However, the area of foreshore which once served as the landing area for the Horse Ferry (to the right of Wentzell's) does appear to have been filled in. This image was reproduced by kind permission of Lambeth Archives department.

the poor, the number of deaths were a reminder to everyone of the suffering and depravation of the poor. Cochrane therefore recommended that they should make a deputation to the Archbishop of Canterbury to ask for his help.

Those present at the meeting also discussed a recommendation to commence house-to-house visits and to ask the Lambeth Board of Guardians to instruct the parochial medical officers not only to visit the poor but also to be able to give out meat and bread. It was also hoped that the Board of Guardians would press Parliament to improve drainage and cleansing, and to provide "proper baths and washhouses for the poor."[127] A final request at the meeting was to ask Mr. Maudslay's and Mr. Field's permission to use their "immense premises" for the next meeting.

By the middle of September cholera continued to rage in Lambeth, particularly in Fore Street and the surrounding area, and the disposal of the dead had become a problem. The poor would often keep their dead in their homes because they could not afford to bury them, or as was the custom for many of the Irish immigrants, they did not bury their deceased quickly. In Lambeth this practice was particularly worrying in the densely populated tenements, and exacerbated by the lack of space to bury the dead. Lambeth Burial Ground was bursting at the seams, as were many in London, with around 3,000 burials taking place in the metropolis every week.[128] The use of quicklime to rapidly dissolve the tissues of corpses had not been popular in the 1832 epidemic and Chadwick had heard that "The slum population was fast losing its head, some even believing that the doctors were poisoning the wells to thin off the population and that the inspectors were there merely to see that the victims were not chosen too wantonly."[129] So, by September 14, the Board of Health decided to close some of the burial grounds in London, but Lambeth's remained open.

On September 11, the daughter of a builder died at number 1 Vauxhall Walk. Farr commented, "At the back of this house is a court called white Lion-yard, a wretched place, inhabited by Irish; a number of half-starved pigs are kept; they have no drainage and the stench is very great. The filth from the sties is thrown under the railway arches adjoining."[130] On the same day the son of a publican died at number 20 Jurston Street. Farr commented, "A very dirty, crowded street, with a long open sewer behind it. This is the child of Jewish parents. Although persons of that persuasion are rather numerous in this district, it is the first death from cholera amongst them."[131]

On September 12 there was yet another victim at 3 Grove Place, when the son of a laborer died, and the following day, in Hampshire Street, the widow of a ship's carpenter succumbed to the disease. Farr noted that of the eight houses in Hampshire Street, cholera had struck every household. At number 3 cholera had killed four children and their mother, who was about to give birth. The husband, overwhelmed with grief, had fled.[132] The land-lord of the premises relet their home to another family who contracted cholera almost immediately, their daughter dying within a few hours.

At the Board of Health, Henry Austin, Dr. Thomas Southwood Smith and Edwin Chadwick all fell ill with fever or diarrhea. Chadwick was the worst affected and in his two-day absence, Lord Ashley conducted business in his place.[133] On his return, Chadwick discovered further complications had arisen with the appointment of his new inspectors. Doubting the legality of the board to make such appointments, the Treasury would not allow funding. Lord Ashley took charge and appointed them himself, but then faced an additional problem with hostility over the closure of the graveyards from the local Boards of Guardians. Chadwick, in his usual fashion, wasted no time and had summonses drawn up against the boroughs which refused to comply with the Board's orders, but in doing so entered into an unpleasant legal battle and, by the end of September, the wishes of the Boards of Guardians were upheld. The graveyards remained open and "disinfectants" (perhaps including quick-lime) were employed.[134] The furore had a damaging effect, and a Society for the Abolition of Burials in the Cities and Towns was set up by Dr. G. A. Walker, President, Mr. Thicke, Dr. Powell and the Member of Parliament, Mr. G. Thompson.[135]

On September 18, Robert Taylor, Lambeth's church warden, wrote to *The Times* regarding the day of prayer which the Bishop of Winchester had requested for the following day, a Wednesday. Mr. Taylor reported that the Rev. C. B. Dalton, the rector of Lambeth and Rural Dean of Southwark, had asked that collections should be made to help the poor, especially the widows and children of the dead; a followup letter printed on September 21 showed that this had been well responded to. The same week, the Board of Health, by the orders of Chief Clerk Henry Austin,[136] ordered the house-to-house visits in London, which included Lambeth. Dr. King commented in the *Gazette*, as re-reported by *The Times*, that the visits had definitely helped the poor of Lambeth by preventing their diarrhoea develop into full-blown cholera.

In the same article, the suggestion was made that "there are instances in which the sanitary condition of localities and houses is so bad, and so incapable of instantaneous improvement, that the only means of saving the susceptible part of the population is the temporary removal of the inhabitants in the worst places to houses of refuge until their own wretched abodes can be cleansed and purified."[137]

The Board of Health cited areas around the country, such as Cornwall, where this had taken place and poor people had been relocated in tents. In areas such as Lambeth, it was suggested that they could be located to the workhouse or other public buildings, but there was resistance to this idea at a local level in London and from the Poor Law Board. Indeed, the Board of Health went on to attack the Boards of Guardians further by pointing out that their recommendations to improve conditions, as in the Lambeth District Sanitary Reports, had not been carried out. "The only motive for delay apparent, on inquiry, to the inspectors has been the hope on the part of the guardians that the epidemic would have passed before the orders were executed, and that, therefore, the expense might possibly be saved."[138]

The article went on to discuss the various reasons why Boards of Guardians had not carried out the instructions of the Board of Health. Complacency and laziness seemed to be the two main culprits:

> A very large proportion of the boards of guardians have pursued a course of action founded on the presumption that the preventative measures directed by the General Board of Health were applicable not to the people generally, but only to a limited portion of the population — the regular pauper population — and that these measures were to be applied according to the ordinary practice in which relief is only given when applied for.
>
> The most common argument against the immediate and energetic adoption of the previous measures directed by the General Board of Health is their expenses. The epidemic is seen by the ignorant as an evil with which it is useless to grapple; and among the better informed, a false economy, which in some instances led to the most fatal results, has been the ground of resistance to measures which were instantly necessary to save life.[139]

In other words, there were some members of the Boards of Guardians who held a fatalistic view of the epidemic and others who simply felt it was not worth spending money on the poor. It is also important to remember that the working population was not represented in Parliament and many of those in authority simply did not consider themselves to be accountable to the poor: "The ratepayers should be informed that the want of compliance with the orders of the General Board of Health on the part of the boards of guardians of the metropolis has already entailed enormous and lasting expenditure on the parishes, and that this expenditure is daily augmenting in a vastly greater ratio than the whole amount required to carry out the needful preventative measures. The parish of Lambeth, for example, was up to August 27, already burdened with 61 cholera widows and 226 cholera orphans, who must for years remain a costly burden on the parish."[140]

The article concluded with a discussion that the supply of water to the poorest houses was indeed sporadic, but that the quality of the water played a role in the spread of infection in the areas of greatest infection by cholera. The General Board of Health cited the example of a well contaminated by a cesspool and badly drained road. There was no doubt in their minds that this was part of the cause of the outbreak of cholera, and cited this discovery by

Dr. Snow, "a medical gentleman who has taken considerable interest."[141] The board stated that "the leakage of privies, cesspools, or sewers, even in very small quantities, is known to render well-water poisonous."[142]

On September 19 the son of a laborer died at 35 Hooper Street. Farr commented on this area, "A long, narrow, densely crowded street; the dirtiest spot in the district, in close connexion with filthy ditches, and surrounded by an unwholesome neighbourhood, in which many deaths have occurred; inhabited by costermongers etc."[143]

By September 20, cholera was still raging in Lambeth, and on the 24th of the month, James Osmotherly, aged 42 years and working as a coal heaver, also died of the disease. Following the death of his wife Ann in July, their eldest daughter, Emma, aged about 19, must have taken charge of the running of the household, and her name was on her father's death certificate, having been present at his death at 11 Princes Street. James' death certificate showed that he suffered from cholera for a full week before succumbing to the disease.

On September 25, 1849, a third person died at St. Mary's Buildings in the Waterloo area, a domestic servant aged 25. On September 27, there was another death in Barrett Street, this time the 46-year-old widow of a candle maker at number 11 Albion Cottages. William Farr noted there were more deaths from cholera among women over the age of 16, at a ratio of 99 to 50, perhaps because pregnant women were more vulnerable to the disease (which has recently been shown to be a fact), but also because women tended to be the ones who nursed the sick. It is also interesting to note that on at least one occasion, Farr mentioned that a woman had died after washing out the clothes of a victim; this also would have been a common way for women to have contracted the disease.

By the end of the month, the epidemic began to wane, though in Lambeth deaths from cholera continued. Albion Cottages in Barrett Street was particularly badly affected in the first week of October and many children died The houses in the area were in a dreadful condition, the privies being dirty and shared by many large families who paid 4/- (20p) and 4/6d (22½p) a week in rent. Nevertheless, in the space of a week, by October 3, deaths had fallen from 117 the previous week to 50. The temperature was still warm for the time of year, averaging 62.2°F.[144]

According to a report on October 5, 1849, in *The Times*, the house-to-house visitations had been an enormous success in Lambeth and Newington. "After fifteen weeks of unwatched and unabated pestilence, 2,193 cases of diarrhoea and 67 verging on collapse were discovered in seven days, and not one passed into cholera."[145] Action had finally been taken to start house-to house visitation when the Board of Guardians realized they now had to take responsibility of 61 women and 226 children left without fathers: they did not want to have to be responsible for many more. In *The Times*, the October 5 article also discussed how the Board of Health had decided to take legal proceedings against the St. Pancras Board of Guardians for not commencing house-to-house visitations. The author of the article criticized the parties who were trying to make little of the poverty in London and who said that the situation in Lambeth, Bermondsey and St. Olave were extremes and that the poverty elsewhere was not as bad. He knew of a court in the city where 200 residents were dependent on one single standpipe for which the supply of water was sporadic. The article blamed the authorities and the London landowners who for far too long had drawn rents but not provided an infrastructure for their tenants. The writer noted that the preservation of public health would also "confirm political tranquillity."[146]

By the beginning of October, the number of cholera cases in Lambeth began to abate, and in the first nine days there were only 21 deaths, though terrible stories continued to be published in the newspapers. On October 5, *The Times* reported the case of a mother and daughter of a sawyer at number 14 Manners Street in the Waterloo Road area, which had been ravaged by cholera. William Farr related the same story: a mother nursing her daughter had died on the first day of the month; the daughter had followed her on the third.[147]

From August to October, Farr noted that the deaths were especially bad at Lower Marsh, James Street, Granby Street, Charles Street, Frances Street, Jurston Street, Gibson Street, Anne Street, Thomas Street, Apollo Buildings, Oakley Street and Belvedere Road; in fact, most of the areas which had been noted as a problem in the Lambeth District Sanitary Reports.

On October 9, *The Times* reported another case in Lambeth at White Lion Court in Vauxhall, which illustrated the dreadful conditions of the poor: "A gulley-hole in the middle of this narrow court receives all the slops and washings of the place, the houses are much dilapidated, and are crowded with inmates. The poor deceased was lying upon what had once been a bedstead, with only some coarse rugs to cover her, and such was the poverty and destitution, that the husband had not a halfpenny to purchase a candle, which from the darkness of the place, was necessary to enable me to see the patient."[148]

On October 12 a 47-year-old man died in Wickham Street. He had worked as a molder at an engineering works in Lambeth, and Farr said of the area in which he lived, "This street is in a very bad condition, no drainage, badly ventilated and crowded. In winter the roadway is impassable to passengers, there being accumulated a quantity of mud and stagnant water, quite green. The inhabitants are obliged to form a gutter to prevent the surplus water from running into the lower rooms of their houses, which are below the crown of the road."[149]

By October 17 there had only been seven deaths recorded that week in Lambeth, and the mean temperature was 46.7°F, which was below average for the time of year. The drop in temperature was most certainly a factor in the decline of cases of cholera, and indeed other infectious diseases in the capital. By October 26, *The Times* reported that the epidemic was at an end but that out of a population in London of around two million, 14,538 had perished. In England, William Farr calculated that 53,293 deaths had been reg-

BURIAL-GROUND NEAR THE PARISH CHURCH, LAMBETH.

Lambeth Burial Ground. As the factory chimneys continue to spew out their smoke and foul smells, a burial takes place and another one arrives. Meanwhile, at the gates to the cemetery, life goes on as normal. This image was reproduced by kind permission of Lambeth Archives department.

istered from cholera and 18,887 from diarrhea: a total death toll of over 70,000 people.

In the first week of October, the burial ground at Lambeth had again been inspected by the Board of Health, where *The Times* reported over 600 had been buried.[150]

Thomas Tenison (1636–1715), Archbishop of Canterbury, gave the ground to be used for burials to Lambeth in the early 1700s. Later the burial ground was added to and in June 1815, it was divided into four sections, the part farthest from the street being reserved for the poor; the new ground was consecrated on February 3, 1816.[151] The burial ground was ordered to be closed on October 31, 1853,[152] following the Metropolitan Burial Act forbidding any more burials in central London. However, a report in *The Times* the following January[153] revealed that burials were still taking place, and bodies were even being brought to Lambeth from other parishes whose burial grounds had already closed. The order for closure was extended to May 31, 1854. By

Another view of Lambeth Burial Ground showing a distinct mound. It is impossible to tell if the mound is an earthwork due to the excessive burials in 1849 or if it is a result of landscaping carried out in the 1980s. Photograph by the author.

1880 the ground had become unsightly and Lambeth Vestry decided to convert the space to a recreational ground. The gravestones were removed to the boundary walls, which is where most of them still are today, as the area is still used as a playing field for the children of the area.

The ground was landscaped in 1985 and as the gravestones had all been removed to the outer walls of the ground, it is impossible to tell exactly where burials are situated, however, some of the mounds are noticeably high and may well be an indication of the positions of the many burials which took place in 1849. At the public meeting which took place in Lambeth in September 1849, at the height of the epidemic, it was stated that the average number of burials per day was 40 to 45, and even before the peak of the epidemic it was around 20. To bury this number of individuals is a considerable problem, and the bodies of the poor would not have been buried individually, but in large pits left open till they were full. The authorities were reluctant to use quicklime on a large scale, though it is possible its use may have been adopted at some point to disinfect and dissolve more rapidly the tissues of the corpses. However, even if this were the case, it could not have been particularly effective as Farr includes a comment in his account of the effluvia emanating from the graveyard in August 1849.

That "over 600" had been buried in Lambeth Burial Ground is a rough observation. In 1848 and 1849 the 1,894 victims of cholera and diarrhea would

Burial Ground at Millbank Prison (from a photograph by Herbert Watkins, 179 Regent Street); Westminster may be seen in the background. City of Westminster Archives Centre.

not have been the only deaths in the area. It is possible that every one of these people was buried in the parish burial ground, but as the graveyards in London became more crowded throughout the epidemic, there is a likelihood that people were buried elsewhere. The sewers and the Thames were unofficial dumping grounds for the dead,[154] and certainly some cholera victims were buried at Seward Street in Islington, the burial

The playground at Millbank Primary School, built roughly on the site of the Millbank Penitentiary graveyard. The photograph has been taken from a similar perspective to the illustration of the burial ground above. Reproduced with the kind permission of Ms. Alyson Russen, head teacher, Millbank Primary School, London.

ground for paupers treated at St. Bart's Hospital. The burial ground for Millbank Penitentiary was close to Lambeth and when Henry Mayhew and John Binney visited the prison in the 1860s, they were told of the graveyard, "In the cholera of 1848, so many corpses were interred there that the authorities thought it unhealthy."[155] Perhaps only convicts were buried at Millbank's graveyard, but some of the poor from Lambeth and the areas surrounding Millbank Penitentiary may also have been interred there. When the Millbank site was redeveloped, the area to the rear of the prison was acquired for residential use. The area formerly used as the graveyard was not built on and today it too is a children's playground, for the pupils of Millbank Primary School.

8

The Aftermath

On November 16, 1849, London came to a standstill when a General Thanksgiving Day was held to remember the dead of the cholera epidemic. Shops and businesses closed and churches all over the capital, including St. Paul's and Westminster Abbey, were packed with those giving thanks to God that the worst now appeared to be over. Collections were taken for those who had been left destitute and in their sermons the clergy urged the wealthy to help the poor particularly by the improvement of social and sanitary conditions. According to *The Times*, the church bells rang out all day.[1]

At Lambeth, services were held at St. Mary's "with particular solemnity."[2] Almost 500 parishioners took Holy Communion at the services held at 8:30 A.M., 11 A.M., 3 P.M. and 6:30 P.M. The morning sermon was read by the Reverend C.B. Dalton and the church was so full that people had to stand outside. The vicar declared that sin had been the primary cause of Lambeth's great suffering; the secondary cause, he preached to his parishioners, was the lack of sanitation and cleansing facilities, and he blessed those who promoted such improvements. The Rev. Dalton added, "Let our streets be clean and wholesome, and our dwellings well drained and ventilated; but if impurity ran through our streets as a river the wrath of God would come down upon us. Nothing but spiritual holiness and the cleansing of the inner man would avail to avert such visitations, and these were only to be accomplished by the ministry of the word."[3]

In the evening, the sentiments of the morning were repeated by the Reverend J. Cave Brown. Collections were not made at St. Mary's as they had been in the other richer districts of the metropolis, but *The Times* newspaper noted that there had been a warm response to the vicar's proposal to build a new church in the district.[4] While the people of Lambeth were relieved that the epidemic was at an end, everyone in the community knew someone who had died. Families had been ripped apart and, in some cases, eradicated. For those living in the waterfront area, the sight of the graveyard brimming over with freshly buried corpses was a constant reminder.

For some families, the collections made in church were no doubt welcome, but for a woman left widowed with children it was no substitute for the wage of a husband. For many the only solution was the workhouse and the meager support the Poor Law could offer. Families who had lost both parents, such as the Osmotherlys, were split up. Today tracing the movements of the survivors of the epidemic is difficult. The early censuses had many omissions, and while the 1851 Census was more accurate and comprehensive than that of 1841, the many mistakes in the spelling of surnames makes the tracing of individuals arduous, and in some cases impossible.

With regard to the Osmotherly family, six children had been orphaned: Emma, Sarah, James, Mary, Hannah and George. There is no trace in subsequent censuses of Emma and Sarah. It is possible that they too may have died of cholera, but their deaths do not appear to have occurred in Lambeth during the 1848 to 1849 outbreak. If they did survive, it is likely they married, though, again, no record of their marriages has been found. Mary, like many young women, may have gone into domestic service, as in the 1861 Census there is a Mary A. *Osmor* (a popular abbreviation of the family name) listed at 188 Tottenham Court Road, London, working as a general servant at the house of Elizabeth Johnson, a stay maker. The two youngest children, George and Hannah, were returned to the Hoo Peninsula, but were separated. George, the youngest child, went to live with his grandparents in High Halstow, and Hannah went to live with her uncle, her father's brother, George Phillips Osmotherly, and his wife Hannah, née Eldridge. George Phillips Osmotherly's family had nine children, and life was hard as George worked as an agricultural laborer. The instability his job offered is reflected in the movement of the family from one farm to another, from High Halstow to Hoo St. Mary, to Stoke and then to Allhallows. James William Osmotherly remained in Lambeth and in the 1851 Census he is registered as James *Osmore*, lodging at 20 Frances Street, one of the most impoverished areas of Lambeth, with the family of Robert Wain. James was working as a potter, however, shortly after this he joined the 7th Royal Fusiliers and by January 1855, Sergeant James Osmotherly was fighting in the Crimea. In November 1855, he gave evidence at the court martial of a deserter to the Russians, Private Thomas Tole, with whom he had shared a tent. After the war, James returned to Lambeth, only moving to Edmonton, London, in his final years; he died in 1902.[5]

As the cholera epidemic subsided the call for sanitary reform continued. In *The Times* in November 1849, Dr. John Simon of the new Board of Health, and the first Medical Officer of the City of London, called for a review of the drainage and sewage system in London. He deplored the putrefying industries in the capital and the practice of burying London's dead within the metropolis.[6]

By the summer of 1850, it was clear that in Lambeth little had changed. A letter to *The Times* complained of the dreadful stench of the industries along the Lambeth waterfront.[7] On July 19, 1850, a public meeting was held "of the parishioners and ratepayers of Lambeth and the liberties adjacent ... at the Vestry-hall, Church-street, for the purpose of taking into consideration the grievous condition of the parish for the want of proper drainage, and to petition Parliament to afford them that redress which they sought for in vain at the hand of the Metropolitan Commissioners of Sewers."[8] Mr. Robert Taylor, the church warden, led the meeting and condemned the behavior of the Metropolitan Commission of Sewers, which all those present agreed was worse than the previous commission. Since the autumn of 1849, Lambeth had paid the Commission between £15,000 and £25,000 in sewer rates, the parish having been assessed at 8d (about 3½p) in the pound.[9] Yet nothing had been done, and even the ditches which for years many had demanded should be covered over remained open.

In January 1849 a new set of members had been selected for the Metropolitan Commission of Sewers, of which Lord Morpeth was to be chairman. The members included army engineers Sir John Burgogyne and Captain Vetch (of the Tidal Harbour Commission), Captain Dawson of the Ordnance Survey, Professor Airey (Astronomer Royal), Cuthbert Johnson, (an authority on manure), Morgan Cowie (head of the College of Civil Engineers), the lawyers E. Lawes and Mr. Hodgson, Alexander Bain, Dr. Thomas Southwood Smith, and consultant engineer Henry Austin.[10] Edwin Chadwick wanted members to consider drawing up plans for London's drainage. A scheme for Westminster had been devised as early as 1847 and the commission had already considered "an intercepting sewer ... near to and parallel with the river, to deliver itself some distance from the town."[11]

It was Henry Austin who had thought the problem through, perhaps as a result of his work on the new Houses of Parliament. He knew that engineers could not rely on gravity to overcome the drainage problems suffered in low-lying areas like Lambeth and Westminster. He proposed the digging of sumps and steam power to pump the sewage into the river. Liquid sewage could then be pumped to farms, an idea Chadwick had long favored and considered financially viable. Indeed the Sewage Manure Committee had confirmed that the product would sell at £12 per acre and make a net profit of £100,000 per annum.[12] However, Chadwick's plan was not well thought through. He was right that there was a need throughout Europe and America for cheap fertilizer to increase crop yields, but this had already been fulfilled by the establishment of trading houses in the 1840s to ship cheap bird manure, or guano, to Britain from Peru in South America.[13]

Chadwick's opponent, John Phillips, proposed another plan, to build a 20-mile tunnel under the Thames, 100 feet below the river, on the north and south banks, which would follow the river from Kingston to Essex. He believed this would cost less than £200,000.[14] *The Times* supported Phillips' plan, and the committee remained in chaos, and continued with its in-fighting, which only served to create a negative image of a commission where indecision and inactivity reigned. By the end of 1849, the three bodies which represented London's sanitary interests were at loggerheads. "The Commission defied the Board and challenged the vestries. The vestries strove to destroy the unrepresentative Commission and the equally unrepresentative Board. The Board strove to throttle the vestries with one hand and the Commission with the other."[15] It was not an atmosphere in which much progress could be made.

In January 1852 the Lambeth Waterworks finally moved from the polluted waters of Lambeth to a new works at Thames Ditton which drew water from much farther upstream, beyond the tidal stretch of the Thames: "The company have now large filtering-beds at Thames-Ditton through which the entire supply passes into the engine wells before it is pumped to the districts."[16] Yet by October 1852, nothing had changed in Lambeth. On the 23rd of the month, a meeting, chaired by the church warden Mr. Robert Taylor, was held at the Vestry Hall in Church Street to discuss the situation. *The Times* reported the proceedings, including the inability of the Metropolitan Commission of Sewers to make a decision. The meeting discussed how, since 1823, it was estimated the borough had paid £140,000 towards new sewers, but had received £40,000 worth of work. The Health of Towns Commission had shown that Lambeth had 62 miles of roads, courts and alleys but only six miles of brick sewers and less than 12 miles of pipe sewers. The City of London on the other hand had a mile of sewer for each mile of street; Lambeth still had 12 open ditches.[17]

The meeting determined to petition Parliament and on November 3, 1852, Lambeth's Member of Parliament, Mr. William Williams, Mr. Murrough M.P., Robert Taylor, the church warden, the surgeon Mr. John Sewell, Mr. Denyer, the overseer, and the surveyors of highways, delivered their grievances on the lack of sanitation in Lambeth to the Home Secretary, Spencer Horatio Walpole (1806–1898). Walpole accepted the deputation's protestations and assured them that when the matter were next discussed in Parliament, the dreadful situation in Lambeth would be raised.[18]

By the autumn of 1853, cholera had returned to England, at Newcastle. In October, the parish guardians held a meeting at Lambeth workhouse in Princes Road and appointed two Inspectors of Nuisances, Mr. George Sutton and Mr. Henry Stevens, to commence house-to-house visitations to try to remove some of the nuisances.[19] By the summer of 1854, cholera was again raging in London, but in Lambeth the rate of mortality was not as high as it had been in 1849. In November 1853, *The Times* gave an overview of the state of the different water companies in London, noting that the Lambeth Waterworks had moved and that the source of their supply had changed: "From the above reports it appears that cholera finds London, as regards water, in the situation in which it left it. This holds true with reference to all except the Lambeth Waterworks Company, who changed their source of supply nearly two years ago from Lambeth to Thames Ditton; and ... it will be seen that the results of the present epidemic in the districts supplied by that company ... are rather more satisfactory than they were in 1849."[20]

Statistics gathered by the Registrar General's office and published in *The Times* in October 1854 showed that in Lambeth, in 1849, 1,618 had died from cholera, whereas in the 14 weeks up to the week ending October 14, 1854, 904 had died.

Nevertheless it would appear that the supply of water was still not all that it should have been, as a letter to *The Times* from a factory owner in Lambeth revealed. "[We] refilled the [water] tanks with water fresh from the main, in four days' time the surface was completely covered with larvae, insects and worms — in fact one moving mass."[21] The reason for the variation of supply in Lambeth was first because the waterfront areas still had no supply at all, and second because a large area of Lambeth was now being supplied by the Southwark and Vauxhall Water Company, which drew its supplies, "the most impure water,"[22] at the southern tip of Lambeth, in an area as polluted as the northern end, where the Lambeth waterworks once drew their supply. *The Times* explained, "The pipes of the two companies [Lambeth and Southwark] which were once in active competition often run down the same streets and through the same sub-districts, so that alternate streets or houses in the same sub-districts are supplied with the pure and impure waters."[23]

The physician Dr. John Snow (1813–1858) was already certain that cholera was caused by the drinking of contaminated water. He had been interested in how the 1848 to 1849 epidemic had erupted and spread in Lambeth and returned to the area during this period to conduct further investigations to prove his hypothesis. Snow discovered, as reported in *The Times*, that in the seven weeks up to August 26, 1854, of the 600 deaths from cholera in Lambeth, 475 occurred in houses supplied by the Southwark and Vauxhall Water Company, 80 in houses supplied by the Lambeth Company, 13 in houses supplied by pumps, wells and springs, and eight in houses which took their water from the Thames and ditches. Snow met with considerable difficulty in obtaining this information, as in many cases no one had any idea which company supplied which houses or how cholera victims obtained their water. Out of 3,805 instances, in 766 cases the water source remained unknown.[24] However, what was certain was that of 3,039 cases, 2,284 deaths did occur from drinking Thames water: "The total number of houses supplied by the Southwark Company is stated to be 40,046; by the Lambeth

Company to be 26,107; consequently there were in six weeks 57 deaths in every 1,000 houses supplied by impure water, and 11 in every 1,000 supplied by the less impure or comparatively impure water."[25]

The article in *The Times* on the private water companies which supplied Lambeth appeared to be a turning point in the thinking of how cholera was transmitted. While the inquiries were conducted by Dr. John Snow, the report and statistics were compiled by William Farr, the Compiler of Abstracts for the General Register Office. The article concludes: "The important inquiry [by Dr Snow] can only be made complete in all its parts by the Board of Health, who have requested the respective [water] companies to furnish street lists in every sub-district of the houses that they supply.... The effects of elevation and other causes may be thus eliminated, and the fatal effects of impure water be precisely determined."[26] Indeed, by 1866, Farr had conceded to every aspect of Snow's theory, as he discussed in his own 1868 *Report on the Cholera Epidemic of 1855 in England,* referring to Snow's research of 1849 and 1855.[27] There were still some, including Florence Nightingale, a miasmist to her death,[28] who disputed Snow's theories and believed cholera to be transmitted through the air by the poisonous noxious smells emanating from polluted water, though public opinion appeared to be stacking up in Snow's favor.

Despite a somewhat reluctant acceptance of Snow's theory that cholera was waterborne many still thought that the *vibriones,* as they called the pathogenic particles, were passed through the air. An experiment was conducted in 1855 by Dr. Thompson and Mr. Rainey to try to capture the particles in the air. They isolated some particles from the air in a ward filled with cholera patients. However, they were unable to find the same particles in the breathing passages of patients suffering from cholera.[29]

In a letter to *The Times* in June 1856, Dr. John Snow criticized Dr. Simon's report on the 1854 epidemic, saying that his statistics on the mortality of those supplied with water by the Southwark and Vauxhall Water Company were incorrect. Simon had said that they were three-and-a-half times greater than those supplied by the Lambeth Company, when in fact they were six times greater. Snow explained that many of those who died had been supplied by the Southwark and Vauxhall Water Company but had been removed to Lambeth Workhouse, which was supplied by the Lambeth Waterworks.[30] Snow was well aware that in order to prove his theory that cholera was waterborne, any research and evidence needed to be accurate.

Many of the leading surgeons and scientists in London and elsewhere were endeavoring to find the cause of cholera before the disease could strike again. Dr. William Baly, the physician at Millbank Penitentiary, had witnessed first-hand the suffering of prisoners and had experimented with various remedies and methods to try and alleviate the symptoms of the disease.

Baly wrote many reports on his theories on disease and by 1854 he had been appointed Assistant Physician at St. Bartholomew's Hospital in London. He became Physician Extraordinary to Queen Victoria in 1859 and was nominated to the General Medical Council as Crown Representative. He was also Censor for the Royal College of Physicians from 1858 to 1859.[31] In much of his research, Baly collaborated with William Withey Gull (1816–1890). In the 1850s, Gull was a distinguished surgeon, Resident Physician at Guy's Hospital and a Fellow at the Royal College of Physicians. He treated Queen Victoria's consort, Prince Albert, during his fatal illness from typhoid fever in 1861.

In 1849 Baly and Gull wrote the *Report on the Nature and Import of Certain Microscopic Bodies Found in the Intestinal Discharges of Cholera* for the Cholera Committee of the Royal College of Physicians in London. This was followed in 1854 by *Reports on epidemic cholera: for the Cholera Committee of the Royal College of Physicians*, bringing together the current research on the disease.

Report on the Nature and Import of Certain Microscopic Bodies Found in the Intestinal Discharges of Cholera began with a discussion of the work by Dr. Joseph Griffith Swayne (1819–1895), a physician obstetrician from 1853 at Bristol General Hospital, his colleague Dr. Frederick Brittan, and Dr. William Budd (1811–1880), a graduate of Edinburgh's medical school, consulting physician to the Bristol Royal Infirmary from 1847, and Fellow of The Royal Society from 1871. Bristol's Medico-Chirurgical Society had set up a subcommittee for "the microscopic investigation of cholera evacuations."[32] Budd published his *Malignant Cholera: Its Mode of Propagation and Prevention*, just after Snow published his *On the Mode* in late 1849, and was in agreement with the theory that cholera originated in the intestines and the disease was spread by water contaminated with human evacuations. Unlike Snow, Budd still thought that airborne contagion by a fungus may play a part in the spread of the disease, and it was this "agent" which had been isolated by Swayne and Brittan.[33]

Baly and Gull had been unable to find any such particles in their investigations of condensed air. They had seen some sort of cell structure in water, but could draw no definite conclusions. Baly and Gull investigated water from many different sources, even from the cisterns of Millbank Prison and from samples given to them by Dr. John Snow. Their conclusions were as follows:

> 1. Bodies presenting the characteristic forms of the so-called Cholera fungi are not to be detected in the air and as far as our experiments have gone, not in the drinking water of infected places.
> 2. It is established that, under the term, *annular bodies, Cholera cells*, or *Cholera fungi*, there have been confounded many objects of various, and totally distinct, natures.

3. A large number of these have been traced to substances taken as food or medicine.

4. The origin of others is still doubtful, but these are clearly not fungi.

5. All the more remarkable forms are to be detected in the intestinal evacuations labouring under diseases totally different in their nature from Cholera.

Lastly ... the general conclusion, that the bodies found by Messrs. Brittan and Swayne are not the cause of Cholera and have no exclusive connexion with that disease ... the whole theory of the disease which has recently been propounded, is erroneous as far as it is based on the existence of the bodies in question.[34]

In October 1853, the Royal College of Physicians put out the following instruction to the public:

DURING THE PREVALENCE OF CHOLERA,—

1. No degree of looseness of the bowels should be neglected for a single hour. Medical advice should be at once sought when the looseness begins; and previous to the arrival of a medical attendant, some of the medicines, at other times used for checking diarrhoea, should be taken; for example; the chalk mixture; the compound cinnamon powder; or the compound chalk powder with opium, in doses of from 20 to 40 grains for an adult.

2. No saline aperients or drastic purgatives should be taken without the advice of a medical man.

3. Intemperance in eating or drinking is highly dangerous. But the moderate use of vegetable as well as animal food may be recommended; and in general, such a plan of diet as each individual has found by experience to be most conducive to his health. For any considerable change in the diet to which a person has been accustomed, is seldom advisable during the prevalence of an Epidemic.

4. Debility, exhaustion, and exposure to damp, render the poor especially subject to the violence of the disease. The Committee urge upon the rich the necessity of supplying those in need with food, fuel and clothing.

5. The extreme importance of removing or counteracting all impurities, whether in air, water, or soil, as by ventilation, cleanliness and the free use of Chloride of Lime or Chloride of Zinc, cannot be too strongly insisted upon.[35]

The inability to confirm the existence of a cholera microorganism was probably due to a lack of sophistication in the instruments used, as *Vibrio cholerae* measure 0.3 micron (a micron being one thousandth of a millimeter) in diameter and 1.3 microns in length.[36] However, Budd was sure that even though his results were inconclusive, he and Snow were on the right track, and it was Budd who established the preventative measures which were to become commonplace in the prevention of the disease: the boiling of water and milk, and the disinfection of patient's bedding, clothes and of corpses. He gave evidence to the Sanitary Commission in 1871 and proposed a Public Health Service.[37]

John Snow was the eldest son of a Yorkshire coal yard laborer and was apprenticed to a doctor in Newcastle upon Tyne at the age of 14. His work with coal miners gave him his first insight into the workings of cholera in 1831.[38] Snow moved to London in 1836. In order to practice as a surgeon and apothecary in London he needed to fulfill the requirements of the Royal College of Surgeons and the Society of Apothecaries. He studied at the Hunterian School of Medicine in Great Windmill Street in Soho, London, a school which had been set up by Edinburgh University graduate William Hunter (1718–1783) with his brother John (1728–1793). Snow was admitted as a member to the Royal College of Surgeons in 1838. He graduated from the University of London in 1844 and was admitted to the Royal College of Physicians in 1850. His unorthodox entry into the profession and his lowly origins did not endear him to the established medical community in London and no doubt prejudiced their view of his theories.[39] However, Snow persisted and persevered with his many interests and theories, which did not extend merely to cholera. He also pioneered the use of anesthetics, experimenting on animals with ether and chloroform.[40] There was much suspicion over the use of these chemicals on humans until Queen Victoria decided to try chloroform for the birth of Prince Leopold in 1853 and Princess Beatrice in 1857,[41] such was her fear of childbirth.

Snow's 1849 and 1854 work, *On the Mode of Communication of Cholera*, set out his theories on the disease and gave an insight into his meticulous research and logical step-by-step thought process. One of the main debates of the day was whether or not cholera was contagious. Snow had observed, as had many in the medical community, that doctors attending cholera patients did not necessarily catch the disease. He logically concluded, therefore, that "if cholera were a catching or communicable disease, it must be spread by effluvia given off from the patient into the surrounding air, and inhaled by others into the lungs."[42] He also understood how the disease was transmitted from person to person through lack of personal hygiene, and because the evacuations were colorless and odorless they could easily be transmitted from hand to mouth.[43]

Snow realized that cholera must be transmitted by water: "If the cholera had no other means of communication than those which we have been considering, it would be constrained to confine itself chiefly to the crowded dwellings of the poor, and would be continually liable to die out accidentally in a place, for want of the opportunity to reach fresh victims; but there is often a way open for it to extend itself more widely, and to reach the well-to-do classes of the community; I allude to the mixture of the cholera evacuations with the water used for drinking and culinary purposes, either by permeating the ground, and getting into wells, or by running along channels and sewers into the rivers from which entire towns are sometimes supplied with water."[44]

Snow based many of his ideas on his observations. In 1849, he had visited the scene of the outbreak of cholera in Horsleydown in Southwark and had noticed that a channel containing human effluent had become mixed with the water from an overflowing well from which residents obtained their drinking water. He deduced that the first cases in the area had arisen from drinking contaminated river water, but that the disease had spread in their evacuations, which had entered the channel and then the well. He noted that in Wandsworth Road, the pipes for drinking water, the sewers and cesspools were all situated close together and that their contents easily mixed together when there was heavy rain, such as occurred on July 26, 1849, flooding the dwelling houses in the process, as was also often the case in Lambeth.

Snow's place in medical history came with the cholera outbreak of 1854. At this time he was living in Sackville Street and practicing in the Soho area of London. He became interested in the spread of the disease in Broad Street (now Broadwick Street) in August and September, which claimed the lives of some 500 victims in ten days. Many fled the area and houses were closed up. Snow said that he immediately suspected the water pump to be the source of the outbreak, but could find nothing untoward with the water when he examined it. However, he continued to take samples of the water over the following days and noticed that the quality of it varied.

A description of these events is included in his *On the Mode of Communication of Cholera,* including how he then visited the General Register Office to view the records of the 89 deaths which had taken place during the week ending December 2. It was fortunate for Snow that William Farr was so meticulous in the compilation of his statistics, as Snow was able to deduce the exact day on which the outbreak must have started, a Thursday. Snow then returned to Broad Street and realized that all of the deaths had taken place just a short distance from the water pump.

> In five of these cases the families of the deceased persons informed me that they always sent to the pump on Broad Street, as they preferred the water to that of the pump which was nearer. In three other cases, the deceased were children who went to school near the pump in Broad Street. Two of them were known to drink the water; and the parents of the third think it probable that it did so. With regard to the deaths occurring in the locality belonging to the pump, there were sixty-one instances in which I was informed that the deceased persons used to drink the pump-water from Broad-street, either constantly or occasionally.
>
> The water [from the pump] was used for mixing with spirits in all the public houses around. It was used likewise at dining-rooms and coffee-shops. The keeper of a coffee-shop in the neighbourhood ... was already

aware nine of her customers who were dead. The pump-water was also sold in various little shops with a teaspoonful of effervescing powder in it, under the name of sherbet.... The pump was frequented much more than is usual, even for a London pump in a populous neighbourhood.[45]

The pump was situated on a site where it was frequented by a diverse range of people and Snow noted, "The mortality appears to have fallen pretty equally amongst all classes.... Masters are not distinguished from journeymen...."[46]

At the workhouse in Poland Street, a short distance from the pump and surrounded by the houses of cholera victims, only five died of the disease out of a number of some 535 inmates; they had obtained their water from a well.

A replica of the water pump in Soho's Broadwick Street. In the background is the John Snow public house. Almost directly under the sign on the right wall of the pub is a pink granite curbstone which identifies the original position of the pump. Photograph by the author.

In the brewery nearby, it was a similar situation; of 70 workmen none had suffered from cholera, as none of them ever drank water. Snow noted case after case of victims who had drunk from the pump and had subsequently fallen ill with cholera. An officer in the army who lived to the north of London in St. John's Wood had died after drinking water from the pump at a restaurant in Wardour Street, and a mother and two children who moved to Gravesend the day after drinking water from the pump all suffered, though the children survived. A gentleman from Brighton had come to see his brother in Poland Street, who was dying of cholera. The gentleman ate his lunch and drank a small glass of brandy with water from the pump, and died the following day. The most famous case of all was of a lady who had moved from the Broad Street area to Hampstead West End, but sent a cart daily to the pump "as she preferred it."[47] The water which was collected from the pump on August 31 not only killed the woman but also her niece, who lived "in a high and healthy part of Islington."[48] There were no other cases of cholera in Hampstead or Islington at the time.

Snow decided to talk to the Board of Guardians in the parish of St. James, where Broad Street was situated, and they agreed to remove the handle of the water pump the very next day, September 8, 1854. "On September the 8th — the day when the handle of the pump was removed — there were twelve attacks; on the 9th, eleven; on the 10th, five; on the 11th, five; on the 12th, only one; and after this time, there were never more than four attacks on one day."[49] Snow subsequently asked for the pump well to be investigated but no obvious source of contamination could be found. However, on further investigation it was discovered that the base of the well passed through gravel and clay above which ran a sewer. Some contamination had clearly taken place, and Snow later discovered that cesspools "sunk in the gravel will often go for twenty years without being emptied, owing to the soluble matters passing away into land-springs by percolation."[50]

Snow gave a sample of the water from the pump to his friend Dr. Arthur Hill Hassall (1817–1894). Hassall was concerned with the quality of the food sold in London shops, and made a name for himself with the publication of his findings.[51] Snow knew Hassall would be able to examine the water: "Dr Hassall ... informed me that these particles [observed in the water] had no organised structure, and he thought they probably resulted from decomposition of other matter. He found a great number of very minute oval animalcules in the water, which are of no importance, except as an additional proof that the water contained organic matter on which they lived."[52]

Snow had been convinced since the previous epidemic in 1848 and 1849 that cholera was a waterborne disease, and his observations in Lambeth had helped form this theory. Snow had noted, as discussed above, that there was

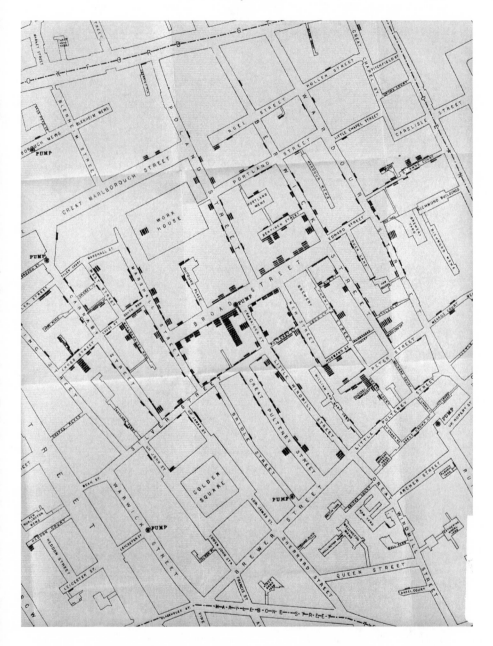

Dr. John Snow's map of the Broad Street area showing the high incidence of deaths (shown by thick black lines) around the pump he suspected was contaminated with raw sewage. The map was included in Snow's On the Mode of Communication of Cholera *to illustrate his theory. Wellcome Library, London.*

a correlation in this outbreak between mortality rates and water suppliers, such as in the case of the Southwark and Vauxhall and the Lambeth water companies. He also noted that residents who took their supply directly from the river, such as those in Fore Street, Lambeth, suffered particularly badly.

Snow knew from all his observations of the disease that "cholera invariably commences with the affection of the alimentary canal."[53] He went on to suggest that if this was where the infection started then the poison which caused cholera must necessarily enter the body through the mouth. Snow saw the outbreak of cholera in 1854 as an opportunity to finally prove his theory to the medical community: "I resolved to spare no exertion which might be necessary to ascertain the exact effect of the water supply on the progress of the epidemic.... I had no reason to doubt the correctness of my conclusions ... but I felt that the circumstance of the cholera-poison passing down the sewers into a great river, and being distributed through miles of pipes, and yet producing its specific effects, was a fact of so startling a nature, and of so vast importance to the community...."[54]

Snow was well aware of the objections to his theory, and realized that some of these were well-founded, he also wanted to be absolutely certain that he had not missed any crucial evidence. Some researchers had noted that there were cases of people who had drunk water known to be contaminated with cholera who had not become ill. Snow countered this with the acknowledgement that "several conditions may be requisite to the communication of cholera with which we are as yet unacquainted."[55]

Snow compared cholera with a seed which does not germinate, realizing that the disease must be organic and have some sort of reproductive cycle. In addition, he realized that not every drop of water taken from the Thames would necessarily contain the cholera pathogen, as water quality would differ from place to place and might also depend on how long it had been stored. Snow disputed once again the theories of wind, miasma and effluvia, noting that often the smelliest places were the least affected by cholera. He also discussed the results of some research in the United States. This showed that the worst outbreaks of cholera had been in areas supplied with hard rather than soft water. The conclusion drawn from this was that the minerals in the water had played some part. Snow was interested in this view but also noted that the hard water originated from a river and the soft water from a spring or rainwater.

Snow also considered the correlation between high population and the duration of an epidemic. He noted that in England epidemics reached their climax in the latter part of the summer whereas in Scotland epidemics would continue in the winter. Snow realized that in England, the population tended to drink unboiled water only in the summer to quench the thirst, but drank "tea, coffee, malt liquor or some other artificial beverage"[56] at mealtimes. The Scots on the other hand mixed unboiled cold water with spirits, and if they drank it without water, then they would often drink water afterwards to quench their thirst. Snow also realized that the weather and temperature might also be a factor and that flies and insects would also have a role in the spread of the disease in the summertime.

Snow commented on Farr's discovery that mortality was higher among women. He attributed this to the fact that women stayed at home and would be more susceptible to localized outbreaks of the disease, they tended to drink water rather than beer, and that they also tended the sick.

Snow gave a series of proposals to prevent the spread of cholera, which can be condensed as follows:

1. Cleanliness when caring for the sick.
2. Washing and drying of contaminated bed linen, preferably to a temperature of 212°F or above.
3. Care should be taken not to drink water which has been contaminated with human excrement; if there is doubt, water should be boiled and also filtered.

   London must be supplied with clean water, obtained above Teddington Lock, as the Lambeth Water Company has done. The pump handles of pumps connected to shallow wells should be removed and a supply of clean water should be provided for shipping.
4. When cholera is prevalent, care should be taken with food preparation with provisions washed in clean water and heated to a temperature of 212°F.
5. In cases of illness, the healthy should be separated from the sick.
6. With regard to the working hours of coal miners, shifts of four hours should be introduced to allow miners to eat and relieve themselves.
7. The communicability of cholera should not be hidden from the public, but they should be informed in order to understand it cannot be "caught."
8. Better drainage.
9. A better and uncontaminated water supply.
10. Provide better accommodation for the poor.
11. Educate the public as to the merits of personal and domestic cleanliness.
12. Segregate the sick on ships arriving in ports.[57]

In the conclusion of these proposals, Snow stated, "I feel confident ... that by attending to the above-mentioned precautions, which I consider to be based on a correct knowledge of the cause of cholera, this disease may be rendered extremely rare, if indeed it may not be altogether banished from civilised countries."[58]

While the majority of Snow's theories would later be proven to be correct, the medical community of the day did not share his confidence. In 1849, following the publication of his initial observations, *The London Medical Gazette* commented: "There is, in our view, an entire failure of proof that the occurrence of any one case could be clearly and unambiguously assigned to water.... Notwithstanding our opinion that Dr. Snow has failed in proving that cholera is communicated in the mode in which he supposes it to be, he deserves the thanks of the profession for endeavouring to solve the mystery. It is only by close analysis of facts and the publication of new views, that we can hope to arrive at the truth."[59]

While the London and Bristol medical communities were arguing over whether the cholera pathogen was a fungus or if it were transmitted by air or water, in Italy in 1854, Filippo Pacini (1812–1883), Professor of Anatomy at the University of Florence, was carrying out his own investigations. In 1831 he had already identified the existence of "corpuscles" and was certain that microscopic investigation was the key to discovering the cause of contagious disease.[60] During the cholera epidemic of 1854 in Florence, Pacini isolated the intestinal mucosa of cholera patients. Under a microscope he observed a comma-shaped bacillus which he named a *vibrio*, and then described the damage to the intestinal lining which he attributed to the pathogen. In the same year, Pacini published his work *Osservazioni Microscopiche e Deduzioni Patologiche sul Cholera Asiatico,* but despite many further publications of his work, he was largely ignored by the scientific community in Italy and elsewhere.[61]

The year after Pacini's death, a similar study was undertaken by the German Heinrich Hermann Robert Koch (1843–1910). Though unaware of Pacini's work, Koch eventually was to confirm his findings. Robert Koch had studied at the University of Göttingen, where he was influenced by the theories of the Professor of Anatomy, Jacob Henle. Henle was of the belief that "infectious diseases were caused by living parasitic organisms."[62] It was while Koch was working on the causes of tuberculosis in 1883 at the Reichs-Gesundheitsamt, or Imperial Health Bureau, in Berlin that he was sent to Egypt as the head of the German Cholera Commission.[63] It was in Alexandria, and then in Calcutta in India, that he became convinced the cholera pathogen was that found in the intestines and feces of infected patients.[64]

Koch's work was systematically published by the German medical and national press, which undoubtedly helped to establish confidence in his theories in some parts of the scientific community, though in Germany too there was still skepticism. Koch observed living and dead victims of the disease and he compared his findings in Alexandria and Calcutta. Finally, in January 1884, he identified the same bacillus in all cases and isolated it in culture. Like Pacini, he described the bacillus as comma-like, "ein wenig gekrümmt, einem Komma ähnlich."[65]

Koch also noted that the bacillus was able to survive and grow on moist linen and damp earth, and was susceptible to drying and weak acidic solutions. Moreover he discovered that in the early stages of the disease, the numbers of bacilli were few in the feces and vomit of victims, but increased rapidly in number up to the stage where stools resembled rice water.[66] In his article for the *British Medical Journal* to celebrate the centenary of Koch's discovery, Norman Howard-Jones concluded, "Posthumous recognition came to Pacini 82 years after his death when the judicial commission of the international committee on bacteriological nomenclature adopted *Vibrio cholerae Pacini 1854* as the correct name of the cholera vibrio."[67] Koch was awarded the Nobel Prize for medicine in 1905.

Despite the work of Snow, Pacini and Koch, medical opinion was still divided as to whether the cholera pathogen was the sole cause of the disease. Work was therefore slow in trying to develop a vaccine to protect the poor and vulnerable, who were still susceptible to outbreaks of the disease. The Russian scientist Waldemar Mordecai Wolfe Haffkine (1860–1930), born Vladimir Aronovich Havkin, worked on developing a vaccine during his time at the Pasteur Institute in Paris. In 1888 cholera was raging once more in Asia and Europe and the need to develop a vaccine was prominent in the minds of the scientific community, and in Paris Haffkine worked with his mentor Elie Metchnikoff (1845–1916) and Louis Pasteur (1822–1895). Haffkine succeeded in isolating an attenuated form of the cholera bacterium by exposing it to blasts of hot air.[68] He continued experimentation on a vaccine with animals, but by 1892 he was so confident that his vaccine would work, he inoculated himself, injecting himself with a dose four times more potent than that which was eventually used in the vaccine.[69]

The results of his test were reported to the Biological Society of Paris, though his findings were greeted with skepticism. Haffkine trialed his vaccine in India, where another epidemic had erupted, and the results were successful; further trials were to follow. Haffkine's work was tainted in 1902 when 19 Punjabi villagers died of tetanus, and the resulting inquiry almost destroyed his reputation and his career. However, further investigations proved that sterile conditions had not been in place when one of the bottles of vaccine had been opened, and Haffkine was finally exonerated. The surgeon Lord Joseph Lister (1827–1912), who had pioneered the use of antiseptics and sterilization, and was also influenced by the work of Pasteur, hailed Haffkine as "a saviour of humanity."[70]

A Royal Commission in 1853 recommended a governing body for London, not including the City, to coordinate London's infrastructure. The Metropolitan Board of Works was created by the passing of the Metropolis Local Management Act of 1855, which in 1858 was amended by Benjamin Disraeli (1804–1881) to speed up reforms to the sewage system. The Board of Works replaced the Metropolitan Board of Sewers and the Metropolitan Buildings Office, and created a system of local government consisting of vestries and district boards of works based on existing parish boundaries. These 36 areas were the same metropolitan registration districts as those defined in the 1851 Census, and therefore useful for the compilation of statistics.[71]

Members to the Board of Works were appointed by nominations from the local vestries, and the first chairman was John Thwaites (1815–1870).[72] However, clauses were inserted into the bill which meant that large-scale work, particularly on the sewage system, had to be approved by the Commissioners of Work and in some cases by Parliament, effectively wrenching local control away from the vestries. The following year the railway engineer Joseph Bazalgette was appointed Chief Engineer to the Board, in preference to Isambard Kingdom Brunel and Robert Stephenson.[73]

The Metropolitan Board of Works argued over the plans and costs for a new sewage system which would take waste out of London and deposit it farther downstream in the Thames estuary, and from there out to sea. Matters came to a head in the summer of 1858 when a period of hot weather caused the Thames to smell intolerably, and which was nicknamed the Great Stink. Parliament could tolerate no more and Disraeli ensured that his amendment to the 1855 Metropolis Local Management Act contained a clause which settled once and for all that the new sewers would not drain into the River Thames within the capital.[74]

Bazalgette began more or less straightaway, but the entire project was to take almost 20 years to complete. The project was complex and fraught with difficulties, one of the hardest being that the land bordering the Thames was low-lying. To keep costs low, Bazalgette's system needed to employ gravity as much as possible to drain water away. Despite the problems at Lambeth with disease and flooding, the area south of the river was not considered as important or prestigious as that to the north. Indeed the design for the Victoria Embankment, which would link some of the most important and historic parts of London, was grander and a larger sum of money was allocated to the scheme, the final cost of which was £1,156,981.[75] The Victoria Embankment was built to enhance the northern bank and would include a new wide road to accommodate London's growing traffic, pavements, trees and elegant street lamps. In addition, it would create a space for the new sewage system and tunnels for the London Underground railway.

Bazalgette built large brick-lined intercepting sewers to link many of the old systems together. Waste flowed into these sewers through salt-glazed ceramic pipes produced at Lambeth by Henry Doulton's works. The high quality water-resistant Portland cement which Bazalgette also employed originated in Northfleet,[76] to the west of the Medway Towns and the Hoo Peninsula in Kent. Work to improve the sanitation of Lambeth continued into the twentieth century, however, Bazalgette's original plan incorporated the Effra as the main sewer. The Thames' tributary was linked at Vauxhall Bridge to a sewer which originated in Putney. The path of the sewer avoided the waterfront area and at Kennington Oval turned east along Albany Street, and then south at the junction to the Old Kent Road. The sewer continued south to Deptford Pumping Station, opened in 1864, where it was joined by sewers from Wimbledon, Balham, Brixton, Norwood and Dulwich. From the pumping station a single sewer followed the river, across Greenwich marshes to the Southern Outfall at Crossness. The outlet for the northern system was a short distance upstream at Becton. Sewage was pumped into reservoirs by massive engines designed by James Watt's company, and then discharged into the river at high tide.[77]

Lambeth's Albert Embankment was to be entirely utilitarian, though the section in front of St. Thomas' Hospital facing the Houses of Parliament was similar in style to that of the north bank. St. Thomas' left Southwark in 1862, when the site was redeveloped by the railway, and moved to Lambeth in 1871. The cost of the plot of land which was sold to the hospital helped to offset the cost of the building of the new Albert Embankment.[78]

To the south of the hospital, and along the waterfront area of Fore Street, the area was too low-lying for the embankment to include the sewage system, but a flood barrier was needed to protect Lambeth. An additional issue was the view and the smell from Westminster. Letters had continued to appear in *The Times* and other press deploring the state of Lambeth's waterfront: "Sir, are any steps being taken towards the removal of all those abominable nuisances in that seat of poison, Princes-street, Lambeth, consisting of bone-boilers, potteries, starch-makers and several of a like abominable nature? A person cannot now pass within a quarter of a mile without feeling ... sickness ... the poisonous vapours are carried ... into the very heart of the metropolis. If the whole of these wretched hovels and filthy factories were swept away altogether ... it would be a downright boon to the parish."[79]

Robert Taylor, Lambeth's church warden, had "pleaded year after year for them [the Metropolitan Board of Works] to come to the rescue of Lambeth, and protect not only the property from being submerged by the tides which overflowed the banks of the Thames, but the lives of the inhabitants living near to them, and it was only on these urgent representations that the southern embankment was undertaken."[80]

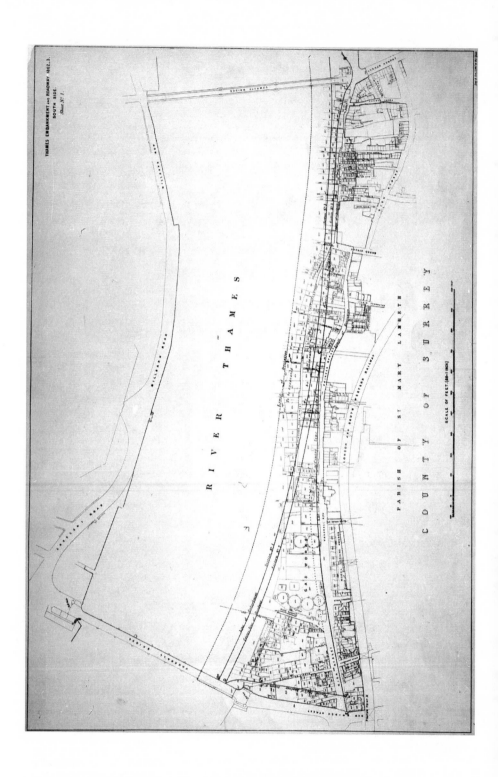

RIVER THAMES

PARISH OF ST MARY LAMBETH

COUNTY OF SURREY

SCALE OF FEET (80÷1 INCH)

Since 1809, plans had been in place to erect a bridge on the site of the old Horse Ferry at Lambeth. Finally, in 1861, the Lambeth Bridge Act made the plans a reality to connect Church Street Lambeth with Market Street, today's Horseferry Road, on the opposite bank at Westminster. The first bridge (which was later demolished) was built by P.W. Barlow "at a cost of £48,924.... The bridge was of stiffened suspension type, 828 feet long, divided into three spans,"[81] and opened in November 1862. When the bridge first opened, there was a toll to pay, but in 1877 it was bought by the Metropolitan Board of Works under the Metropolitan Toll Bridges Act for £35,974 and the toll was abolished. The bridge was to be incorporated into the new Albert Embankment. The first reading of the Thames Embankment (South Side) Bill took place in March 1863. "To enable the Metropolitan Board of Works to embank that portion of the River Thames opposite the Houses of Parliament extending between Westminster Bridge and the Gasworks near Vauxhall on the south side of the River."[82]

Little progress had been made in alleviating the problems in Lambeth. The Metropolitan Burial Act had ordered the closure of St. Mary's Burial Ground in Lambeth on October 31, 1854 (see Chapter 7), but a report in *The Times* the following January revealed that burials were still taking place, and that the order had been extended to May 31, 1854. The report in the newspaper deplored the situation, particularly as, with the closure of other graveyards, Lambeth had become "the receptacle for other parishes."[83] The new Lambeth cemetery did eventually open at Blackshaw Road in Tooting, a few miles to the south of Lambeth.

In 1859, the writer George Augustus Sala depicted the area around New Cut and the Victoria Theatre as "sordid, squalid ... disreputable ... gorged with vile, rotten tenements.... Everything is second-hand, except the leviathan gin-shops.... It is the paradise of the lowliest of costermongers, and often the saturnalia of the most emerited thieves. Women appear there in their most unlovely aspect: brazen, slovenly, dishevelled, brawling, muddled with beer or fractious with gin."[84]

By 1865 Lambeth Vestry was at least finally able to prosecute people for *nuisances*,[85] and while the move by Lambeth Waterworks to Thames Ditton had been lauded — and even established the link between contaminated water and cholera — Lambeth's water supply was still sporadic and ceased altogether on Sundays.[86] A change in government's attitude to social and sanitary reform had been slow and in response to financial rather than welfare concerns. Yet

Opposite: *One of the original plans for the Albert Embankment, dated 1862–63, showing the proposed line of the new waterfront area and the demolition to be undertaken. This image was reproduced by kind permission of Lambeth Archives department.*

as international trade expanded, the welfare of workers became more important to protect the supply of goods. There was still strong resistance to central control and a move away from localized government. However, many of the reforms necessary to improve the conditions in towns and cities were simply too expensive for local authorities to fund, though by the late 1860s, provision was made in law to make this easier. The Reform Act of 1867 continued the work of the 1832 Act and gave the vote to all male adult householders, which included those paying over £10 rent, extending the vote to over one-and-a-half million of the population and thereby including some members of the working class.[87]

The building of the Albert Embankment was seen as a solution to Lambeth's problems. It would prevent the frequent flooding of the area. The problem of how to provide sanitation for those along the waterfront was also resolved by demolishing the entire area. The businesses and people who lived in the waterfront area had little choice but to move out and reestablish themselves elsewhere. In March 1867, businesses began selling off their equipment. Advertisements appeared in *The Times* for auctions "instructed by the Metropolitan Board of Works." Items for sale included a 12-horsepower, high-

Building the Albert Embankment in the area of Lower Fore Street, circa 1867, looking towards Lambeth Palace. From the Woolley Collection. Photograph by William Strudwick. Reproduced by kind permission of Lambeth Archives department.

pressure, grasshopper steam engine, a Cornish boiler, 4 feet wide and 12 feet long, a flour dressing machine (from a flour mill), gun-metal lift pump, brickwork, a sheet lead rolling mill, hydraulic lead pipe making machines, an 8-horsepower oscillating steam engine, two cast-iron lead melting furnaces, smiths' tools, and weighing machines.

Construction on the Albert and Victoria Embankments began in 1864. The building of the Victoria Embankment went downstream from Westminster Bridge towards the City, and at the Albert Embankment it went upstream from Westminster Bridge to Vauxhall.[88]

The Albert Embankment was the first of the two embankments to open, on November 24, 1869. The ceremony was not as grand as that which had been planned for the grander Victoria Embankment and was attended by the chairman of the Metropolitan Board of Works, Joseph Bazalgette and the architect George Vulliamy. A band played *See the Conquering Hero Comes*,[89] the piece Handel had composed to celebrate the role played by the Duke of Cumberland in the defeat of the Jacobite Rebellion.

Building the Albert Embankment in the area of Upper Fore Street, circa 1867; note the pottery kilns in the background of the middle section of the photograph. From the Woolley Collection. Photograph by William Strudwick. Reproduced by kind permission of Lambeth Archives department.

In 1871, during a meeting of the Metropolitan Board of Works, the Works and General Purposes committee considered an appeal from Lambeth Vestry. Under the Thames Embankment (South) Act, the maintenance of the entire length of the Albert Embankment had become the Vestry's responsibility. The Vestry wanted it noted that they had lost a considerable amount of revenue in rates after the removal of the manufacturing industries and wharves along the Lambeth waterfront and therefore they could not afford to maintain the "paving, repairing, cleansing, lighting and watching."[90] Lambeth Vestry also noted that this consideration had already been given to the District Boards of the Strand and Westminster on the north bank of the Thames with regard to the Victoria Embankment. The board responded that the Victoria Embankment was of "almost national character," while the Albert Embankment was of "local character."[91] Moreover, Lambeth had lost a value of around £20,000 in rates from the houses which had been demolished but had gained around £24,000 in rates from St. Thomas' Hospital and the surrounding buildings. The Vestry disputed the board's opinion, stating that the new embankment was not used by the people of Lambeth but as a thoroughfare for others from Battersea and Wandsworth going to London Bridge and the City. In addition, the rateable value of St. Thomas' Hospital would not equal that of a private dwelling. A bitter argument ensued and when a vote was taken, Lambeth Vestry lost by 17 votes to 14.[92]

9

Conclusion

At least 2,000 people died from cholera and diarrhea in Lambeth throughout 1848 and 1849, creating an atmosphere of fear and hopelessness, particularly in the waterfront area. Yet there is no memorial to the dead, except perhaps a mound in Lambeth Burial Ground, which may be an indication of the site of the mass grave. While the epidemic devastated many lives, the episode was brief and has been overshadowed by the 1854 epidemic, when Dr. John Snow was able to prove that cholera was a waterborne disease. Yet it was Snow's observations in Lambeth which led him to this conclusion. Snow noted how the people of Fore Street had to obtain their drinking water from the Thames with a bucket, and how it was in this same street and the surrounding area that the epidemic erupted so violently. Snow also noted how the incidences of cholera and diarrhea diminished when the Lambeth Waterworks later moved to Thames Ditton. Lambeth played a crucial role in the understanding of cholera.

With hindsight there was an inevitability about the cholera epidemic. Every aspect of Lambeth which made it attractive for the development of business also made it prone to disease. Here the giants of the industrial age, such as James Watt and Matthew Boulton, were able to experiment at the hub of a communications network where the river not only provided transportation but also an unlimited source of water for coal-fired steam engines. While Lambeth's riverside position was beneficial for business, it was the worst place for human habitation. As the factories and potteries expanded so workers moved in to live in back-to-back tenements devoid of sanitation and hastily erected on the flood-prone, marshy ground.

Life in the countryside was not much better. Since the enclosure of land and the introduction of a fixed price for grain, many were without work and starving. In the early days of the Industrial Revolution, many preferred to stay in a more familiar environment, taking what work there was and moving from farm to farm. Others took their chances in places like Lambeth, for although living conditions were harsh, there was work to be had. In addition there was the prospect of apprenticeships for male children and with this came the faint possibility of social elevation.

By the end of the eighteenth century, death rates in England and Wales had fallen, however, as rural workers began to move to areas like Lambeth, they began to rise again in urban areas[1] and, by 1841, most males in England and Wales did not live beyond the age of 49.[2]

The living conditions of the working population were conducive to the spread of disease. Tuberculosis, for example, was more prevalent in urban environments, where it thrived in the undernourished population and in damp, unventilated living conditions. The disease was not widely understood in the nineteenth century and accepted as part of life, and in London deaths from tuberculosis peaked in the period from 1780 to 1830.[3] In Lambeth, houses built on the low-lying marshy swampland were damp and poorly ventilated, packed tightly together. While there was some running water supplied by hand pumps in the streets away from the waterfront, the supply was sporadic. In the waterfront streets, such as Fore Street and Princes Street, there was no water supply at all, and throughout the entire area there was no adequate system for the disposal of sewage or industrial and domestic waste products.

Living conditions in the poor areas of London were no different to how they had been in medieval times, moreover, while some advances were being made, medical understanding had also improved little. The medical establishment was convinced that disease was spread through foul smells, and in airborne particles like fungal spores, and when physicians like Dr. John Snow suggested otherwise, they were dismissed out of prejudice and arrogance. If disease was spread by nasty smells, then demands to clean the streets and flush the sewers could be justified, but dirty water and a lack of personal hygiene were not seen as a threat to public health. Reform of the sanitary infrastructure in London throughout the first half of the nineteenth century was slow, and as time went on, the task became almost impossible. Sir Edwin Chadwick and Sanitary Committees like those in Lambeth were quite right in saying that something needed to be done, but their recommendations were hard to put into practice as the structure of local government was still in its infancy and its role was still not clearly defined. The worst areas in London, such as Lambeth, were also the poorest, and the working class had no representation at a local or parliamentary level, indeed, the idea that they should have any representation at all was seen as subversive and was not encouraged. Improving conditions for the poor could even lead to revolution, as sanitary reform would acknowledge that the poor had a right to certain services, even to education, and for some this was simply unacceptable. The Agrarian and Industrial Revolutions created a watershed in British society. Britain could not go back to an economy based on agriculture and cottage industries, but neither could it move forward to become a fully industrialized nation if changes were not made. Slowly governments realized that the welfare of workers was important for production levels, but it was to take over half a century before the rights of the working population were properly recognized.

In the 1840s, trade was essential to the British economy and to the expansion of the Empire, and the welfare of the working population came second to the demands of the factory owners, who were also landlords and members of the parish committees. A letter to *The Times* from "A Working Man" of Lambeth (in reality, no doubt, someone giving the working man a voice) illustrated the frustration and hopelessness of the situation: "There is an inspector of nuisances appointed by the parish; but to expect anything from a parochial officer, who is, to a certain extent, the servant of the influential proprietors of the manufactories in question is in vain. The Board of Health may be doing great things in other quarters (although we do not hear where), but a more fruitful field for its staff to be 'up and doing' can scarcely be found."[4]

If disease were spread by foul smells then it is likely that the factory owners would do everything in their power to prevent the closure of their businesses, which might be held responsible. This is shown in another letter to *The Times* at the height of the cholera epidemic in 1849: "Mr Grainger, the inspector of the Board of Health, has, I believe, with others, inspected these places [the bone-boiling factories], but nothing has been done to remedy the evil. The proprietor of one of these premises resides on the spot, and may, perhaps, have represented to the officers that he and his family enjoy good health, and that consequently it cannot be injurious; but the public think differently and complaints are very numerous."[5]

Lambeth had grown too quickly and people had flooded into the area who were not used to living in a crowded city, particularly the Irish immigrants escaping from famine. The extreme poverty and deprivation was simply too much for the parish authorities to cope with, even those with a social conscience, which included the surgeons and some members of the religious community. On August 4, 1849, a letter appeared in *The Times* from Mr. J. T. Mitchell of Kennington Common regarding the conduct of the Lambeth Board of Guardians, their medical officers and the help given by them to the poor of the district. Mr. Mitchell, a medical officer of the parish for some 18 years, and two assistants were appointed by the Lambeth Board of Guardians, which he pointed out included a medical man, as directed by the Board of Health. He stated that in the last week of July they had attended the homes of 1,028 inhabitants of the area, which included 59 cases of Asiatic cholera, and 141 cases of diarrhea and "ordinary" cholera. The distinction between the three types of illness being that Asiatic cholera was the most serious and had symptoms which were likely to be fatal. Whether there was any real difference between the three is impossible to tell. Mitchell related how he and his assistants worked night and day and were so exhausted one of the assistants had resigned. He complained that his salary was too low and barely covered the cost of the medicines he was expected to provide. Worse, when he appealed to the Board of Guardians on July 26 to recruit another assistant and to ask for help from other medical professionals in the tending of the poor, he had been met with indifference. By the Tuesday morning, which was the same day as the next meeting of the board, Mitchell decided to tender his conditional resignation, no doubt in the hope that this might spur the board into action; his resignation was immediately accepted. Mitchell's conclusion was that the Board of Guardians of Lambeth should not have the responsibility for the poor and that this should be entrusted to the government. Mitchell added that despite the fact he was no longer employed by the board, he would continue to work with the poor until a successor was found.[6]

The task was huge, and the Lambeth parish authorities knew that the only way to solve the growing problem was to spend money, but who was responsible and where such vast sums of money would come from remained unresolved, and as the Lambeth District Sanitary Sub Committee of St. Mark's District reported in 1848: "It would appear that all parties would gladly avail themselves of the advantage of the Common sewers but that the expense of doing so deters them, and the unwillingness of tenants to lay out money upon the landlord's property.

"The use of cesspools being in most cases resorted to in order to avoid the expense of carrying to the main drainage, or sewers, altho' these latter are in many parts available for the purpose while others for want of this or of suitable cesspools are in a very bad state."[7]

The Lambeth District Sanitary Reports show that in 1848 the parish authorities were aware cholera could return, but save providing a clean running water supply for every resident, there was little that could be done to stop it. Epidemics had already broken out overseas, however, it is likely that a strain, or even strains, of *Vibrio cholerae* were already endemic in the River Thames. Cholera was at its most virulent during the summers of 1832, 1849, 1852 and 1866, years characterized by high pressure, high air and water temperatures and low rainfall, but in the intervening time, those who drank the river water still suffered from cholera-like diarrhea. The observations of Parkes, Snow and Farr indicate that endemic cholera is a likely scenario, as does one final letter from *The Times* newspaper of 1855: "It would appear that there is no longer any doubt that diarrhea and cholera, when they prevail together endemically, are different degrees of the same disease, produced by the same causes, and aggravated by the same influences."[8]

The working people of Lambeth were most at risk. Undernourished with a diet supplemented in many cases with alcohol, they were not healthy enough

An artist's drawing for the White Hart Dock Public Art and Community Engagement Project, Albert Embankment, Lambeth. Illustration by Joe Tenner, with the kind permission of Handspring Design.

to withstand the cholera infection, neither were their gastric juices acidic enough to kill the bacteria. The living conditions in Lambeth were low-lying, damp and insanitary so there was ample opportunity for the disease to spread through poor hygiene and on the feet of rats, mice and flies. Lambeth's water supply came from a brackish river teeming with algae, copepods, crustaceans, insects, and the eggs of midges and gnats, the ideal breeding ground for the free-swimming *Vibrio cholerae* brought to England in the holds and bilges of ships and boats, and with the ability to lie dormant when conditions were unfavorable. However, in the hot epidemic summers, the Thames, and those drinking its waters, were the perfect environments to activate the pathogenic virus and to recommence the bacterium's deadly cycle. However, by the 1860s, most had accepted Snow's theory that cholera was a waterborne disease and, as a result, many lives were saved by prevention rather than cure.

It is hardly surprising that the only solution to disease and poverty in Lambeth was to raze the waterfront area to the ground. The building of the Albert Embankment was seen as a solution to Lambeth's problems. It would prevent the frequent flooding of the area and solve the problem of how to provide sanitation for the waterfront area. The building of the southern stretch of the Albert Embankment completed the work that the London and South Western Railway started and destroyed much of the charm and character of the area, a job which was completed in the Blitz in World War II. However, in 2004, the London Borough of Lambeth began work on a project to restore one of the waterfront's ancient docks. The White Hart Dock was incorporated into the original building of the Albert Embankment to enable Doulton's pottery works to continue loading and unloading goods. The dock was situated at the junction of Broad Street, today's Black Prince Road, and in more recent times has been obscured by a concrete wall. It is hoped that the new development will begin the process of bringing the Lambeth waterfront area back to life and may even be a memorial to those who needlessly died in the cholera outbreak of 1848 to 1849.

Chapter Notes

Introduction

1. Ancestry.co.uk.
2. *Lambeth District Sanitary Reports*, Ref.: P3, 73–75, 1848–1878, Lambeth Archives.
3. S.E. Finer, *The Life and Times of Edwin Chadwick* (London: Methuen, 1952).
4. Department of Epidemiology, University of California Los Angeles (UCLA), School of Public Health, Box 951772, Los Angeles, California, 90095–1772; www.ph.ucla.edu.
5. Ibid.
6. *Lambeth Parish and Vestry Committee Minutes* (Ref.: P3); *Lambeth District Sanitary Reports* (Ref: P3, 73–75, 1848–1878), Lambeth Archives.

Chapter 1

1. www.nationalarchives.gov.uk and www.knowingbritishhistory.co.uk.
2. www.statistics.gov.uk and E.A. Wrigley and R.S. Schofield, *The Population History of England 1541–1871: A Reconstruction* (London: Edward Arnold, 1981).
3. www.statistics.gov.uk and Office of Population Census and Surveys, *1991 Census Historic Tables — Great Britain* (London: OPCS, 1993).
4. www.statistics.gov.uk.
5. Monarchs: www.en.wikipedia.org; Prime Ministers: Dr. Marjorie Bloy's *A Web of English History*, www.historyhome.co.uk.
6. www.historyhome.co.uk.
7. Gregory Fremont-Barnes, *Encyclopedia of the Age of Political Revolutions and New Ideologies, 1760–1815* (Westport, CT: Greenwood, 2007).
8. Ibid.
9. Clive Emsley, "The London 'Insurrection' of December 1792: Fact, Fiction or Fantasy?" *The Journal of British Studies* XVII (1978), 66–86. www.jstor.org.
10. Druin Burch, *Digging up the Dead, Uncovering the Life and Times of an Extraordinary Surgeon* (London: Vintage, 2007), 86.
11. Ibid., 122.
12. John Mee, "'In private speculation a republican': The Case of John Thelwall 1794–5," paper given at University College Oxford, 2006. http://www.english.wisc.edu/midmod/speculative.re publcianism.doc.
13. Druin Burch, *Digging up the Dead, Uncov-*

ering the Life and Times of an Extraordinary Surgeon (London: Vintage, 2007), 122.
14. John Mee, "'In private speculation a republican': The Case of John Thelwall 1794–5," paper given at University College Oxford, 2006. http://www.english.wisc.edu/midmod/speculative.re publcianism.doc.
15. www.historyhome.co.uk.
16. Druin Burch, *Digging up the Dead, Uncovering the Life and Times of an Extraordinary Surgeon* (London: Vintage, 2007), 137–139.
17. Ibid., 141.
18. www.historyhome.co.uk.
19. Druin Burch, *Digging up the Dead, Uncovering the Life and Times of an Extraordinary Surgeon* (London: Vintage, 2007), 143.
20. www.historyhome.co.uk.
21. http://www.victorianweb.org/history/riots/pentrich.html.
22. http://en.wikipedia.org/wiki/Cato_Street_Conspiracy.
23. Charles Barrow, *Industrial Relations Law*, 2d ed., revised (London: Cavendish, 2002), 8.
24. http://en.wikipedia.org/wiki/The_Making_of_the_English_Working_Class, referring to E. P. Thompson, *The Making of the English Working Class* (London: Victor Gollancz, 1963).
25. Adrian Randall, *Riotous Assemblies: Popular Protest in Hanoverian England* (Oxford: Oxford University Press, 2006).
26. www.historyhome.co.uk.
27. www.saburchill.com/history/.
28. R.J. Unstead, *Freedom and Revolution* (London: Macdonald, 1972), 56.
29. www.thehistorychannel.co.uk.
30. Ibid.
31. Coling G. Pooley, and Jean Turnbull, *Migration and Mobility in Britain Since the 18th Century* (London: Routledge, 1998), 14.
32. Robert Clark, "Famine; Speenhamland System of Poor Relief," *The Literary Encyclopedia*, May 18, 2005. www.litencyc.com.
33. Adrian Randall, *Riotous Assemblies: Popular Protest in Hanoverian England* (Oxford: Oxford University Press, 2006).
34. www.historyhome.co.uk.
35. Robert Clark, "Famine; Speenhamland System of Poor Relief," *The Literary Encyclopedia*, May 18, 2005. *www.litencyc.com.*
36. Ibid.
37. Edwin Chadwick, *Report on The Sanitary Condition of the Labouring Population of Great*

Britain, edited with an introduction by M.W. Flinn (1842; rpt. Edinburgh: Edinburgh University Press, 1965), 7.

38. www.historyhome.co.uk.

39. Ibid.

40. Norman Longmate, *King Cholera. The Biography of a Disease* (London: Hamish Hamilton, 1966), 93.

41. Edwin Chadwick, *Report on The Sanitary Condition of the Labouring Population of Great Britain,* edited with an introduction by M.W. Flinn (1842; rpt. Edinburgh: Edinburgh University Press, 1965), 36.

42. www.robert-owen-museum.org.uk.

43. http://thedorsetpage.com/history/tolpuddle_martyrs/tolpuddle_martyrs.htm.

44. www.unionhistory.info.

45. http://www.manchester2002-uk.com/history/victorian/Victorian2.html.

46. Ibid.

47. http://www.economicexpert.com/a/Corn:Laws.htm.

48. http://www.manchester2002-uk.com/history/victorian/Victorian2.html.

49. http://en.wikipedia.org/wiki/Six_Acts.

50. www.historyhome.co.uk.

51. William Page and William Ashley, *Commerce and Industry. A Historical Review of the Economic Conditions of the British Empire from the Peace of Paris in 1815 to the Declaration of War in 1914, Based on Parliamentary Debates* (Boston: Adamant Media Corporation, 2005), Chapter IV.

52. "National Union of the Working Classes," in D.J. Rowe, ed., *London Radicalism 1830–1843: A selection of the papers of Francis Place* (London Record Society, 1970), 29–34. http://british-history.ac.uk/report.aspx?compid=39483.

53. Patricia Hollis, *Class and Conflict in Nineteenth-Century England, 1815–1850* (London: Routledge & Kegan Paul, 1973), 132–133.

54. "National Union of the Working Classes," in D.J. Rowe, ed., *London Radicalism 1830–1843: A selection of the papers of Francis Place* (London Record Society, 1970), 64–72. http://british-history.ac.uk/report.aspx?compid=39483.

55. Ibid.

56. Ibid.

57. Ibid.

58. The National Archives. http://www.learningcurve.gov.uk/politics/g6/.

59. Patricia Hollis, *Class and Conflict in Nineteenth-Century England, 1815–1850* (London: Routledge & Kegan Paul, 1973), 126.

60. http://en.wikipedia.org/wiki/Reform_Act_1832.

61. Ibid., and www.historyhome.co.uk.

62. William Page and William Ashley, *Commerce and Industry. A Historical Review of the Economic Conditions of the British Empire from the Peace of Paris in 1815 to the Declaration of War in*

1914, *Based on Parliamentary Debates* (Boston: Adamant Media Corporation, 2005), Chapter IV.

63. Ibid.

64. www.historyhome.co.uk.

65. Ibid.

66. Ibid.

67. Ibid.

68. Ibid.

69. Ibid.

70. John Breuilly, "The TLTP History Courseware Consortium," University of Birmingham. http://web.bham.ac.uk/.

71. www.historyhome.co.uk.

72. Ibid.

73. Catalogue reference HO 44/32/114 (1839). www.nationalarchives.gov.uk.

74. Ibid.

75. Ibid.

76. www.spartacus.schoolnet.co.uk.

77. www.historyhome.co.uk.

78. Edwin Chadwick, *Report on The Sanitary Condition of the Labouring Population of Great Britain,* edited with an introduction by M.W. Flinn (1842; rpt. Edinburgh: Edinburgh University Press, 1965), 36.

79. http://en.wikipedia.org/wiki/Factory_Acts.

80. www.historyhome.co.uk.

81. http://commons.wikimedia.org/wiki/File:Chartist_Demonstration.jpg, taken from Rodney Mace, *British Trade Union Posters: An Illustrated History* (Stroud, Gloucestershire: Alan Sutton, 1999).

82. www.historyhome.co.uk.

Chapter 2

1. Edwin Chadwick, *Report on The Sanitary Condition of the Labouring Population of Great Britain,* edited with an introduction by M.W. Flinn (1842; rpt. Edinburgh: Edinburgh University Press, 1965), 13.

2. Ibid., 5.

3. Ibid., 7.

4. Ibid., Chapter III.

5. Ibid., 11, and J. Brownlee, "An Investigation into the Epidemiology of Phthisis in Great Britain and Ireland," *Special Reports Series,* no. 18 (Medical Research Council, 1918), Table XXV.

6. *Stedman's Medical Dictionary,* 23rd ed. (Baltimore: Williams and Wilkins, 1979), 1,393.

7. *Bodies Dissected at St. Bartholomew's Hospital Medical School; 1832–1964,* Ref.: GB 0405 MS 81, Volume III (sub-fonds of St. Bartholomew's Hospital Medical School records), 1851–1852.

8. M. Whitehead, "William Farr's Legacy to the Study of Inequalities in Health," *Bulletin of the World Health Organization,* 78.1 (2000): 86–7.

9. Edwin Chadwick, *Report on The Sanitary Condition of the Labouring Population of Great*

Britain, edited with an introduction by M.W. Flinn (1842; rpt. Edinburgh: Edinburgh University Press, 1965), 28–29; and William Farr, *First Annual Report of the Registrar-General, 1839.*

10. William Farr, *Report on the Mortality of Cholera in England 1848–49; Section I. Vitality of England and Wales and Average Amount of Sickness: Experienced by the Results of Mr. Neison* (London: W. Clowes and Sons, 1852), 11.

11. Edwin Chadwick, *Report on The Sanitary Condition of the Labouring Population of Great Britain,* edited with an introduction by M.W. Flinn (1842; rpt. Edinburgh: Edinburgh University Press, 1965), 29; and William Farr, *Tenth Annual Report of the Registrar-General* (1847), xvii.

12. Certified Copy of an Entry of Death, General Register Office, England.

13. Allan Cherry, *A Pictorial History of Cooling and Cliffe, Looking back from the Millennium* (Kent: Martins News, 1998).

14. Charles Dickens, *Great Expectations* (London and Glasgow: Collins, 1965), 15.

15. S.W. Lindsay, and S.G. Willis, "Foresight. Infectious Diseases: preparing for the future." T8.10: "Predicting future areas suitable for vivax malaria in the United Kingdom" (Office of Science and Innovation, Institute of Ecosystem Science, School of Biological and Biomedical Sciences, University of Durham). http://www.foresight.gov.uk/Infectious%20Diseases/t8_10.pdf.

16. C.H. Collins, M.A., D.Sc., F.R.C.Path., "Cholera and Typhoid Fever in Kent," Kent Archaeological Society online. www.kentarchaeology.ac.

17. David A. Sack, R. Bradley Sack, G. Balakrish Nair, and A. K. Siddique, "Cholera," *The Lancet,* Vol. 363 (January 17, 2004): 229. http://www.ph.ucla.edu/epi/snow/lancet363_223_233_2004.pdf.

18. Norman Longmate, *King Cholera. The Biography of a Disease* (London: Hamish Hamilton, 1966), 83.

19. Ibid., 95.

20. John G. Avery, *The Cholera Years. An Account of the Cholera Outbreaks in our Ports, Towns and Villages* (Southampton: Beech Books, 2001).

21. Norman Longmate, *King Cholera. The Biography of a Disease* (London: Hamish Hamilton, 1966), 89.

22. Ibid.

23. Edwin Chadwick, David Gladstone, and Samuel Edward Finer, *Edwin Chadwick: Nineteenth-century Social Reform* (London: Routledge, 1997), 342.

24. Times Online archive, August 23, 1855. http://archive.timesonline.co.uk/tol/archive/.

25. Ibid.

26. www.experiencefestival.com/a/Cholera—Pathology/id/1287591.

27. www.kcom.edu/faculty/chamberlain/website/lectures/tritzid/INFGAS.htm.

28. Richard A. Finkelstein, "General Concepts, Cholera and *Vibrio cholerae.*" gsbs.utmb.edu/microbook/ch024.htm.

29. Dartmouth Electron Microscope Facility, Dartmouth College. Scanning electron microscope image of *Vibrio cholerae* bacteria, which infect the digestive system. Zeiss DSM 962 SEM; T.J. Kirn, M.J. Lafferty, C.M.P. Sandoe and R.K. Taylor, "Delineation of pilin domains required for bacterial association into microcolonies and intestinal colonization," *Molecular Microbiology,* 35.4 (2000): 896–910; Ronald Taylor, Tom Kirn, and Louisa Howard (Wikimedia Commons).

30. www.mrc-lmb.cam.ac.uk/genomes/madanm/articles/cholera.htm.

31. www.kcom.edu/faculty/chamberlain/website/lectures/tritzid/INFGAS.htm.

32. http://en.wikipedia.org/wiki/Enterotoxin.

33. Richard A. Finkelstein, General Concepts, "Cholera and *Vibrio cholerae.*" gsbs.utmb.edu/microbook/ch024.htm.

34. Matthew K. Waldor and John J. Mekalanos, "Lysogenic Conversion by a Filamentous Phage Encoding Cholera Toxin," *Science,* 272.5270 (June 28, 1996): 1,910–1,914. http://www.sciencemag.org/cgi/content/abstract/sci;272/5270/1910?maxtoshow=&HITS=10&hits=10&RESULTFORMAT=&fulltext=cholera&searchid=1&FIRSTINDEX=0&resourcetype=HWCIT.

35. www.mrc-lmb.cam.ac.uk/genomes/madanm/articles/cholera.htm.

36. Michael L. Bennish, "Cholera: Pathophysiology, Clinical Features and Treatment," in I. Kaye Wachsmuth, Paul A. Blake, and Ørjan Olsvik, eds., Vibrio cholerae *and Cholera. Molecular to Global Perspectives* (Washington, D.C.: American Society for Microbiology, 1994), 231.

37. Michael L. Bennish, "Cholera: Pathophysiology, Clinical Features and Treatment," in I. Kaye Wachsmuth, Paul A. Blake, and Ørjan Olsvik, eds., Vibrio cholerae *and Cholera. Molecular to Global Perspectives* (Washington, D.C.: American Society for Microbiology, 1994), 235.

38. Kenneth Todar, www.textbookofbacteriology.net (University of Wisconsin-Madison Department of Bacteriology, 2005).

39. Michael L. Bennish, "Cholera: Pathophysiology, Clinical Features and Treatment," in I. Kaye Wachsmuth, Paul A. Blake, and Ørjan Olsvik, eds., Vibrio cholerae *and Cholera. Molecular to Global Perspectives* (Washington, D.C.: American Society for Microbiology, 1994), 231.

40. www.mrc-lmb.cam.ac.uk/genomes/madanm/articles/cholera.htm.

41. Michael L. Bennish, "Cholera: Pathophysiology, Clinical Features and Treatment," in I. Kaye Wachsmuth, Paul A. Blake, and Ørjan Olsvik, eds., Vibrio cholerae *and Cholera. Molecular to Global Perspectives* (Washington, D.C.: American Society for Microbiology, 1994), 237.

42. http://en.wikipedia.org/wiki/Interstitial_fluid.

43. J.N. Hays, *Epidemics and Pandemics: Their Impacts on Human History* (Santa Barbara, CA: ABC-CLIO, 2005), 193.

44. Mary Dobson, *The Extraordinary Stories behind History's Deadliest Killers* (London: Quercus, 2007), 44–45.

45. Rita R. Colwell and Anwarul Hug, "Vibrios in the Environment: Viable but Nonculturable *Vibrio cholerae*," in I. Kaye Wachsmuth, Paul A. Blake, and Ørjan Olsvik, eds., Vibrio cholerae *and Cholera. Molecular to Global Perspectives* (Washington, D.C.: American Society for Microbiology, 1994), 120 and 124, citing Rita R. Colwell, P.A. West, D. Maneval, E.F. Remmers, E.L. Elliot, and N.E. Carlson, "Ecology of Pathogenic Vibrios in Chesapeake Bay," 367–387, in Rita R. Colwell, ed., *Vibrios in the Environment* (New York: John Wiley and Sons, 1984), 367–387.

46. I. Kaye Wachsmuth, Paul A. Blake, and Ørjan Olsvik, eds., Vibrio cholerae *and Cholera. Molecular to Global Perspectives* (Washington, D.C.: American Society for Microbiology, 1994); Rita R. Colwell and Anwarul Huq, *Vibrios in the Environment* (New York: John Wiley and Sons, 1984), 121.

47. I. Kaye Wachsmuth, Paul A. Blake, and Ørjan Olsvik, eds., Vibrio cholerae *and Cholera. Molecular to Global Perspectives* (Washington, D.C.: American Society for Microbiology, 1994); Rita R. Colwell and Anwarul Huq, *Vibrios in the Environment* (New York: John Wiley and Sons, 1984), 120, citing Anwarul Huq, R.R. Colwell, R. Rahman, A. Ali, M.A.R. Chowdhury, S. Parveen, D.A. Sack, and R. Russek-Cohen, "Detection of Vibrio cholerae in the Aquatic Environment by Fluorescent-monoclonal Antibody and Culture Methods," *Applied Environmental Microbiology*, 56 (1990): 2370–2373.

48. I. Kaye Wachsmuth, Paul A. Blake, and Ørjan Olsvik, eds., Vibrio cholerae *and Cholera. Molecular to Global Perspectives* (Washington, D.C.: American Society for Microbiology, 1994); Rita R. Colwell and Anwarul Huq, *Vibrios in the Environment* (New York: John Wiley and Sons, 1984), 3, citing P. Baumann, A.L. Furniss, and J.V. Lee, "Genus I. Vibrio Pacini 1854, 411AL," 518–538, in N.R. Krieg and J.G. Jolt, eds., *Bergey's Manual of Systematic Bacteriology* (Baltimore: Williams and Wilkins, 1984), vol.1, 518–538; and P. Baumann, and R.H.W Schubert, "Family II; Vibrionaceae Veron 1965, 5245AL," in Krieg and Jolt, eds., vol. 1, 516–517.

49. David A. Sack, R. Bradley Sack, G. Balakrish Nair, A. K. Siddique, "Cholera," *The Lancet*, vol. 363 (January 17, 2004). http://www.ph.ucla.edu/epi/snow/lancet363_223_233_2004.pdf.

50. I. Kaye Wachsmuth, Paul A. Blake, and Ørjan Olsvik, eds., Vibrio cholerae *and Cholera. Molecular to Global Perspectives* (Washington,

D.C.: American Society for Microbiology, 1994); Rita R. Colwell and Anwarul Huq, *Vibrios in the Environment* (New York: John Wiley and Sons, 1984), 119.

51. I. Kaye Wachsmuth, Paul A. Blake, and Ørjan Olsvik (edited by), Vibrio cholerae *and Cholera. Molecular to Global Perspectives* (Washington, D.C.: American Society for Microbiology, 1994); Rita R. Colwell and Anwarul Huq, *Vibrios in the Environment* (New York: John Wiley and Sons, 1984), 120.

52 I. Kaye Wachsmuth, Paul A. Blake, and Ørjan Olsvik, eds., Vibrio cholerae *and Cholera. Molecular to Global Perspectives* (Washington, D.C.: American Society for Microbiology, 1994); Rita R. Colwell and Anwarul Huq, *Vibrios in the Environment* (New York: John Wiley and Sons, 1984), 119.

53. I. Kaye Wachsmuth, Paul A. Blake, and Ørjan Olsvik, eds., Vibrio cholerae *and Cholera. Molecular to Global Perspectives* (Washington, D.C.: American Society for Microbiology, 1994); Rita R. Colwell and Anwarul Huq, *Vibrios in the Environment* (New York: John Wiley and Sons, 1984), 119, citing R.V. Citarella, and R.R. Colwell, "Polyphasic taxonomy of the genus Vibrio: polynucleotide sequence relationships among selected Vibrio species," *Journal of Bacteriology*, 104 (October 1970):434–442.

54. Edmund A. Parkes, M.D., Assistant Physician to University College Hospital, *An Inquiry into the bearing of the Earliest Cases of Cholera, which occurred in London During the Present Epidemic, On the Strict Theory of Contagion*, Part Third, Original Reports (London: Printed by C. & J. Adlard, 1849), 273.

55. I. Kaye Wachsmuth, Paul A. Blake, and Ørjan Olsvik, eds., Vibrio cholerae *and Cholera. Molecular to Global Perspectives* (Washington, D.C.: American Society for Microbiology, 1994); Rita R. Colwell and Anwarul Huq, *Vibrios in the Environment* (New York: John Wiley and Sons, 1984), 125, citing M.L. Tamplin, and R.R. Colwell, "Effects of the microcosm salinity and organic substrate concentration on production of Vibrio cholerae enterotoxin," *Applied Environmental Microbiology*, 52 (1986): 297–301.

56. I. Kaye Wachsmuth, Paul A. Blake, and Ørjan Olsvik, eds., Vibrio cholerae *and Cholera. Molecular to Global Perspectives* (Washington, D.C.: American Society for Microbiology, 1994); Rita R. Colwell and Anwarul Huq, *Vibrios in the Environment* (New York: John Wiley and Sons, 1984), 125, citing C.J. Miller, B.S. Drasar, R.G. Feacham, and R.J. Hayes, "The impact of physicochemical stress on the toxigenicity of Vibrio cholerae," *Journal of Hygiene* 93 (1986):475–495.

57. I. Kaye Wachsmuth, Paul A. Blake, and Ørjan Olsvik, eds., Vibrio cholerae *and Cholera. Molecular to Global Perspectives* (Washington, D.C.: American Society for Microbiology, 1994);

Rita R. Colwell and Anwarul Huq, *Vibrios in the Environment* (New York: John Wiley and Sons, 1984), 125, citing M.S. Islam, "Seasonality and toxigenicity of *Vibrio cholerae* non–01 during survival with a green algae, *Rhizoclonium fontanum*," *Journal of Tropical Medicine and Hygiene*, 92 (1992): 396–401.

58. M.S. Islam, "Increased toxin production by Vibrio cholerae O1 during survival with a green alga, Rhizoclonium fontanum, in an artificial aquatic environment," Department of Tropical Hygiene, London School of Hygiene and Tropical Medicine. Available online at www.pubmed. gov, a service of the U.S. National Library of Medicine and the National Institutes of Health. http://www.ncbi.nlm.nih.gov/pubmed/2266879?dopt=Abstract.

59. Times Online archive, August 23, 1855. http://archive.timesonline.co.uk/tol/archive/.

60. Tim Stephens, UC Santa Cruz, http://www.sciencedaily.com/releases/2000/02/000 227142140.htm, adapted from materials provided by San Francisco State University.

61. David A. Sack, R. Bradley Sack, G. Balakrish Nair, A. K. Siddique, "Cholera," *The Lancet*, vol. 363 (January 17, 2004): 228. http://www.ph.ucla.edu/epi/snow/lancet363_223_233_2004.pdf.

62. Ibid.

63. Ibid., 228–229.

64. K. Eric Wommack, and Rita R. Colwell, "Virioplankton: Viruses in Aquatic Ecosystems," *American Society for Microbiology, Microbiology and Molecular Biology Reviews*, 64.1 (2000): 69–114.

65. World Health Organization, "Guidelines for Drinking-water Quality. Second Edition. Addendum Microbiological agents in drinking water" (2002): 131.

66. William Farr, *Report on the Mortality of Cholera in England 1848–49* (London: W. Clowes and Sons, 1852), lix.

67. Ibid.

68. Charles Dickens, *Our Mutual Friend* (Ware, Hertfordshire: Wordsworth Editions, 1998), 3–4.

69. J.W. Parker, *The Saturday Magazine* (Oxford: Oxford University, 1837).

70. http://www.victorianlondon.org.

71. I. Kaye Wachsmuth, Paul A. Blake, and Ørjan Olsvik, eds., Vibrio cholerae *and Cholera. Molecular to Global Perspectives* (Washington, D.C.: American Society for Microbiology, 1994); Rita R. Colwell and Anwarul Huq, *Vibrios in the Environment* (New York: John Wiley and Sons, 1984), 124.

72. I. Kaye Wachsmuth, Paul A. Blake, and Ørjan Olsvik, eds., Vibrio cholerae *and Cholera. Molecular to Global Perspectives* (Washington, D.C.: American Society for Microbiology, 1994); Rita R. Colwell and Anwarul Huq, *Vibrios in the Environment:* (New York: John Wiley and Sons,

1984), 121, citing M.L. Tamplin, A.L. Gauzens, A. Huq, D.A. Sack, and R.R. Colwell, "Attachment of *V. cholerae* serogroup 01 to zooplankton and phytoplankton of Bangladesh waters," *Applied Environmental Microbiology* 56 (1990): 1977–1980.

73. I. Kaye Wachsmuth, Paul A. Blake, and Ørjan Olsvik, eds., Vibrio cholerae *and Cholera. Molecular to Global Perspectives* (Washington, D.C.: American Society for Microbiology, 1994); Rita R. Colwell and Anwarul Huq, *Vibrios in the Environment* (New York: John Wiley and Sons, 1984), 121, citing R.R. Colwell, P.R. Brayton, D.J. Grimes, D.R. Roszak, S.A. Huq, and L.M. Palmer, "Viable but non-culturable Vibrio cholerae and related pathogens in the environment: implication for release of genetically engineered microorganisms," *Bio/Technology* 3 (1985) 817–820.

74. Ibid.

75. Ibid.

76. World Health Organization, "Guidelines for Drinking-water Quality. Second Edition. Addendum Microbiological agents in drinking water (2002): 131.

77. C.B. Munn, *Marine Microbiology, Ecology and Applications* (London and New York: Garland Science/BIOS Scientific Publishers, 2004).

78. I. Kaye Wachsmuth, Paul A. Blake, and Ørjan Olsvik, eds., Vibrio cholerae *and Cholera. Molecular to Global Perspectives* (Washington, D.C.: American Society for Microbiology, 1994); Eric D. Mintz, Tanja Popovic, and Paul A. Blake, "Transmission of Vibrio cholerae 01," in Wachsmuth, Blake and Olsvik, eds., 349.

79. Saul Roseman (2003), 5, in Karin L. Meibom, Xibing B. Li, Alex T. Nielsen, Cheng-Yen Wu, Saul Roseman, and Gary K. Schoolnik, "The Vibrio cholerae chitin utilization program" (Stanford: Department of Medicine, Division of Infectious Diseases and Geographic Medicine, and Department of Microbiology and Immunology, Stanford University School of Medicine, 2004, and Baltimore: Department of Biology and McCollum-Pratt Institute, Johns Hopkins University, 2004). http://www.pnas.org/content/101/8/25 24.full.pdf.

80. D.R. Nalin, V. Daya, A. Reid, M.M. Levine, and L. Cisneros, "Adsorption and Growth of Vibrio cholerae on Chitin" (Baltimore: Center for Vaccine Development, Division of Infectious Diseases, Department of Medicine, University of Maryland School of Medicine, 1979).

81. I. Kaye Wachsmuth, Paul A. Blake, and Ørjan Olsvik, eds., Vibrio cholerae *and Cholera. Molecular to Global Perspectives* (Washington, D.C.: American Society for Microbiology, 1994); Eric D. Mintz, Tanja Popovic, and Paul A. Blake, "Transmission of Vibrio cholerae 01," in Wachsmuth, Blake and Olsvik, eds., 349.

82. I. Kaye Wachsmuth, Paul A. Blake, and Ørjan Olsvik, eds., Vibrio cholerae *and Cholera.*

Molecular to Global Perspectives (Washington, D.C.: American Society for Microbiology, 1994); Rita R. Colwell and Anwarul Huq, *Vibrios in the Environment:* (New York: John Wiley and Sons, 1984), 126–130.

83. Edmund A. Parkes, M.D., Assistant Physician to University College Hospital, *An Inquiry into the bearing of the Earliest Cases of Cholera, which occurred in London During the Present Epidemic, On the Strict Theory of Contagion,* Part Third, Original Reports (London: C. & J. Adlard, 1849), 272–273.

84. http://www.who.int/topics/cholera/control/en/index.html.

85. www.mrc-lmb.cam.ac.uk/genomes/madanm/articles/cholera.htm.

86. "Surgeons' report book, including cases of puerperal fever, 1824, cholera, 1825, typhoid, 1826, consumption, 1826, and smallpox, against which several children were vaccinated, only to have it in a worse form." 1823 to 1826. 1 small volume. Medway Archives and Local Studies Centre, Kent.

87. Archibald Billing, M.D., A.M., F.R.S., "On The Treatment of Asiatic Cholera," 2d ed., revised (London: S. Highley, 1848), from William Baly, *Reports on Epidemic Cholera: Drawn up at the desire of the Cholera Committee of the Royal College of Physicians*, Cholera Committee, Royal College of Physicians (London: J. Churchill, 1854), Ref. SLTr80.

88. Ibid.

89. E. Manby, surgeon, *Dissertation, with Practical Remarks, on Cholera Morbus,* (London: Burgess and Hill, 1831), from William Baly, *Reports on Epidemic Cholera: Drawn up at the desire of the Cholera Committee of the Royal College of Physicians*, Cholera Committee, Royal College of Physicians (London: J. Churchill, 1854), Ref. SLTr80.

90. Ibid.

91. "Cholera and choleraic diarrhoea casebook of St. Thomas's Hospital, 1853–1854," Sub-fonds of St. Thomas's Hospital Medical School, 1 volume, ref. GB 0100 TH/CLR 2, King's College London College Archives.

92. "Cholera and Choleraic Diarrhoea Casebook of St. Thomas's Hospital, 1853–1854"; "Casebook of St. Thomas's Hospital, 1854," recording details of 149 cases of cholera and choleraic diarrhoea admitted to the Hospital, by an unidentified compiler. Archives and Corporate Records Services, Information Services and Systems, King's College London.

93. Times Online archive, September 11, 1849. http://archive.timesonline.co.uk/tol/archive/.

94. Ibid., September 12, 1849.

95. Ibid, September 24, 1849.

96. Ibid., September 19, 1849.

97. John Parkin, M.D., and William H. Allen, *Statistical Report of the Epidemic Cholera in Jamaica* (London, 1852); from William Baly, *Reports on Epidemic Cholera: Drawn up at the desire of the Cholera Committee of the Royal College of Physicians,* Cholera Committee, Royal College of Physicians (London: J. Churchill, 1854), Ref. SLTr80.

98. http://archives.ucl.ac.uk.

99. Edwin Chadwick, *Report on The Sanitary Condition of the Labouring Population of Great Britain,* edited with an introduction by M.W. Flinn (1842; Edinburgh: Edinburgh University Press, 1965), 31, citing David Roberts, *Victorian Origins of the British Welfare State* (New Haven: Yale University Press, 1960).

100. Edwin Chadwick, *Report on The Sanitary Condition of the Labouring Population of Great Britain,* edited with an introduction by M.W. Flinn, first published 1842 (Edinburgh: Edinburgh University Press, 1965), 1.

101. Ibid., 30.

102. http://archives.ucl.ac.uk.

103. Edwin Chadwick, *Report on The Sanitary Condition of the Labouring Population of Great Britain,* edited with an introduction by M.W. Flinn (1842; Edinburgh: Edinburgh University Press, 1965), 16.

104. Druin Burch, *Digging up the Dead, Uncovering the Life and Times of an Extraordinary Surgeon* (London: Vintage, 2007), 88–89.

105. Ibid., p.89.

106. en.wikipedia.org/wiki/Scottish_Enlightenment and www.scotland.org/about/innovation-and-creativity/features/culture/alliance.html.

107. Druin Burch, *Digging up the Dead, Uncovering the Life and Times of an Extraordinary Surgeon* (London: Vintage, 2007), 38.

108. Edwin Chadwick, *Report on The Sanitary Condition of the Labouring Population of Great Britain,* edited with an introduction by M.W. Flinn (1842; Edinburgh: Edinburgh University Press, 1965), 22, citing David Roberts, *Victorian Origins of the British Welfare State* (New Haven: Yale University Press, 1960).

109. en.wikipedia.org.

110. Edwin Chadwick, *Report on The Sanitary Condition of the Labouring Population of Great Britain,* edited with an introduction by M.W. Flinn (1842; Edinburgh: Edinburgh University Press, 1965), 22.

111. Ibid., 23, 63–64.

112. Druin Burch, *Digging up the Dead, Uncovering the Life and Times of an Extraordinary Surgeon* (London: Vintage, 2007), 94.

113. Ibid., 224.

114. Edwin Chadwick, *Report on The Sanitary Condition of the Labouring Population of Great Britain,* edited with an introduction by M.W. Flinn (1842; Edinburgh: Edinburgh University Press, 1965), 32.

115. Ibid., 17.

116. Ibid, 32, 44.

117. Ibid., 26.

118. Ibid., 33.

119. www.bbc.co.uk/whodoyouthinkyouare/past-stories/jeremy-paxman.shtml.

120. Edwin Chadwick, *Report on The Sanitary Condition of the Labouring Population of Great Britain,* edited with an introduction by M.W. Flinn (1842; Edinburgh: Edinburgh University Press, 1965), 33.

121. Ibid., 34.

122. Ibid., 34–35.

123. Ibid., 16

124. Ibid., 45.

125. Ibid., 37.

126. Ibid., 39.

127. Gatze Lettinga and Grietje Zeeman, *Decentralised Sanitation and Reuse: Concepts, Systems and Implementation* (London: IWA, 2001), 18.

128. Edwin Chadwick, *Report on The Sanitary Condition of the Labouring Population of Great Britain,* edited with an introduction by M.W. Flinn (1842; Edinburgh: Edinburgh University Press, 1965), 46.

129. Ibid., 47–52.

130. Ibid., 55.

131. Gatze Lettinga and Grietje Zeeman, *Decentralised Sanitation and Reuse: Concepts, Systems and Implementation* (London: IWA, 2001), 18.

132. Edwin Chadwick, *Report on The Sanitary Condition of the Labouring Population of Great Britain,* edited with an introduction by M.W. Flinn (1842; Edinburgh: Edinburgh University Press, 1965), 57.

133. Gatze Lettinga and Grietje Zeeman, *Decentralised Sanitation and Reuse: Concepts, Systems and Implementation* (London: IWA, 2001), 18.

134. Edwin Chadwick, *Report on The Sanitary Condition of the Labouring Population of Great Britain,* edited with an introduction by M.W. Flinn (1842; Edinburgh: Edinburgh University Press, 1965), 60.

135. Ibid.

136. Ibid.

137. Ibid, 61.

138. Ibid.

139. Ibid., 67–68.

140. Henry Hurrell Clay, *Clay's Handbook of Environmental Health: Theory, Methods and Measuring Instrumentation,* ed. W.H. Bassett (Philadelphia: Taylor & Francis, 1992), 8.

141. Edwin Chadwick, *Report on The Sanitary Condition of the Labouring Population of Great Britain,* edited with an introduction by M.W. Flinn (1842; Edinburgh: Edinburgh University Press, 1965), 69.

142. Ibid., 68.

143. Ibid., 70.

144. Stephen Halliday, *The Great Stink of London. Sir Joseph Bazalgette and the Cleansing of the Victorian Metropolis* (Stroud, Gloucestershire: Sutton, 2007), 49–50.

145. Henry Hurrell Clay, *Clay's Handbook of Environmental Health: Theory, Methods and Measuring Instrumentation,* ed. W.H. Bassett (Philadelphia: Taylor & Francis, 1992), p. 8.

146. Great Britain Metropolitan Sanitary Commission, *[First—Third]: Report of the Commissioners appointed to inquire whether any and what special means may be requisite for the improvement of the health of the metropolis* (London: W. Clowes and Sons, for Her Majesty's Stationery Office, 1848), item notes: v. 1–3, vi–xiv.

147. Ibid., item notes: v. 1–3, 262.

148 Anthony S. Wohl, *The Eternal Slum: Housing and Social Policy in Victorian London* (London: Transaction, 2002); Edwin Chadwick, David Gladstone, and Samuel Edward Finer, *Edwin Chadwick: Nineteenth-century Social Reform* (London: Routledge, 1997), 355.

149. Edwin Chadwick, David Gladstone, and Samuel Edward Finer, *Edwin Chadwick: Nineteenth-century Social Reform* (London: Routledge, 1997), 355.

150. uk.encarta.msn.com.

151. Edwin Chadwick, *Report on The Sanitary Condition of the Labouring Population of Great Britain,* edited with an introduction by M.W. Flinn (1842; Edinburgh: Edinburgh University Press, 1965), 70–71.

152. Edwin Chadwick, David Gladstone, and Samuel Edward Finer, *Edwin Chadwick: Nineteenth-century Social Reform* (London: Routledge, 1997), 330.

153. *Lambeth Parish and Vestry Committee Minutes* (Ref.: P3), *Lambeth District Sanitary Reports* (Ref: P3, 73–75, 1848–1878); Lambeth Archives.

154. Times Online archive, October 23, 1852. http://archive.timesonline.co.uk/tol/archive/.

155. Great Britain Metropolitan Sanitary Commission, *[First—Third]: Report of the Commissioners appointed to inquire whether any and what special means may be requisite for the improvement of the health of the metropolis* (London: W. Clowes and Sons, for Her Majesty's Stationery Office, 1848), item notes: v. 1–3, 272.

156. Edwin Chadwick, David Gladstone, and Samuel Edward Finer, *Edwin Chadwick: Nineteenth-century Social Reform* (London: Routledge, 1997), 335.

157. Ibid., 337.

158. Ibid.

159. Edwin Chadwick, *Report on The Sanitary Condition of the Labouring Population of Great Britain,* edited with an introduction by M.W. Flinn (1842; Edinburgh: Edinburgh University Press, 1965), 72–73; http://www.schoolshistory.org.uk/publichealth/publichealthact1848.htm; http://www.historyhome.co.uk/peel/p-health/phact.htm; http://en.wikipedia.org/wiki/Local_board_of_health.

160. Edwin Chadwick, *Report on The Sanitary*

Condition of the Labouring Population of Great Britain, edited with an introduction by M.W. Flinn (1842; Edinburgh: Edinburgh University Press, 1965), 73.

161. Anthiny S. Wohl, *The Eternal Slum: Housing and Social Policy in Victorian London* (London: Transaction, 2002), 18.

Chapter 3

1. Colin G. Pooley, and Jean Turnbull, *Migration and Mobility in Britain Since the 18th Century* (London: Routledge, 1998).

2. *Survey of London: Volume 23: Lambeth: South Bank and Vauxhall,* edited by Sir Howard Roberts and Walter H. Godfrey (1951), Chapter 16, "The County Hall," 62–65. http://www.british-history.ac.uk/report.aspx?compid=47045.

3. http://www.victorianlondon.org, Lee Jackson's Victorian Dictionary.

4. http://www.british-history.ac.uk/report.aspx?compid=47049, British History Online.

5. Jane Sidell, Jonathan Cotton, Louise Rayner, and Lucy Wheeler, *The Prehistory and Topography of Southwark and Lambeth* (London: Museum of London Archaeology Service, 2002), monograph 14.

6. Ordnance Survey, *Historical Map and Guide, Roman Britain,* 5th ed. (Southampton: Ordnance Survey, 2001).

7. Geoffrey Chaucer, *The Canterbury Tales* (Middlesex, England: Penguin, 1975), 19–20.

8. *A History of the County of Surrey: Volume 4,* ed. H.E. Malden (1912), "Lambeth: The parish," 50–64. http://www.british-history.ac.uk/report.aspx?compid=43031.

9. Charles Dickens, *David Copperfield* (Ware: Wordsworth, 2000).

10. David Mountfield, *Stage and Mail Coaches* (Princes Risborough, Buckinghamshire: Shire, 2003), 4.

11. en.wikipedia.org/wiki/Turnpike_Trusts.

12. *Survey of London: Volume 26: Lambeth: Southern area,* gen. ed. F. H. W. Sheppard (1956), General Introduction, 1–17. http://www.british-history.ac.uk/report.aspx?compid=49753.

13. David Mountfield, *Stage and Mail Coaches* (Princes Risborough, Buckinghamshire: Shire, 2003), 9–10.

14. *Survey of London: Volume 26: Lambeth: Southern area,* gen. ed. F. H. W. Sheppard (1956), General Introduction, 1–17. http://www.british-history.ac.uk/report.aspx?compid=49753.

15 http://www.victorianlondon.org, Lee Jackson's Victorian Dictionary.

16. David Mountfield, *Stage and Mail Coaches* (Princes Risborough, Buckinghamshire: Shire, 2003), 4.

17. Ibid.

18. en.wikipedia.org/wiki/Thames_and_Medway_Canal.

19. J.G. Wright, *Wright's Topography of Rochester, Chatham, Strood, Brompton etc. and Directory of the Clergy, Gentry, Tradesmen etc.* (1838). Medway Archives and Local Studies Centre, Strood, Kent.

20. David Feldman, "History in Focus; The Boundaries of Welfare," Birkbeck College, University of London. www.history.ac.uk/ihr/Focus/Migration/articles/feldman.html.

21. Colin G. Pooley, and Jean Turnbull, *Migration and Mobility in Britain Since the 18th Century* (London: Routledge, 1998).

22. Ibid.

23. Ibid.

24. www.visionofbritain.org.uk/data.

25. Ancestry.co.uk.

26. Kieron Tyler, Ian Betts, and Roy Stephenson, *London's Delftware Industry. The tin-glazed pottery industries of Southwark and Lambeth* (London: Museum of London Archaeology Service, 2008), Monograph 40.

27. Hannah Renier, *Lambeth Past, Kennington, Vauxhall, Waterloo* (London: Historical, 2006).

28. *www.dorsetlife.co.uk.*

29. *Ancestry.co.uk.*

30. http://www.bookrags.com/wiki/London_and_South_Western_Railway.

31. www.gosport.info.

32. http://freespace.virgin.net/roger.hewitt/iwias/history.htm.

33. R.H. Clark, *A Southern Region, Chronology and Record, 1803–1965* (Tanglewood, Surrey: Oakwood Press, 1964).

34. Cormac O'Grada, *Ireland's Great Famine* (Dublin: University College Dublin Press, 2006).

35. Ibid.

36. David B. Grigg, *Population Growth and Agrarian Change: An Historical Perspective* (CUP Archive, 1980).

37. *Lambeth Parish and Vestry Committee Minutes* (Ref.: P3), *Lambeth District Sanitary Reports* (Ref: P3, 73–75, 1848–1878); Lambeth Archives.

38. Edwin Chadwick, *Report on The Sanitary Condition of the Labouring Population of Great Britain,* edited with an introduction by M.W. Flinn (1842; Edinburgh: Edinburgh University Press, 1965), 15.

39. Ibid.; and *Report of the Poor Inquiry (Ireland) Commission, App. G,* "Report of the State of the Irish Poor in Great Britain," P.P. 1836, XXXIV, pp. 6, xi.

Chapter 4

1. www.compulink.co.uk/~museumgh/local%20history, The Museum of Garden History, Lambeth.

2. *Lambeth Parish and Vestry Committee Minutes* (Ref.: P3), *Lambeth District Sanitary Reports* (Ref: P3, 73–75, 1848–1878); Lambeth Archives.

3. www.visionofbritain.org.uk/data.

4. *A History of the County of Surrey: Volume 4*, ed., H.E. Malden (1912), "Lambeth: The parish," 50–64. http://www.british-history.ac.uk/report. aspx?compid=43031.

5. Henry Mayhew and John Binny, *The Criminal Prisons of London and Scenes of Prison Life* (1862; London: Frank Cass, 1968).

6. www.compulink.co.uk/~museumgh/ index.htm, The Museum of Garden History, Lambeth.

7. Hannah Renier, *Lambeth Past, Kennington, Vauxhall, Waterloo* (London: Historical Publications, 2006).

8. *A History of the County of Surrey: Volume 4*, ed. H.E. Malden (1912), "Lambeth: The parish," 50–64. http://www.british-history.ac.uk/report. aspx?compid=43031.

9. Hannah Renier, *Lambeth Past, Kennington, Vauxhall, Waterloo* (London: Historical Publications, 2006).

10. Ibid.

11. *A History of the County of Surrey: Volume 4*, ed. H.E. Malden (1912), "Lambeth: The parish," 50–64. http://www.british-history.ac.uk/report. aspx?compid=43031.

12. Hannah Renier, *Lambeth Past, Kennington, Vauxhall, Waterloo* (London: Historical Publications, 2006).

13. www.compulink.co.uk/~museumgh/index. htm, The Museum of Garden History, Lambeth.

14. *Survey of London: Volume 26: Lambeth: Southern area*, gen. ed. F. H. W. Sheppard, (1956), General Introduction, 1–17. http://www.british-history.ac.uk/report.aspx?compid=49753.

15. London Metropolitan Archives B/NTG/ 1499–1515.

16. *Survey of London: Volume 26: Lambeth: Southern area*, gen. ed. F. H. W. Sheppard, (1956), General Introduction, 1–17. http://www.british-history.ac.uk/report.aspx?compid=49753.

17. Hannah Renier, *Lambeth Past, Kennington, Vauxhall, Waterloo* (London: Historical Publications, 2006).

18. London Metropolitan Archives; Ref. B/ NTG.

19. *Survey of London: Volume 23: Lambeth: South Bank and Vauxhall*, eds. Sir Howard Roberts and Walter H. Godfrey (1951), Chapter 34, "The Albert Embankment," 148–149. http://www. british-history.ac.uk/report.aspx?compid=47063.

20. Hannah Renier, *Lambeth Past, Kennington, Vauxhall, Waterloo* (London: Historical Publications, 2006).

21. Thomas Allen, *The History and Antiquities of the Parish of Lambeth, and the Archiepiscopal Palace: Including Biographical Sketches* (London: J. Allen, 1826).

22. Hannah Renier, *Lambeth Past, Kennington, Vauxhall, Waterloo* (London: Historical Publications, 2006).

23. Ibid.

24. *Survey of London: Volume 23: Lambeth: South Bank and Vauxhall*, eds. Sir Howard Roberts and Walter H. Godfrey (1951), Chapter 34, "The Albert Embankment," 148–149. http://www. british-history.ac.uk/report.aspx?compid=47063.

25. www.geocities.com/rbeaufoy/hbhb.html.

26. www.nationaltheatre.org.uk/.

27. www.archbishopofcanterbury.org/.

28. http://www.icons.org.uk/.

29. Lambeth Landmark imagebase, Ref. 762, Lambeth Archives.

30. Thomas Allen, *A History of the County of Surrey; Comprising Every Object of Topographical, Geological, or Historical Interest; Vol. I.* (London: Hinton, 1831).

31. John Richardson, *The Annals of London. A Year-by-Year Record of a Thousand Years of History* (London: Cassell, 2001).

32. Hannah Renier, *Lambeth Past, Kennington, Vauxhall, Waterloo* (London: Historical Publications, 2006).

33. http://www.neo-tech.com.

34. www.compulink.co.uk/~museumgh/ local%20history, Museum of Garden History, Lambeth.

35. Thomas Allen, *A History of the County of Surrey; Comprising Every Object of Topographical, Geological, or Historical Interest; Vol. I* (London: Hinton, 1831).

36. Hannah Renier, *Lambeth Past, Kennington, Vauxhall, Waterloo* (London: Historical Publications, 2006).

37. www.compulink.co.uk/~museumgh/local %20history, Museum of Garden History, Lambeth.

38. Ibid.

39. Hannah Renier, *Lambeth Past, Kennington, Vauxhall, Waterloo* (London: Historical Publications, 2006).

40. www.clayheritage.org/, The Ball Clay Heritage Society.

41. www.dorsetlife.co.uk.

42. *Survey of London: Volume 23: Lambeth: South Bank and Vauxhall*, eds. Sir Howard Roberts and Walter H. Godfrey (1951), Chapter 11, "No. 55 Belvedere Road," 50. http://www.british-history. ac.uk/report.aspx?compid=47040.

43. *Survey of London: Volume 23: Lambeth: South Bank and Vauxhall*, eds. Sir Howard Roberts and Walter H. Godfrey (1951), Chapter 12, "The Lambeth Waterworks and Lion Brewery," 51–54. http://www.british-history.ac.uk/report.aspx?com pid=47041.

44. Hannah Renier, *Lambeth Past, Kennington, Vauxhall, Waterloo* (London: Historical Publications, 2006).

45. Kieron Tyler, Ian Betts, and Roy Stephen-

son, *London's Delftware Industry. The tin-glazed pottery industries of Southwark and Lambeth* (London: Museum of London Archaeology Service, 2008), Monograph 40.

46. Centre for Kentish Studies, Maidstone, Ref.: CKS — P12/28/4. Details of a court case at Quarter Sessions in Maidstone between the Churchwardens and overseers of the poor in Aylesford and the lessees of claypits in the parish; 18th March 1775. Courtesy of Dr. Andrew Hann, English Heritage.

47. Centre for Kentish Studies, Maidstone, Ref.: U234/E21; Aylesford Atlas. Courtesy of Dr. Andrew Hann, English Heritage.

48. Kieron Tyler, Ian Betts, and Roy Stephenson, *London's Delftware Industry. The tin-glazed pottery industries of Southwark and Lambeth* (London: Museum of London Archaeology Service, 2008), Monograph 40.

49. woolvey.com/royal_doulton_history.php.

50. www.purewatergazette.net/doultonhistory.

51. Hannah Renier, *Lambeth Past, Kennington, Vauxhall, Waterloo* (London: Historical Publications, 2006).

52. www.dorsetlife.co.uk/.

53. Ibid.

54. www.purewatergazette.net/doultonhistory.

55. Lambeth Archives, Lambeth Landmark imagebase, ref. 7115.

56. Pigot and Company Directory of 1832–34; Medway Archives and Local Studies Centre, Strood, Kent.

57. www.compulink.co.uk/~museumgh/ocal%20history, The Museum of Garden History, Lambeth.

58. Hannah Renier, *Lambeth Past, Kennington, Vauxhall, Waterloo* (London: Historical Publications, 2006).

59. www.vauxhallsociety.org.uk/Doulton.

60. woolvey.com/royal_doulton_history.

61. Lambeth Archives; Lambeth Landmark imagebase refs.: 7348; 4757; and http://freepages.genealogy.rootsweb.ancestry.com/~dutillieul/ZOtherPapers/S&WJJan171825.html.

63. *The Post Office London Directory of* 1848, Lambeth Archives.

64. Hannah Renier, *Lambeth Past, Kennington, Vauxhall, Waterloo* (London: Historical Publications, 2006).

65. Lambeth Archives, Lambeth Landmark imagebase, ref. 2099.

66. Ibid., ref. 7474.

67. Ibid., ref. 8177.

68. Hannah Renier, *Lambeth Past, Kennington, Vauxhall, Waterloo* (London: Historical Publications, 2006).

69. *A History of the County of Surrey: Volume 4*, ed. H.E. Malden (1912), "Lambeth: The parish," 50–64. http://www.british-history.ac.uk/report.aspx?compid=43031.

70. Hannah Renier, *Lambeth Past, Kennington,*

Vauxhall, Waterloo (London: Historical Publications, 2006).

71. www.victorianlondon.org.

72. *Survey of London: Volume 26: Lambeth: Southern area*, gen. ed. F. H. W. Sheppard, (1956), General Introduction, 1–17. http://www.british-history.ac.uk/report.aspx?compid=49753.

73. *Survey of London: Volume 26: Lambeth: Southern area*, gen. ed. F. H. W. Sheppard, (1956), "Vauxhall and South Lambeth: Vauxhall Escheat," 73–80. http://www.british-history.ac.uk/report.aspx?compid=49762.

74. http://www.bookrags.com/wiki/London_and_South_Western_Railway.

75. Ibid.

76. http://freespace.virgin.net/roger.hewitt/iwias/history.htm.

77. www.gosport.info/History/Gosport_Railway_History/Gosport_Railway_History_Page_2.

78. Ibid.

79. www.compulink.co.uk/~museumgh/local%20history, The Museum of Garden History, Lambeth.

80. Ibid.

81. R.H. Clark, *A Southern Region, Chronology and Record, 1803–1965* (Yanglewood, Surrey: Oakwood Press, 1964).

82. www.compulink.co.uk/~museumgh/local%20history, The Museum of Garden History, Lambeth.

83. www.workhouses.org.uk.

84. Druin Burch, *Digging up the Dead, Uncovering the Life and Times of an Extraordinary Surgeon* (London: Vintage, 2007).

85. Hannah Renier, *Lambeth Past, Kennington, Vauxhall, Waterloo* (London: Historical Publications, 2006).

86. www.compulink.co.uk/~museumgh/local%20history, The Museum of Garden History.

87. http://www.victorianlondon.org, Lee Jackson's Victorian Dictionary.

88. www.geocities.com/rbeaufoy, taken from Gwendolyn Beaufoy, *Leaves from a Beech Tree* (Oxford: Printed for the author by B. Blackwell, 1930).

89. Lambeth Archives, Lambeth Landmark imagebase, ref. 4225.

90. www.victorianlondon.org/education/ragged schools.

91. *Survey of London: Volume 23: Lambeth: South Bank and Vauxhall*, ed. Sir Howard Roberts and Walter H. Godfrey (1951), Chapter 30, "Water Lambeth," 142–143. http://www.british-history.ac.uk/report.aspx?compid=47059.

92. www.buildingconservation.com/articles/terracotta/terracotta.

93. Catherine Edwards and Karl Hulka in "The Millbank Penitentiary: Excavations at the Chelsea School of Art and Design," *London Archaeologist*, Winter 2006.

94. Peter McRorie Higgins, M.Ch., Ph.D., F.R.C.S., "The Scurvy Scandal at Millbank Peni-

tentiary: A Reassessment," *Medical History*, 50.4 (2006): 513–34, Wellcome Institute for the History of Medicine, ISSN 00257273. http://www.pubmedcentral.nih.gov/articlerender.fcgi?artid=15 92637.

95. www.ph.ucla.edu/epi/snow/1859map/millbank prison a2.html.

96. Peter McRorie Higgins, M.Ch., Ph.D., F.R.C.S., "The Scurvy Scandal at Millbank Penitentiary: A Reassessment," *Medical History*, 50.4 (2006): 513–34, Wellcome Institute for the History of Medicine, ISSN 00257273. http://www.pubmedcentral.nih.gov/articlerender.fcgi?artid=15 92637.

97. J. David Hirschel, and William O. Wakefield, *Criminal Justice in England and the United States* (Westport, CT: Greenwood, 1995).

98. www.vauxhallsociety.org.uk/Millbank.

99. www.45millbank.com/history-of-45-millbank.

100. Michael Baker and the Baker Family Tree, "Strood's New Church in 1812: Which Mr Baker?" *The Clock Tower*, August 2008, Friends of Medway Archives and Local Studies Centre.

101. Catherine Edwards, and Karl Hulka in "The Millbank Penitentiary: Excavations at the Chelsea School of Art and Design," *London Archaeologist*, Winter 2006; Joseph Mordaunt Crook, "Sir Robert Smirke: A Pioneer of Concrete Construction," *Transactions of the Newcomen Society*, 38, 1968 for 1965–6, 5–22.

102. Michael Baker and the Baker Family Tree; "Strood's New Church in 1812: Which Mr Baker?" *The Clock Tower*, August 2008, Friends of Medway Archives and Local Studies Centre.

103. Henry Mayhew, and John Binney, *The Criminal Prisons of London and Scenes of Prison Life* (1862; London: Frank Cass, 1968).

104. Royal College of Physicians, London, Heritage Collections, Ref. 715/330.

105. Henry Mayhew and John Binney, *The Criminal Prisons of London and Scenes of Prison Life* (1862; London: Frank Cass, 1968), 199 and 209.

106. *hansard.millbanksystems.com/commons.*

107. Peter McRorie Higgins, M.Ch., Ph.D., F.R.C.S., "The Scurvy Scandal at Millbank Penitentiary: A Reassessment," *Medical History*, 50.4 (2006): 513–34, Wellcome Institute for the History of Medicine. http://www.pubmedcentral.nih.gov/articlerender.fcgi?artid=1592637.

108. Henry Mayhew, and John Binney, *The Criminal Prisons of London and Scenes of Prison Life* (1862; London: Frank Cass, 1968), 267.

109. Catherine Edwards, and Karl Hulka in "The Millbank Penitentiary: Excavations at the Chelsea School of Art and Design," *London Archaeologist*, Winter 2006.

110. Henry Mayhew and John Binney, *The Criminal Prisons of London and Scenes of Prison Life* (1862; London: Frank Cass, 1968), 261.

111. Charles Dickens, *David Copperfield* (Ware: Wordsworth, 2000), Chapter XLVII, 578.

112. William Farr, *Report on the Mortality of Cholera in England 1848–49* (London: W. Clowes and Sons, for Her Majesty's Stationery Office, 1852), 170–171.

113. Peter McRorie Higgins, MCh, Ph.D., FRCS, "The Scurvy Scandal at Millbank Penitentiary: A Reassessment," *Medical History* 50(4): 513–534. http://www.pubmedcentral.nih.gov/articlerender.fcgi?artid=1592637.

114. Peter McRorie Higgins, M.Ch., Ph.D., F.R.C.S., "The Scurvy Scandal at Millbank Penitentiary: A Reassessment," *Medical History*, 50:4 (2006), 513–34, Wellcome Institute for the History of Medicine. http://www.pubmedcentral.nih.gov/articlerender.fcgi?artid=1592637.

115. Ibid.

116. Ibid.

117. Royal College of Physicians, London; Heritage Collections, Ref. 716/15.

118. William Baly, M.D., F.R.S., Physician to Millbank Prison, "Report on the Cause and Mode of Diffusion of Epidemic Cholera." (London: Woodfall and Kinder, 1853). Royal College of Physicians, London, Heritage Collections.

119. freepages.genealogy.rootsweb.ancestry.com/~folkestonefamilies, contributed by Maureen Cate.

120. www.45millbank.com/history-of-45-millbank.

121. John Richardson, *The Annals of London. A Year-by-Year Record of a Thousand Years of History* (London: Cassell, 2001).

122. www.parliament.uk/parliament/guide/palace.

123. www.countyhalllondon.com/the-south-bank-london/local-attractions/174-the-palace-of-westminster.html.

124. City of Westminster Archives, Ref. F942.1341; RA/KA1004.

125. www.bbc.co.uk/history/trail/church_state/westminster_later/westminster_new_palace.

126. *The Gentleman's Magazine*, published by F. Jefferies (1835), Item notes: v.158.

127. hansard.millbanksystems.com.

128. *Contracts Relative to the New Houses of Parliament*, City of Westminster Archives F942.1341; RA/KA1004.

129. Ibid.

130. *Metropolitan Commission of Sewers, January 1849, Reports and Correspondence Respecting the Drainage of the New Palace at Westminster*, City of Westminster Archives, q942.1341, A (Ref) (West), [628.3], 3.

131. Ibid., 11.

132. Ibid., 19.

133. Ibid., 12 and 8.

134. Ibid., 2 -3.

135. Ibid., 8.

136. Ibid., 13.

137. Ibid., 23.

138. Great Britain Metropolitan Sanitary Commission, [*First—Third*]: *Report of the Commissioners appointed to inquire whether any and what special means may be requisite for the improvement of the health of the metropolis* (London: W. Clowes and Sons, for Her Majesty's Stationery Office, 1848), Item notes: v. 1–3, 263.

139. Thomas Allen, *A History of the County of Surrey; Comprising Every Object of Topographical, Geological, or Historical Interest, Vol. I* (London: Hinton, 1831).

140. *Survey of London: Volume 23: Lambeth: South Bank and Vauxhall*, eds. Sir Howard Roberts, and Walter H. Godfrey (1951), Chapter 12, "The Lambeth Waterworks and Lion Brewery," 51–54. http://www.british-history.ac.uk/report.aspx?compid=47041.

141. John Snow, M.D., *On the Mode of Communication of Cholera*, 2d ed. (Washington, D.C.: Delta Omega), 37. http://www.deltaomega.org.

142. Luke Hebert, *Comprehending Practical Illustrations of the Machinery and Processes Employed In Every Description of Manufacture of the British Empire; The Engineer's and Mechanic's Encyclopaedia, Vol. I* (London: Thomas Kelly, 1849).

143. John Snow, M.D., *On the Mode of Communication of Cholera*, 2d ed. (Washington, D.C.: Delta Omega), 41. http://www.deltaomega.org.

144. Henry Mayhew, *London Labour and the London Poor*, selections made and introduced by Victor Neuburg (1849; London: Penguin, 1985); and http://www.victorianlondon.org, The Victorian Dictionary.

145. Hannah Renier, *Lambeth Past, Kennington, Vauxhall, Waterloo* (London: Historical Publications, 2006).

Chapter 5

1. www.channel4.com/history/microsites/T/timeteam/vauxhall.

2. Jane Sidell, Jonathan Cotton, Louise Rayner, and Lucy Wheeler, *The Prehistory and Topography of Southwark and Lambeth* (London: Museum of London Archaeology Service, 2002).

3. Ibid.

4. Ibid.

5. M. Whitehead, "William Farr's legacy to the study of inequalities in Health," www.who.intbulletinarchives78(1)86.pdf.

6. William Farr, *Report on the Mortality of Cholera in England 1848–49* (London: W. Clowes and Sons for Her Majesty's Stationery Office, 1852), "The Thames and Water Supply," lviii, Wellcome Library, London.

7. Graham Gower and Kieron Taylor, *Lambeth Unearthed. An Archaeological History of Lambeth*, Museum of London Archaeology Service on behalf of the London Borough of Lambeth's Archive Department, 2003.

8. Great Britain Metropolitan Sanitary Commission, [*First—Third*]: *Report of the Commissioners appointed to inquire whether any and what special means may be requisite for the improvement of the health of the metropolis* (London: W. Clowes and Sons, for Her Majesty's Stationery Office, 1848), Item notes: v. 1–3, 263.

9. www.teddington-lock.co.uk.

10. http://www.the-river-thames.co.uk/, Floating down the River. The River Thames and Boaty Things.

11. John Snow, M.D., *On the Mode of Communication of Cholera*, 2d ed. (Washington, D.C.: Delta Omega). www.deltaomega.org.

12. *Metropolitan Commission of Sewers, January 1849, Reports and Correspondence Respecting the Drainage of the New Palace at Westminster*, City of Westminster Archives, q942.1341, A (Ref) (West), [628.3], 3.

13. William Farr, *Report on the Mortality of Cholera in England 1848–49* (London: W. Clowes and Sons for Her Majesty's Stationery Office, 1852), "The Thames and Water Supply," lx, Wellcome Library, London.

14. John Snow, M.D., *On the Mode of Communication of Cholera*, 2d ed. (Washington, D.C.: Delta Omega), 60. www.deltaomega.org.

15. John G. Avery, *The Cholera Years. An Account of the Cholera Outbreaks in our Ports, Towns and Villages* (Southampton: Beech, 2001).

16. Nicholas Barton, *The Lost Rivers of London* (London: Historical Publications, 2005).

17. Times Online archive, August 6, 1849. http://archive.timesonline.co.uk/tol/archive/.

18. John G. Avery, *The Cholera Years. An Account of the Cholera Outbreaks in our Ports, Towns and Villages* (Southampton: Beech, 2001).

19. The Archives of St. Bartholomew's Hospital, London, Medical records, MR5, Registers of Deaths 1847–52; full version of register, MR5/8. Position of tributaries made with reference to Nicholas Barton, *The Lost Rivers of London* (London: Historical Publications, 2005).

20. William Farr, *Report on the Mortality of Cholera in England 1848–49* (London: W. Clowes and Sons for Her Majesty's Stationery Office, 1852), "The Thames and Water Supply," lix, Wellcome Library, London.

21. Ibid.

22. Ibid., lxi–lxii.

23. Ibid., lxvi.

24. Ibid., lxix — lxxii.

Chapter 6

1. Times Online archive, July 24, 1849. http://archive.timesonline.co.uk/tol/archive/.

2. *Lambeth Parish and Vestry Committee Minutes* (Ref.: P3), *Lambeth District Sanitary Reports* (Ref: P3, 73–75, 1848–1878); Lambeth Archives.

3. Ibid.
4. Ibid.
5. Ibid.
6. Ibid.
7. Ibid.
8. Ibid.
9. Ibid.
10. Ibid.
11. Ibid.
12. Ibid.
13. Ibid.
14. Ibid.
15. Ibid.
16. Ibid.
17. Ibid.
18. Ibid.
19. Ibid.
20. Ibid.
21. Ibid.
22. Ibid.
23. Ibid.
24. Ibid.
25. Ibid.
26. Ibid.
27. Ibid.
28. Ibid.
29. Ibid.
30. Ibid.
31. Ibid.
32. Ibid.
33. Ibid.
34. Ibid.
35. Ibid.
36. Ibid.
37. Ibid.
38. Ibid.
39. Ibid.
40. Ibid.
41. Ibid.
42. Ibid.
43. Ibid.
44. Ibid.
45. Ibid.
46. Ibid.
47. Ibid.
48. Ibid.
49. Times Online archive, July 24, 1849. http://archive.timesonline.co.uk/tol/archive/.
50. Ibid., August 4, 1849.

Chapter 7

1. William Farr, *Report on the Mortality of Cholera in England 1848–49* (London: W. Clowes and Sons for Her Majesty's Stationery Office, 1852), "Deaths Registered from Cholera Weekly," clxxiv.

2. Edwin Chadwick, *Report on The Sanitary Condition of the Labouring Population of Great Britain,* edited with an introduction by M.W. Flinn (1842; Edinburgh: Edinburgh University Press, 1965) 27.

3. M. Whitehead, "William Farr's legacy to the study of inequalities in Health," www.who.intbulletinarchives78(1)86.pdf.

4. Edwin Chadwick, *Report on The Sanitary Condition of the Labouring Population of Great Britain,* edited with an introduction by M.W. Flinn (1842; Edinburgh: Edinburgh University Press, 1965), 27.

5. M. Whitehead, "William Farr's legacy to the study of inequalities in Health," www.who.intbulletinarchives78(1)86.pdf; William Farr, Letter to the Registrar General, *First annual report of the Registrar General* (London: Her Majesty's Stationery Office, 1839).

6. *The Registrars General 1836–1945*; Farr and the Census and BMD; www.statistics.gov.ukcensus2001bicentenarypdfregistrars.pdf.

7. Edwin Chadwick, *Report on The Sanitary Condition of the Labouring Population of Great Britain,* edited with an introduction by M.W. Flinn (1842; Edinburgh: Edinburgh University Press, 1965), 29.

8. P. Bingham, P., N.Q. Verlander, M.J. Cheal, "John Snow, William Farr and the 1849 outbreak of cholera that affected London: a reworking of the data highlights the importance of the water supply," *Journal of the Royal institute of Public Health,* 2004. www.ph.ucla.eduepisnow public health118_387_394_2004.pdf.

9. John Snow, M.D., *On the Mode of Communication of Cholera,* 2d ed., (Washington, D.C.: Delta Omega), 772. www.deltaomega.org.

10. Ibid.

11. William Farr, *Report on the Mortality of Cholera in England 1848–49* (London: W. Clowes and Sons for Her Majesty's Stationery Office, 1852), "Deaths Registered from Cholera Weekly," clxxiv.

12. Ibid.

13. Edwin Chadwick, David Gladstone, and Samuel Edward Finer, *Edwin Chadwick: Nineteenth-century Social Reform* (London: Routledge, 1997), 347.

14. J.N. Hays, *Epidemics and Pandemics: Their Impacts on Human History* (Santa Barbara, CA: ABC-CLIO, 2005), 193.

15. Mary Dobson, *Disease. The Extraordinary Stories Behind History's Deadliest Killers* (London: Quercus, 2007), 44–45.

16. Norman Longmate, *King Cholera. The Biography of a Disease* (London: Hamish Hamilton, 1966), 158.

17. John G. Avery, *The Cholera Years. An Account of the Cholera Outbreaks in our Ports, Towns and Villages* (Southampton: Beech, 2001).

18. Edmund A. Parkes, M.D., Assistant Physi-

cian to University College Hospital, *An Inquiry into the bearing of the Earliest Cases of Cholera, which occurred in London During the Present Epidemic, On the Strict Theory of Contagion*, Part Third, Original Reports (London: Printed by C. and J. Adlard, 1849), 257.

19. Lambeth District Sanitary Reports 1848–1878, P3 73–75; Lambeth Archives, London.

20. Edmund A. Parkes, M.D., Assistant Physician to University College Hospital, *An Inquiry into the bearing of the Earliest Cases of Cholera, which occurred in London During the Present Epidemic, On the Strict Theory of Contagion*, Part Third, Original Reports (London: Printed by C. and J. Adlard, 1849), 257.

21. Obituary, "Edmund A. Parkes, M.D., F.R.S.," *British Medical Journal*, March 25, 1876.

22. Edmund A. Parkes, M.D., Assistant Physician to University College Hospital, *An Inquiry into the bearing of the Earliest Cases of Cholera, which occurred in London During the Present Epidemic, On the Strict Theory of Contagion*, Part Third, Original Reports (London: Printed by C. and J. Adlard, 1849), 251.

23. I. Kaye Wachsmuth, Paul A. Blake, and Ørjan Olsvik, eds., Vibrio cholerae *and Cholera. Molecular to Global Perspectives* (Washington, D.C.: American Society for Microbiology, 1994), 119.

24. Matthew K. Waldor and John J. Mekalanos, "Lysogenic Conversion by a Filamentous Phage Encoding Cholera Toxin," *Science*, 272.5270 (June 1996): 1,910–1,914.

25. I. Kaye Wachsmuth, Paul A. Blake, and Ørjan Olsvik, eds., Vibrio cholerae *and Cholera. Molecular to Global Perspectives* (Washington, D.C.: American Society for Microbiology, 1994), 119.

26. Ibid., after R.V. Citarella, and R.R. Colwell, "Polyphasic taxonomy of the genus, Vibrio; polynucleotide sequence relationships among selected Vibrio species," *Journal of Bacteriology*, 104 (1970): 434–442.

27. Times Online archive, August 23, 1855. http://archive.timesonline.co.uk/tol/archive/.

28. Edmund A. Parkes, M.D., Assistant Physician to University College Hospital, *An Inquiry into the bearing of the Earliest Cases of Cholera, which occurred in London During the Present Epidemic, On the Strict Theory of Contagion*, Part Third, Original Reports (London: Printed by C. and J. Adlard, 1849), 264.

29. Ibid.

30. John Snow, M.D., *On the Mode of Communication of Cholera*, 2d ed. (Washington, D.C.: Delta Omega), 2. www.deltaomega.org.

31. Edmund A. Parkes, M.D., Assistant Physician to University College Hospital, *An Inquiry into the bearing of the Earliest Cases of Cholera, which occurred in London During the Present Epidemic, On the Strict Theory of Contagion*, Part

Third, Original Reports (London: Printed by C. and J. Adlard, 1849), 258.

32. William Farr, *Report on the Mortality of Cholera in England 1848–49* (London: W. Clowes and Sons for Her Majesty's Stationery Office, 1852), "Deaths Registered from Cholera Weekly," 213.

33. John Snow, M.D., *On the Mode of Communication of Cholera*, 2d ed. (Washington, D.C.: Delta Omega), 14. www.deltaomega.org.

34. I. Kaye Wachsmuth, Paul A. Blake, and Ørjan Olsvik, eds., Vibrio cholerae *and Cholera. Molecular to Global Perspectives* (Washington, D.C.: American Society for Microbiology, 1994), 349.

35. Ibid.

36. Saul Roseman (2003), 5, in Karin L. Meibom, Xibing B. Li, Alex T. Nielsen, Cheng-Yen Wu, Saul Roseman, and Gary K. Schoolnik, "The Vibrio cholerae chitin utilization program" (Stanford: Department of Medicine, Division of Infectious Diseases and Geographic Medicine, and Department of Microbiology and Immunology, Stanford University School of Medicine and Baltimore: Department of Biology and McCollum-Pratt Institute, Johns Hopkins University). http://www.pnas.org/content/101/8/2524.full.pdf.

37. D.R. Nalin, V. Daya, A. Reid, M.M. Levine, and L. Cisneros, "Adsorption and Growth of Vibrio cholerae on Chitin" (Baltimore: Center for Vaccine Development, Division of Infectious Diseases, Department of Medicine, University of Maryland School of Medicine, 1979).

38. I. Kaye Wachsmuth, Paul A. Blake, and Ørjan Olsvik, eds., Vibrio cholerae *and Cholera. Molecular to Global Perspectives* (Washington, D.C.: American Society for Microbiology, 1994), 349.

39. Edmund A. Parkes, M.D., Assistant Physician to University College Hospital, *An Inquiry into the bearing of the Earliest Cases of Cholera, which occurred in London During the Present Epidemic, On the Strict Theory of Contagion*, Part Third, Original Reports (London: Printed by C. and J. Adlard, 1849), 259.

40. John Snow, M.D., *On the Mode of Communication of Cholera*, 2d ed. (Washington, D.C.: Delta Omega), 49. www.deltaomega.org.

41. Edwin Chadwick, David Gladstone, and Samuel Edward Finer, *Edwin Chadwick: Nineteenth-century Social Reform* (London: Routledge, 1997), 339.

42. Ibid., 340.

43. Ibid., 340.

44. Ibid., 340.

45. Edmund A. Parkes, M.D., Assistant Physician to University College Hospital, *An Inquiry into the bearing of the Earliest Cases of Cholera, which occurred in London During the Present Epidemic, On the Strict Theory of Contagion*, Part Third, Original Reports (London: Printed by C. and J. Adlard, 1849), 260.

46. Ibid.

47. Medical Records MR5, Registers of Deaths 1847–52; full version of register, MR 5/8, Archives of St. Bartholomew's Hospital.

48. St. Bartholomew's Hospital Archives; Hal/ 11, 381.

49. St. Bartholomew's Hospital Archives, London.

50. Ancestry.co.uk.

51. Edmund A. Parkes, M.D., Assistant Physician to University College Hospital, *An Inquiry into the bearing of the Earliest Cases of Cholera, which occurred in London During the Present Epidemic, On the Strict Theory of Contagion*, Part Third, Original Reports (London: Printed by C. and J. Adlard, 1849), 272.

52. Times Online archive, October 13, 1848. http://archive.timesonline.co.uk/tol/archive/.

53. Ibid., October 11, 1848.

54. Ibid., October 25, 1848.

55. Edmund A. Parkes, M.D., Assistant Physician to University College Hospital, *An Inquiry into the bearing of the Earliest Cases of Cholera, which occurred in London During the Present Epidemic, On the Strict Theory of Contagion*, Part Third, Original Reports (London: Printed by C. and J. Adlard, 1849), 274.

56. Edwin Chadwick, David Gladstone, and Samuel Edward Finer, *Edwin Chadwick: Nineteenth-century Social Reform* (London: Routledge, 1997), 341.

57. Times Online archive, November 8, 1848. http://archive.timesonline.co.uk/tol/archive/.

58. Ibid., November 15, 1848.

59. Ibid.

60. Ibid., November 22, 1848.

61. Ibid.

62. Ibid., November 24, 1848.

63. Ancestry.co.uk, 1841 Census; http://www.familysearch.org/.

64. William Farr, *Report on the Mortality of Cholera in England 1848–49* (London: W. Clowes and Sons for Her Majesty's Stationery Office, 1852).

65. Ibid.

66. Times Online archive, July 18, 1849. http://archive.timesonline.co.uk/tol/archive.

67. Ibid., October 26, 1849.

68. Ibid., July 18, 1849.

69. Ibid.

70. Ibid.

71. William Farr, *Report on the Mortality of Cholera in England 1848–49* (London: W. Clowes and Sons for Her Majesty's Stationery Office, 1852).

72. Times Online archive, July 24, 1849. http://archive.timesonline.co.uk/tol/archive/.

73. Ibid.

74. Ibid.

75. William Farr, *Report on the Mortality of Cholera in England 1848–49* (London: W. Clowes and Sons for Her Majesty's Stationery Office, 1852).

76. John Snow, M.D., *On the Mode of Communication of Cholera*, 2d ed. (Washington, D.C.: Delta Omega), 18. www.deltaomega.org.

77. Times Online archive, July 25, 1849. http://archive.timesonline.co.uk/tol/archive/.

78. Ibid.

79. William Farr, *Report on the Mortality of Cholera in England 1848–49* (London: W. Clowes and Sons for Her Majesty's Stationery Office, 1852).

80. Ibid., 212.

81. Ibid.

82. Times Online archive, July 30, 1849. http://archive.timesonline.co.uk/tol/archive/.

83. Ibid., August 1, 1849.

84. Ibid., August 2, 1849.

85. Ibid., August 4, 1849.

86. Ibid.

87. Ibid.

88. Ibid.

89. William Farr, *Report on the Mortality of Cholera in England 1848–49* (London: W. Clowes and Sons for Her Majesty's Stationery Office, 1852).

90. Ibid.

91. Edwin Chadwick, David Gladstone, and Samuel Edward Finer, *Edwin Chadwick: Nineteenth-century Social Reform* (London: Routledge, 1997), 348.

92. Ibid.

93. Times Online archive, August 8, 1849. http://archive.timesonline.co.uk/tol/archive/.

94. William Farr, *Report on the Mortality of Cholera in England 1848–49* (London: W. Clowes and Sons for Her Majesty's Stationery Office, 1852).

95. Times Online archive, August 10, 1849. http://archive.timesonline.co.uk/tol/archive/.

96. Ibid., August 11, 1849.

97. William Farr, *Report on the Mortality of Cholera in England 1848–49* (London: W. Clowes and Sons for Her Majesty's Stationery Office, 1852).

98. Ibid.

99. Times Online archive, August 13, 1849. http://archive.timesonline.co.uk/tol/archive/.

100. Ibid.

101. Ibid.

102. William Farr, *Report on the Mortality of Cholera in England 1848–49* (London: W. Clowes and Sons for Her Majesty's Stationery Office, 1852).

103. Ibid., 213.

104. Ibid., 212.

105. Ibid., 214.

106. Ibid.

107. Edwin Chadwick, David Gladstone, and Samuel Edward Finer, *Edwin Chadwick: Nineteenth-century Social Reform* (London: Routledge, 1997), 348.

108. William Farr, *Report on the Mortality of Cholera in England 1848–49* (London: W. Clowes and Sons for Her Majesty's Stationery Office, 1852).

109. Ibid., 212.

110. Ibid.

111. Ibid., 214–15.

112. Ibid., 213.

113. Ibid.

114. Ibid., 214.

115. Ibid., 215.

116. Ibid.

117. Ibid., 213.

118. Times Online archive, September 3, 1849. http://archive.timesonline.co.uk/tol/archive/.

119. Ibid., September 4, 1849.

120. Ibid.

121. Post Office Directory, London, 1848, Ref. 0109; Archive CD Books.

122. Times Online archive, September 4, 1849. http://archive.timesonline.co.uk/tol/archive/.

123. William Farr, *Report on the Mortality of Cholera in England 1848–49* (London: W. Clowes and Sons for Her Majesty's Stationery Office, 1852).

124. Ibid.

125. Times Online archive, September 8, 1849. http://archive.timesonline.co.uk/tol/archive/.

126. Ibid., September 11, 1849.

127. Ibid.

128. Edwin Chadwick, David Gladstone, and Samuel Edward Finer, *Edwin Chadwick: Nineteenth-century Social Reform* (London: Routledge, 1997), 349.

129. Ibid.

130. William Farr, *Report on the Mortality of Cholera in England 1848–49* (London: W. Clowes and Sons for Her Majesty's Stationery Office, 1852).

131. Ibid., 213.

132. Ibid., 215.

133. Edwin Chadwick, David Gladstone, and Samuel Edward Finer, *Edwin Chadwick: Nineteenth-century Social Reform* (London: Routledge, 1997), 349.

134. Ibid., 350–51.

135. Ibid., 352; and Times Online archive, September 19, 1849. http://archive.timesonline.co.uk/tol/archive/.

136. Edwin Chadwick, David Gladstone, and Samuel Edward Finer, *Edwin Chadwick: Nineteenth-century Social Reform* (London: Routledge, 1997), 349.

137. Times Online archive, September 19, 1849. http://archive.timesonline.co.uk/tol/archive/.

138. Ibid.

139. Ibid.

140. Ibid.

141. Ibid.

142. Ibid.

143. William Farr, *Report on the Mortality of Cholera in England 1848–49* (London: W. Clowes and Sons for Her Majesty's Stationery Office, 1852).

144. Times Online archive, October 3, 1849. http://archive.timesonline.co.uk/tol/archive/.

145. Ibid., October 5, 1849.

146. Ibid.

147. Ibid; and William Farr, *Report on the Mortality of Cholera in England 1848–49* (London: W. Clowes and Sons for Her Majesty's Stationery Office, 1852), 213.

148. Times Online archive, October 11, 1849. http://archive.timesonline.co.uk/tol/archive/.

149. William Farr, *Report on the Mortality of Cholera in England 1848–49* (London: W. Clowes and Sons for Her Majesty's Stationery Office, 1852), 214.

150. Times Online archive, October 29, 1849. http://archive.timesonline.co.uk/tol/archive/.

151. Marie P.G. Draper, *Lambeth's Open Spaces—A Historical Account* (London: Borough of Lambeth, 1979). Information supplied by Dr. Iain Boulton.

152. Times Online archive, January 19, 1854. http://archive.timesonline.co.uk/tol/archive/.

153. Ibid.

154. Edwin Chadwick, *Report on The Sanitary Condition of the Labouring Population of Great Britain,* edited with an introduction by M.W. Flinn (1842; Edinburgh: Edinburgh University Press, 1965), 61.

155. Henry Mayhew and John Binney, *The Criminal Prisons of London and Scenes of Prison Life* (1862; London: Frank Cass, 1968), 268.

Chapter 8

1. Times Online archive, October 26, 1849. http://archive.timesonline.co.uk/tol/archive/.

2. Ibid.

3. Ibid.

4. Ibid.

5. Family historian Susan Algar and the O'Smotherly family; Ancestry.co.uk.

6. Times Online archive, November 8, 1849. http://archive.timesonline.co.uk/tol/archive/.

7. Ibid., July 19, 1850.

8. Ibid.

9. Ibid.

10. Edwin Chadwick, David Gladstone, and Samuel Edward Finer, *Edwin Chadwick: Nineteenth-century Social Reform* (London: Routledge, 1997), 364.

11. Ibid., 367; and Metropolitan Sanitary Report (parliamentary papers, 1847–48, xxxii), Minutes of Evidence, 58–59.

12. Ibid., 368–69.

13. J. Fisher, A.P. Cotton, and B.J. Reed,

"Learning from the Past. Delivery of water and sanitation services to the poor in 19th century Britain," Background Report for WELL (Resource centre network for water, sanitation and environmental health), January 2005, 10.

14. Edwin Chadwick, David Gladstone, and Samuel Edward Finer, *Edwin Chadwick: Nineteenth-century Social Reform* (London: Routledge, 1997), 370.

15. Ibid., 381.

16. Times Online archive, November 25, 1853. http://archive.timesonline.co.uk/tol/archive/.

17. Ibid., October 23, 1852.

18. Ibid., November 3, 1852.

19. Ibid., October 6, 1853.

20. Ibid., November 25, 1853.

21. Ibid., October 7, 1854.

22. Ibid., October 19, 1854.

23. Ibid.

24. Ibid.

25. Ibid.

26. Ibid.

27. UCLA School of Public Health, "Invisible to the Naked Eye: John Snow." www.ph.ucla.edu/EPI/snow/gilbert_mappingvictoriasocbody_55_79_2004.pdf.

28. Stephen Halliday, *The Great Stink of London. Sir Joseph Bazalgette and the Cleansing of the Victorian Metropolis* (Stroud, Gloucestershire: Sutton, 2007), 17.

29. Times Online archive, August 23, 1855. http://archive.timesonline.co.uk/tol/archive/.

30. Ibid., June 26, 1856.

31. Royal College of Physicians, London, Fef. GB 0113 MS-BALYW.

32. R.J. Morris, *Cholera 1832—The social Response to an Epidemic* (London: Croon Helm, 1976), Chapter 9, Epilogue.

33. John Powell, "Anaesthesia, Cholera and the Medical Reading Society of Bristol." http://www.johnpowell.net/anchol12.htm.

34. William Baly and William Withey Gull, *Report on the Nature and Import of Certain Microscopic Bodies Found in the Intestinal Discharges of Cholera: Presented to the Cholera Committee of the Royal College of Physicians ... by Their Sub-committee, on the 17th October, 1849*, Cholera Committee, Royal College of Physicians (London: J. Churchill, 1849), 20–21.

35. *Cholera Letters*, TH/CLR1 printed instructions on hygiene practices from the Royal College of Physicians, 1853. Archives and Corporate Records Services, Information Services and Systems, King's College London; Ref.: TH1/CLR/1 S2 a.7.

36. M. Babu, M. Madan and K. Sankaran, "New Strains of V. cholerae" (2000).

37. http://www.bristolmedchi.co.uk/docs/Lecture%20Budd.pdf. Bristol Medico–Chirurgical Society.

38. John Powell, "Anaesthesia, Cholera and the Medical Reading Society of Bristol." http://www.johnpowell.net/anchol12.htm.

39. http://www.ph.ucla.edu/epi/snow/hunterian.html.

40. http://www.bbc.co.uk/history/historic_figures/snow_john.shtml.

41. John Snow, M.D., *On the Mode of Communication of Cholera*, 2d ed. (Washington, D.C.: Delta Omega). *www.deltaomega.org.*

42. Ibid., 6.

43. Ibid., 10.

44. Ibid., 14.

45. Ibid., 24–26.

46. Ibid., 25–26.

47. Ibid., 27.

48. Ibid., 27.

49. Ibid., 32.

50. Ibid., 33.

51. Nigel Paneth, "Commentary: Snow on Rickets," *International Journal of Epidemiology*, 32.3 (2003). http://ije.oxfordjournals.org.

52. John Snow, M.D., *On the Mode of Communication of Cholera*, 2d ed. (Washington, D.C.: Delta Omega), 32. www.deltaomega.org.

53. Ibid., 6.

54. Ibid., 47.

55. Ibid., 70.

56. Ibid., 74.

57. Ibid., 84–85.

58. Ibid., 85.

59. *London Medical Gazette*, 1849. http://www.johnsnowsociety.org/johnsnow/facts.html.

60. Marina Bentivoglio and Paolo Pacini, *Filippo Pacini: A Determined Observer* (Verona and Florence, Italy: Institute of Anatomy and Histology, University of Verona; Department of Anatomy and Histology, University of Florence, 1995). *http://www.sciencedirect.com/.*

61. www.ph.ucla.edu/EPI/snow/brainresearchbul38(2)_161_165_1995.pdf.

62. nobelprize.org/nobel_prizes/medicine/laureates/1905/koch-bio.html.

63. Ibid.

64. Norman Howard-Jones, "Robert Koch and the Cholera Vibrio: a Centenary," *British Medical Journal*, Vol. 288, February 4, 1984.

65. nobelprize.org/nobel_prizes/medicine/laureates/1905/koch-bio.html, 379.

66. Ibid.

67. Ibid., 380.

68. www.whonamedit.com/doctor.cfm/3306.html.

69. Ibid.

70. Ibid.

71. Stephen Halliday, *The Great Stink of London. Sir Joseph Bazalgette and the Cleansing of the Victorian Metropolis* (Stroud, Gloucestershire: Sutton, 2007), 63.

72. en.wikipedia.org/wiki/Metropolitan_Board_of_Works.

73. Stephen Halliday, *The Great Stink of Lon-*

don. *Sir Joseph Bazalgette and the Cleansing of the Victorian Metropolis* (Stroud, Gloucestershire: Sutton, 2007), 64.

74. Ibid., 74.

75. Ibid., 148.

76. Ibid., 150.

77. Ibid., 77–84.

78. Hannah Renier, *Lambeth Past, Kennington, Vauxhall, Waterloo* (London: Historical Publications, 2006), 133.

79. *The Builder*, 8.367, February 16, 1850.

80. Times Online archive, September 19, 1871. http://archive.timesonline.co.uk/tol/archive/.

81. *Survey of London: volume 23: Lambeth: South Bank and Vauxhall*, eds. Sir Howard Roberts and Walter H. Godfrey (1951), Chapter 24, "Lambeth Bridge and its predecessor the Horseferry," 118–121. http://www.british-history.ac.uk/report.aspx?compid=47053.

82. *Hansard,* HC Deb March 17, 1863, vol. 169 cc1584–8; hansard.millbanksystems.com.

83. Times Online archive, January 19, 1854. http://archive.timesonline.co.uk/tol/archive/.

84. George Augustus Sala, *Gaslight And Daylight with Some London Scenes They Shine Upon* (London: Chapman & Hall, 1859); www.victorianlondon.org/publications2/gaslight.htm, The Victorian Dictionary.

85. Times Online archive, October 6, 1865. http://archive.timesonline.co.uk/tol/archive/.

86. Ibid., August 28, 1866.

87. J. Fisher, A.P. Cotton, and B.J. Reed, "Learning from the Past. Delivery of water and sanitation services to the poor in 19th century Britain," Background Report for WELL (Resource centre network for water, sanitation and environmental health), January 2005, 9.

88. *Survey of London: Volume 23: Lambeth: South Bank and Vauxhall*, eds. Sir Howard Roberts and Walter H. Godfrey (1951), Chapter 34, "The Albert Embankment," 148–149. http://www.british-history.ac.uk/report.aspx?compid=47063.

89. Stephen Halliday, *The Great Stink of London. Sir Joseph Bazalgette and the Cleansing of the Victorian Metropolis* (Stroud, Gloucestershire: Sutton, 2007), 156.

90. Times Online archive, September 19, 1871. http://archive.timesonline.co.uk/tol/archive/.

91. Ibid.

92. Ibid.

Chapter 9

1. Edwin Chadwick, *Report on The Sanitary Condition of the Labouring Population of Great Britain*, edited with an introduction by M.W. Flinn (1842; Edinburgh: Edinburgh University Press, 1965), 13.

2. William Farr, *Report on the Mortality of Cholera in England 1848–49* (London: W. Clowes and Sons for Her Majesty's Stationery Office, 1852), Section I, "Vitality of England and Wales and Average Amount of Sickness: Experienced by the Results of Mr. Neison," 11.

3. Edwin Chadwick, *Report on The Sanitary Condition of the Labouring Population of Great Britain,* edited with an introduction by M.W. Flinn (1842; Edinburgh: Edinburgh University Press, 1965), 11; and J. Brownlee, *An Investigation into the Epidemiology of Phthisis in Great Britain and Ireland*, Medical Research Council, Special Reports Series, No. 18 (1918) Table XXV.

4. Times Online archive September 3, 1849. http://archive.timesonline.co.uk/tol/archive/.

5. Ibid., September 4, 1849.

6. Ibid., August 4, 1849.

7. *Lambeth Parish and Vestry Committee Minutes* (Ref.: P3), *Lambeth District Sanitary Reports* (Ref: P3, 73–75, 1848–1878), Lambeth Archives.

8. Times Online archive, August 23, 1855. http://archive.timesonline.co.uk/tol/archive/.

Bibliography

Books

Ackroyd, Peter. *London. The Biography.* London: Vintage, 2001.

Allen, Thomas. *The History and Antiquities of the Parish of Lambeth, and the Archiepiscopal Palace: Including Biographical Sketches.* London: J. Allen, 1826.

_____. *A History of the County of Surrey; Comprising Every Object of Topographical, Geological, or Historical Interest.* Vol. I. London: Hinton, 1831.

_____. *A New and Complete History of the County of Surrey.* London: Hinton, 1830.

Arnold, Catherine. *Necropolis, London and its Dead.* London: Pocket Books, 2006.

Avery, John G. *The Cholera Years. An Account of the Cholera Outbreaks in our Ports, Towns and Villages.* Southampton: Beech, 2001.

Baly, William, and William Withey Gull. *Report on the Nature and Import of Certain Microscopic Bodies Found in the Intestinal Discharges of Cholera: Presented to the Cholera Committee of the Royal College of Physicians ... by Their Sub-committee, on the 17th October, 1849.* Cholera Committee, Royal College of Physicians. London: J. Churchill, 1849.

_____, and _____. *Reports on Epidemic Cholera: Drawn up at the desire of the Cholera Committee of the Royal College of Physicians.* Cholera Committee, Royal College of Physicians. London: J. Churchill, 1854.

Barrow, Charles. *Industrial Relations Law.* 2d ed., revised. London: Cavendish, 2002.

Barton, Nicholas. *The Lost Rivers of London.* London: Historical, 2005.

The Builder. Vol. 8. No. 367. February 16, 1850.

Burch, Druin. *Digging up the Dead, Uncovering the Life and Times of an Extraordinary Surgeon.* London: Vintage, 2007.

Carlyle, Thomas. *Chartism; Past and Present.* Boston: Elibron Classics, 2005.

Chadwick, Edwin. *Report on The Sanitary Condition of the Labouring Population of Great Britain.* Edited with an introduction by M.W. Flinn. 1842; Edinburgh: Edinburgh University Press, 1965.

_____, David Gladstone, and Samuel Edward Finer. *Edwin Chadwick: Nineteenth-century Social Reform.* London: Routledge, 1997.

Chaucer, Geoffrey. *The Canterbury Tales.* Middlesex, England: Penguin, 1975.

Cherry, Allan. *A Pictorial History of Cooling and Cliffe, Looking back from the Millennium.* Kent: Martins News, 1998.

Clark, R.H. *A Southern Region, Chronology and Record, 1803–1965.* Tanglewood, Surrey: Oakwood Press, 1964.

Clay, Henry Hurrell. *Clay's Handbook of Environmental Health: Theory, Methods and Measuring Instrumentation.* Ed. W. H. Bassett. Philadelphia: Taylor & Francis, 1999.

The Clock Tower. The journal of the Friends of Medway Archives and Local Studies Centre. http://www.foma-lsc.org/newsletter.html.

Dickens, Charles. *David Copperfield.* Ware: Wordsworth, 2000.

_____. *Great Expectations.* London & Glasgow: Collins, 1965.

_____. *Oliver Twist.* London: Puffin Books, 1994.

_____. *Our Mutual Friend.* Ware: Wordsworth, 1998.

Dobson, Mary. *Disease. The Extraordinary Stories Behind History's Deadliest Killers.* London: Quercus, 2007.

Draper, Marie P.G. *Lambeth's Open Spaces—A Historical Account.* London: Borough of Lambeth, 1979.

Dudman, Jill. *Britain in Old Photographs. Lambeth, Kennington and Clapham.* Stroud, Gloucestershire: Sutton, 1996.

Engels, Friederich. *The Condition of the Working Class in England.* Gloucester: Dodo Press, 2007.

Farr, William. *Mortality in Mid 19th Century Britain; with an introduction by Richard Wall.* Farnborough, Hampshire: Gregg International, 1974.

_____. *Report on the Mortality of Cholera in England 1848–49*. London: W. Clowes and Sons, for Her Majesty's Stationery Office, 1852.

Fremont-Barnes, Gregory. *Encyclopedia of the Age of Political Revolutions and New Ideologies, 1760–1815*. Westport, CT: Greenwood, 2007.

The Gentleman's Magazine. Item notes: v.158. January to June 1835. Published by F. Jefferies. Original from the University of Michigan.

Gower, Graham, and Kieron Taylor. *Lambeth Unearthed. An Archaeological History of Lambeth*. London: Museum of London Archaeology Service, on behalf of the London Borough of Lambeth's Archive Department, 2003.

Gray, Adrian. *Crime and Criminals of Victorian London*. Chichester, Sussex: Phillimore, 2006.

Great Britain Metropolitan Sanitary Commission. [*First—Third*]: *Report of the Commissioners appointed to inquire whether any and what special means may be requisite for the improvement of the health of the metropolis*. London: W. Clowes and Sons, for Her Majesty's Stationery Office, 1848.

Halliday, Stephen. *The Great Filth. The War Against Disease in Victorian England*. Stroud, Gloucestershire: Sutton, 2007.

_____. *The Great Stink of London. Sir Joseph Bazalgette and the Cleansing of the Victorian Metropolis*. Stroud, Gloucestershire: Sutton, 2007.

Hays, J.N. *The Burdens of Disease. Epidemics and Human Response in Western History*. New Brunswick, NJ: Rutgers University Press, 2003.

_____. *Epidemics and Pandemics: Their Impacts on Human History*. Santa Barbara, CA: ABC-CLIO, 2005.

Hebert, Luke. *Comprehending Practical Illustrations of the Machinery and Processes Employed In Every Description of Manufacture of the British Empire; The Engineer's and Mechanic's Encyclopaedia*. Vol. I. London: Thomas Kelly, 1849.

Hempel, Sandra. *The Medical Detective. John Snow, Cholera and the Mystery of the Broad Street Pump*. London: Granta, 2006.

Hirschel, J. David, and William O. Wakefield. *Criminal Justice in England and the United States*. Westport, CT: Greenwood, 1995.

A History of the County of Surrey: Volume 4. Edited by H.E. Malden. 1912.

Hollis, Patricia. *Class and Conflict in Nineteenth-Century England, 1815–1850*. London: Routledge & Kegan Paul, 1973.

Lambeth District Sanitary Reports, 1848–1878. Ref.: P3 73–75. Lambeth Archives Department.

Lettinga, Gatze, and Grietje Zeeman. *Decentralised Sanitation and Reuse: Concepts, Systems and Implementation*. London: IWA, 2001.

Longmate, Norman. *King Cholera. The Biography of a Disease*. London: Hamish Hamilton, 1966.

Mayhew, Henry. *London Labour and the London Poor*. Selections made and introduced by Victor Neuburg. 1849. London: Penguin Books, 1985.

_____. *The London Underworld in the Victorian Period. Authentic First-Person Accounts by Beggars, Thieves and Prostitutes*. Mineola, NY: Dover, 2005.

_____, and John Binny. *The Criminal Prisons of London and Scenes of Prison Life*. Reprinted from the first edition of 1862. London: Frank Cass, 1968.

Mill, John Stuart. *Principles of Political Economy*. Oxford: Oxford University Press, 1998.

Morris, R.J. *Cholera 1832—The Social Response to an Epidemic*. London: Croon Helm, 1976.

Mountfield, David. *Stage and Mail Coaches*. Princes Risborough, Buckinghamshire: Shire, 2003.

Munn, C.B. *Marine Microbiology, Ecology and Applications*. London and New York: Garland Science/BIOS Scientific Publishers, 2004.

O'Grada, Cormac. *Ireland's Great Famine*. Dublin: University College Dublin Press, 2006.

Ordnance Survey. *Historical Map and Guide, Roman Britain*. 5th Edition. Southampton: Ordnance Survey, 2001.

Ordnance Survey. *Londinium. A Descriptive Map and Guide to Roman London*. Southampton: Ordnance Survey, 1981.

Page, William, and William Ashley. *Commerce and Industry. A Historical Review of the Economic Conditions of the British Empire from the Peace of Paris in 1815 to the Declaration of War in 1914, Based on Parliamentary Debates*. Boston: Adamant Media, 2005.

Parker, J.W. *The Saturday Magazine*. Oxford: Oxford University, 1837.

Parkes, Edmund A., M.D., Assistant Physician to University College Hospital. *An Inquiry into the bearing of the Earliest Cases of*

Cholera, which occurred in London During the Present Epidemic, On the Strict Theory of Contagion. Part Third, Original Reports. London: Printed by C. and J. Adlard, 1849.

Picard, Lisa. *Victorian London. The Life of a City 1840–1870.* London: Phoenix, 2005.

Pooley, Colin G., and Jean Turnbull. *Migration and Mobility in Britain Since the 18th Century.* London: Routledge, 1998.

Porter, Roy. *London: A Social History.* London: Penguin Books, 1994.

Randall, Adrian. *Riotous Assemblies: Popular Protest in Hanoverian England.* Oxford: Oxford University Press, 2006.

Renier, Hannah. *Lambeth Past, Kennington, Vauxhall, Waterloo.* London: Historical Publications, 2006.

Richardson, John. *The Annals of London. A Year-by-Year Record of a Thousand Years of History.* London: Cassell, 2001.

Richardson, Ruth. *Death, Dissection and the Destitute.* London: Penguin, 1988.

Roberts, Stephen, and Dorothy Thompson. *Images of Chartism.* Woodbridge, Suffolk: Merlin Press, 1998.

Sala, George Augustus. *Gaslight And Daylight with Some London Scenes They Shine Upon.* London: Chapman & Hall, 1859.

Salinity on Vibrio cholerae *Growth.* College Park: Department of Microbiology, University of Maryland, 1982.

Sidell, Jane, Jonathan Cotton, Louise Rayner, and Lucy Wheeler. *The Prehistory and Topography of Southwark and Lambeth.* Monograph 14. London: Museum of London Archaeology Service, 2002.

Singleton, F.L., R. Attwell, S. Jangi, and R.R. Colwell. *Effects of Temperature and*

Snow, John, M.D. *On the Mode of Communication of Cholera.* 2d ed. Washington, D.C.: Delta Omega.

Survey of London: Volume 23: Lambeth: South Bank and Vauxhall. Eds. Sir Howard Roberts, and Walter H. Godfrey. 1951. http://www.british-history.ac.uk/report.aspx?compid=47045.

Thomson, John, with Adolphe Smith. *Victorian Street Life in Historic Photographs.* New York: Dover, 1994.

Tyler, Kieron, Ian Betts, and Roy Stephenson. *London's Delftware Industry. The tin-glazed pottery industries of Southwark and Lambeth.* Monograph 40. London: Museum of London Archaeology Service, 2008.

Unstead, R.J. *Freedom and Revolution.* London: Macdonald, 1972.

Wachsmuth, I. Kaye, Paul A. Blake and Ørjan Olsvik, eds. Vibrio cholerae *and Cholera: Molecular to Global Perspectives.* Washington, D.C.: American Society for Microbiology, 1994.

Wohl, Anthony S. *The Eternal Slum: Housing and Social Policy in Victorian London.* London: Transaction, 2002.

Wright, J.G. *Wright's Topography of Rochester, Chatham, Strood, Brompton etc. and Directory of the Clergy, Gentry, Tradesmen etc.* 1838. Strood, Kent: Medway Archives and Local Studies Centre.

Articles

Babu, M. Madan, and K. Sankaran. "New Strains of V. cholerae." 2000.

Baly, William, M.D., F.R.S., Physician to Millbank Prison. *Report on the Cause and Mode of Diffusion of Epidemic Cholera.* London: Woodfall and Kinder, 1853. Royal College of Physicians, London, Heritage Collections.

Billing, Archibald, M.D., A.M., F.R.S. "On The Treatment of Asiatic Cholera." 2d ed., revised. London: S. Highley, 1848. In Baly, William. "Report of Cholera, 1849." Royal College of Physicians, London. Ref. SLTr80.

"Cholera and choleraic diarrhoea casebook of St. Thomas's Hospital, 1853–1854." Subfonds of St. Thomas's Hospital Medical School. One volume. Ref. GB 0100 TH/CLR 2. King's College London College Archives.

"Cholera Letters." TH/CLR1 printed instructions on hygiene practices from the Royal College of Physicians, 1853. Archives and Corporate Records Services, Information Services and Systems, King's College London. Ref.: TH1/CLR/1 S2 a.7.

Clark, Robert. "Famine; Speenhamland System of Poor Relief." *The Literary Encyclopedia.* May 18, 2005.

Collins, C.H, M.A., D.Sc., F.R.C.Path. "Cholera and Typhoid Fever in Kent." Kent Archaeological Society online. www.kentarchaeology.ac.

"Contracts Relative to the New Houses of Parliament." City of Westminster Archives. F942.1341; RA/KA1004.

Crook, Joseph Mordaunt. "Sir Robert Smirke: A Pioneer of Concrete Construction." *Transactions of the Newcomen Society.* 38 (1968).

Edwards, Catherine, and Karl Hulka, contribs. "The Millbank Penitentiary: Excavations at the Chelsea School of Art and Design." *London Archaeologist*, Winter 2006.

Emsley, Clive. "The London 'Insurrection' of December 1792: Fact, Fiction or Fantasy?" *The Journal of British Studies* XVII (1978): 66–86.

Feldman, David. "History in Focus; The Boundaries of Welfare." Birkbeck College, University of London. http://www.history.ac.uk/ihr/Focus/Migration/articles/feldman.html.

Fisher, J., A.P. Cotton, and B.J. Reed. "Learning from the Past. Delivery of water and sanitation services to the poor in 19th century Britain." Background Report for WELL (Resource centre network for water, sanitation and environmental health). January 2005.

Hassall, Dr. A.H. "Report on the Microscopical Examination of Different Waters (principally those used in the Metropolis) during the Cholera Epidemic of 1855." http://www.niph.go.jp/toshokan/koten/Britain/PDF/100718490008.pdf.

Higgins, Peter McRorie, M.Ch., Ph.D., F.R.C.S. "The Scurvy Scandal at Millbank Penitentiary: A Reassessment." *Medical History*, 50.4 (2006): 513–34. Wellcome Institute for the History of Medicine. http://www.pubmedcentral.nih.gov/articlerender.fcgi?artid=1592637.

Howard-Jones, Norman. "Robert Koch and the Cholera Vibrio: a Centenary." *British Medical Journal*. Vol. 288. February 4, 1984.

Islam, M.S. "Increased toxin production by *Vibrio cholerae* O1 during survival with a green alga, *Rhizoclonium fontanum*, in an artificial aquatic environment." Department of Tropical Hygiene, London School of Hygiene and Tropical Medicine. http://www.ncbi.nlm.nih.gov/pubmed/2266879?dopt=Abstract.

Lindsay, S.W., and S.G. Willis. "Foresight. Infectious Diseases: preparing for the future." T8.10: "Predicting future areas suitable for vivax malaria in the United Kingdom." Office of Science and Innovation, Institute of Ecosystem Science, School of Biological and Biomedical Sciences, University of Durham. http://www.foresight.gov.uk/Infectious%20Diseases/t8_10.pdf.

Manby, E., surgeon. "Dissertation, with Practical Remarks, on Cholera Morbus." London: Burgess and Hill, 1831. In Baly, William. *Report of Cholera, 1849*. London: Royal College of Physicians. Ref. SLTr80.

Mee, John. "'In private speculation a republican': The Case of John Thelwall 1794–5." University College Oxford, 2006. www.english.wisc.edu/midmod/speculative.republicanism.doc.

Meibom, Karin L., Xibing B. Li, Alex T. Nielsen, Cheng-Yen Wu, Saul Roseman, and Gary K. Schoolnik. "The Vibrio cholerae chitin utilization program." Stanford: Department of Medicine, Division of Infectious Diseases and Geographic Medicine, and Department of Microbiology and Immunology, Stanford University School of Medicine; and Baltimore: Department of Biology and McCollum-Pratt Institute, The Johns Hopkins University. http://www.pnas.org/content/101/8/2524.full.pdf.

Metropolitan Commission of Sewers. "Reports and Correspondence Respecting the Drainage of the New Palace at Westminster." January 1849. City of Westminster Archives. q942.1341, A (Ref) (West), [628.3].

Nalin, D. R., V. Daya, A. Reid, M.M. Levine, and L. Cisneros. "Adsorption and Growth of Vibrio cholerae on Chitin." Baltimore: Center for Vaccine Development, Division of Infectious Diseases, Department of Medicine, University of Maryland School of Medicine, 1979.

Paneth, Nigel. "Commentary: Snow on Rickets." International Journal of Epidemiology, 2003.

Parkin, John, M.D., and William H. Allen. "Statistical Report of the Epidemic Cholera in Jamaica." London, 1852. In Baly, William. *Report of Cholera, 1849*. London: Royal College of Physicians. Ref. SLTr80.

Powell, John. "Anaesthesia, Cholera and the Medical Reading Society of Bristol." http://www.johnpowell.net/ancholl2.htm.

Sack, David A., R. Bradley Sack, G. Balakrish Nair, and A. K. Siddique. "Cholera." The Lancet. Vol. 363. January 17, 2004. http://www.ph.ucla.edu/epi/snow/lancet363_223_233_2004.pdf.

"Surgeons' report book, including cases of puerperal fever, 1824, cholera, 1825, typhoid, 1826, consumption, 1826, and smallpox, against which several children were vaccinated, only to have it in a worse form." 1823 to 1826. One small volume. Medway Archives and Local Studies Centre, Kent.

UCLA School of Public Health. "Invisible to

the Naked Eye: John Snow." www.ph.ucla. edu/EPI/snow/gilbert_mappingvictoriasoc body_55_79_2004.pdf.

Waldor, Matthew K., and John J. Mekalanos. "Lysogenic Conversion by a Filamentous Phage Encoding Cholera Toxin." *Science* 272.5270.

World Health Organization. "Guidelines for Drinking-water Quality. Second Edition. Addendum Microbiological agents in drinking water." Geneva, 2002.

Web Sites

ancestry.co.uk
archbishopofcanterbury.org/
bbc.co.uk/history/
bbc.co.uk/whodoyouthinkyouare/past-stories/jeremy-paxman.shtml
british-history.ac.uk/report.aspx?compid= 39483
bristolmedchi.co.uk/docs/Lecture%20Budd.p df (Bristol Medico–Chirurgical Society)
channel4.com/history/microsites/T/timeteam/ vauxhall.html (Time Team)
cityark.medway.gov.uk/www.clayheritage.org/ (The Ball Clay heritage Society)
compulink.co.uk/~museumgh/local%20his tory (The Museum of Garden History, Lambeth)
countyhalllondon.com/the-south-bank-london/local-attractions/174-the-palace-of-westminster.html
thedorsetpage.com/history/tolpuddle_mar tyrs/tolpuddle_martyrs.htm
economicexpert.com/a/Corn:Laws.htm
uk.encarta.msn.com
experiencefestival.com/a/Cholera — Pathol ogy/id/1287591
freespace.virgin.net/roger.hewitt/iwias/his tory.htm
geocities.com/rbeaufoy
hansard.millbanksystems.com/commons/
icons.org.uk/
johnsnowsociety.org
landmark.lambeth.gov.uk/Lambeth Archives (Lambeth Landmark imagebase)
manchester2002-uk.com/history/victo rian/Victorian2.html
45millbank.com/history-of-45-millbank
nationalarchives.gov.uk/ (The National Archives)
nationaltheatre.org.uk/
neo-tech.com
nobelprize.org/nobel_prizes/medicine/lau reates/1905/koch-bio.html
parliament.uk/parliament/guide/palace.htm
ph.ucla.edu/EPI/snow/brainresearchbul 38(2)_161_165_1995.pdf
purewatergazette.net/doultonhistory.htm
the-river-thames.co.uk/, Floating down the River (The River Thames and Boaty Things)
robert-owen-museum.org.uk
schoolshistory.org.uk/
teddington-lock.co.uk.
unionhistory.info
vauxhallsociety.org.uk/Doulton.
victorianlondon.org/ (The Victorian Dictio-nary; Jackson, Lee)
en.wikipedia.org
woolvey.com/royal_doulton_history.php.
workhouses.org.uk.

Index

Numbers in *bold italics* indicate pages with photographs.